W9-BLN-167

# DAILY LIGHT ON THE DAILY PATH

# DAILY LIGHT ON THE DAILY PATH

## INSPIRATIONAL THOUGHTS FOR EVERY DAY OF THE YEAR

NEW KING JAMES VERSION

INSPIRATIONAL PRESS
NEW YORK

Published in 1991 by

Inspirational Press
A division of LDAP, Inc.
386 Park Avenue South
New York, NY 10016

Inspirational Press is a registered trademark of LDAP, Inc.
Published by arrangement with Thomas Nelson Publishers.

ISBN: 0-88486-038-8

Printed in the United States of America

*Your word
is a lamp to my feet
And a light to my path*

PSALM 119:105

Father, I desire that they . . . whom You gave Me may be with Me where I am, that they may behold My glory which You have given Me. ◇ I know whom I have believed and am persuaded that He is able to keep what I have committed to Him until that Day. ◇ He who has begun a good work in you will complete it until the day of Jesus Christ.

Do you not know that those who run in a race all run, but one receives the prize? Run in such a way that you may obtain it. ◇ Lay aside every weight, and the sin which so easily ensnares us, and let us run with endurance the race that is set before us, . . . looking unto Jesus.

PHIL 3:13-14.JOHN 17:24.2 TIM 1:12.PHIL 1:6.1 COR 9:24-25.HEB 12:1-2

## January 1

But one thing I do, forgetting those things which are behind and reaching forward to those things which are ahead, . . . I press toward the goal for the prize of the upward call of God in Christ Jesus.

## January 2

**Sing to the Lord a new song.**

Sing aloud to God our strength; make a joyful shout to the God of Jacob. Raise a song and strike the timbrel, the pleasant harp with the lute. ◊ He has put a new song in my mouth—praise to our God; many will see it and fear, and will trust in the Lord.

Be strong and of good courage; do not be afraid, nor be dismayed, for the Lord your God is with you wherever you go. ◊ The joy of the Lord is your strength. ◊ Paul . . . thanked God and took courage.

The night is far spent, the day is at hand. Therefore let us cast off the works of darkness, and let us put on the armor of light. Let us walk properly, as in the day, not in revelry and drunkenness, not in licentiousness and lewdness, not in strife and envy. But put on the Lord Jesus Christ, and make no provision for the flesh, to fulfill its lusts.

IS 42:10.PS 81:1-2.PS 40:3.JOSH 1:9.NEH 8:10.ACTS 28:15.ROM 13:12-14

He led them forth by the right way, that they might go to a city for habitation.

In the wasteland, a howling wilderness, He encircled him, He instructed him, He kept him as the apple of His eye. As an eagle stirs up its nest, hovers over its young, spreading out its wings, taking them up, carrying them on its wings, . . . so the Lord alone led him. ◊ Even to your old age, I am He, and even to gray hairs I will carry you! I have made, and I will bear; even I will carry, and will deliver you.

He restores my soul; He leads me in the paths of righteousness for His name's sake. Yea, though I walk through the valley of the shadow of death, I will fear no evil; for You are with me; Your rod and Your staff, they comfort me.

The Lord will guide you continually, and satisfy your soul in drought, and strengthen your bones; you shall be like a watered garden, and like a spring of water, whose waters do not fail. ◊ For this is God, our God forever and ever; He will be our guide even to death. ◊ Who teaches like Him?

PS 107:7.DEUT 32:10-12.IS 46:4.PS 23:3-4.IS 58:11.PS 48:14.JOB 36:22

## January 4

For as yet you have not come to the rest and the inheritance which the Lᴏʀᴅ your God is giving you.

This is not your rest. ◊ There remains therefore a rest for the people of God. ◊ Behind the veil, where the forerunner has entered for us, even Jesus.

In My Father's house are many mansions; if it were not so, I would have told you. I go to prepare a place for you. And if I go and prepare a place for you, I will come again and receive you to Myself; that where I am, there you may be also. ◊ With Christ, which is far better.

God will wipe away every tear from their eyes; there shall be no more death, nor sorrow, nor crying; and there shall be no more pain, for the former things have passed away. ◊ There the wicked cease from troubling, and there the weary are at rest.

Lay up for yourselves treasures in heaven, . . . for where your treasure is, there your heart will be also. ◊ Set your mind on things above, not on things on the earth.

DEUT 12:9.MIC 2:10.HEB 4:9.HEB 6:19-20.JOHN 14:2-3.PHIL 1:23.REV 21:4.JOB 3:17.MATT 6:20-21.COL 3:2

They . . . weary themselves to commit iniquity. ◊ I see another law in my members, warring against the law of my mind, and bringing me into captivity to the law of sin which is in my members. O wretched man that I am! Who will deliver me from this body of death?

Come to Me, all you who labor and are heavy laden, and I will give you rest. ◊ Having been justified by faith, we have peace with God through our Lord Jesus Christ, through whom also we have access by faith into this grace in which we stand, and rejoice in hope of the glory of God.

He who has entered His rest has himself also ceased from his works. ◊ Not having my own righteousness, which is from the law, but that which is through faith in Christ, the righteousness which is from God by faith. ◊ This is the rest with which you may cause the weary to rest, and, this is the refreshing.

HEB 4:3.JER 9:5.ROM 7:23-24.MATT 11:28.ROM 5:1-2.HEB 4:10.PHIL 3:9.IS 28:12

We who have believed do enter that rest.

## January 6

Let the beauty of the LORD our God be upon us, and establish the work of our hands for us.

"Your beauty, . . . was perfect through My splendor which I had bestowed on you," says the Lord God. ◊ We all, with unveiled face, beholding as in a mirror the glory of the Lord, are being transformed into the same image from glory to glory, just as by the Spirit of the Lord.

Blessed is every one who fears the Lord, who walks in His ways. When you eat the labor of your hands, you shall be happy, and it shall be well with you. ◊ Commit your works to the Lord, and your thoughts will be established.

Work out your own salvation with fear and trembling; for it is God who works in you both to will and to do for His good pleasure. ◊ Our Lord Jesus Christ Himself, and our God and Father, who has loved us and given us everlasting consolation and good hope by grace, comfort your hearts and establish you in every good word and work.

PS 90:17.EZEK 16:14.2 COR 3:18.PS 128:1-2.PROV 16:3.PHIL 2:12-13. 2 THESS 2:16-17

Remember me, my God, for good.

Thus says the Lord: "I remember you, the kindness of your youth, the love of your betrothal, when you went after Me in the wilderness." ◊ I will remember My covenant with you in the days of your youth, and I will establish an everlasting covenant with you. ◊ I will visit you and perform My good word toward you, . . . For I know the thoughts that I think toward you, says the Lord, thoughts of peace and not of evil, to give you a future and a hope.

As the heavens are higher than the earth, so are My ways higher than your ways, and My thoughts than your thoughts. ◊ I would seek God, and to God I would commit my cause—who does great things, and unsearchable, marvelous things without number. ◊ Many, O Lord my God, are Your wonderful works which You have done; and Your thoughts which are toward us cannot be recounted to You in order; if I would declare and speak of them, they are more than can be numbered.

NEH 5:19.JER 2:2.EZEK 16:60.JER 29:10-11.IS 55:9.JOB 5:8-9.PS 40:5

## January 8

Those who know Your name will put their trust in You; for You, LORD, have not forsaken those who seek You.

The name of the Lord is a strong tower; the righteous run to it and are safe. ◇ I will trust and not be afraid; for YAH, the Lord, is my strength and my song; He also has become my salvation.

I have been young, and now am old; yet I have not seen the righteous forsaken, nor his descendants begging bread. ◇ For the Lord loves justice, and does not forsake His saints; they are preserved forever, but the descendants of the wicked shall be cut off. ◇ The Lord will not forsake His people, for His great name's sake, because it has pleased the Lord to make you His people. ◇ [He] delivered us from so great a death, and does deliver us; in whom we trust that He will still deliver us.

Be content with such things as you have. For He Himself has said, "I will never leave you nor forsake you." So we may boldly say: "The Lord is my helper; I will not fear. What can man do to me?"

PS 9:10.PROV 18:10.IS 12:2.PS 37:25.PS 37:28.1 SAM 12:22.2 COR 1:10 HEB 13:5-6

The-Lord-Is-My-Banner. ◊ When the enemy comes in like a flood, the Spirit of the Lord will lift up a standard against him.

We will rejoice in your salvation, and in the name of our God we will set up our banners! ◊ The Lord has revealed our righteousness. Come and let us declare in Zion the work of the Lord our God. ◊ We are more than conquerors through Him who loved us. ◊ Thanks be to God, who gives us the victory through our Lord Jesus Christ.

My brethren, be strong in the Lord and in the power of His might. ◊ [Be] valiant for the truth. ◊ Fight the Lord's battles. ◊ "Be strong, all you people of the land," says the Lord, "and work; . . . do not fear!" ◊ Lift up your eyes and look at the fields, for they are already white for harvest! ◊ For yet a little while, and He who is coming will come and will not tarry.

PS 60:4.EX 17:15.IS 59:19.PS 20:5.JER 51:10.ROM 8:37.1 COR 15:57.EPH 6:10.JER 9:3.1 SAM 18:17.HAG 2:4-5.JOHN 4:35.HEB 10:37

You have given a banner to those who fear You, that it may be displayed because of the truth.

## January 10

May your whole spirit, soul, and body be preserved blameless at the coming of our Lord Jesus Christ.

Christ . . . loved the church and gave Himself for it, . . . that He might present it to Himself a glorious church, not having spot or wrinkle or any such thing, but that it should be holy and without blemish. ◊ Him we preach, warning every man and teaching every man in all wisdom, that we may present every man perfect in Christ Jesus.

The peace of God . . . surpasses all understanding. ◊ Let the peace of God rule in your hearts, to which also you were called in one body.

May our Lord Jesus Christ Himself, and our God and Father, who has loved us and given us everlasting consolation and good hope by grace, comfort your hearts and establish you in every good word and work. ◊ [God] will also confirm you to the end, that you may be blameless in the day of our Lord Jesus Christ.

1 THESS 5:23.EPH 5:25,27.COL 1:28.PHIL 4:7.COL 3:15.2 THESS 2:16-17.1 COR 1:8

For us there is only one God, the Father, of whom are all things, and we for Him; and one Lord Jesus Christ. ◊ All should honor the Son just as they honor the Father. He who does not honor the Son does not honor the Father who sent Him. ◊ Therefore by Him let us continually offer the sacrifice of praise to God, that is, the fruit of our lips, giving thanks to His name. ◊ Whoever offers praise glorifies Me; and to him who orders his conduct aright I will show the salvation of God.

I looked, and behold, a great multitude which no one could number, of all nations, tribes, peoples, and tongues, standing before the throne and before the Lamb, clothed with white robes, with palm branches in their hands, and crying out with a loud voice, saying, "Salvation belongs to our God who sits on the throne, and to the Lamb!" ◊ Amen! Blessing and glory and wisdom, thanksgiving and honor and power and might, be to our God forever and ever. Amen.

PS 65:1.1 COR 8:6.JOHN 5:23.HEB 13:15.PS 50:23.REV 7:9-10.REV 7:12

## January 11

Praise is awaiting You, O God, in Zion.

## January 12

[You] are in Christ Jesus, who became
for us wisdom from God—and
righteousness and sanctification and
redemption. ◊ Can you search out the
deep things of God? Can you find out
the limits of the Almighty? . . . They
are higher than heaven—what can you
do? Deeper than Sheol—what can you
know?

We speak the wisdom of God in a
mystery, the hidden wisdom which God
ordained before the ages for our glory.
◊ The mystery, which from the
beginning of the ages has been hidden
in God who created all things through
Jesus Christ; . . . to the intent that now
the manifold wisdom of God might be
made known by the church to the
principalities and powers in the
heavenly places.

If any of you lacks wisdom, let him
ask of God, who gives to all liberally
and without reproach, and it will be
given to him. ◊ The wisdom that is
from above is first pure, then peaceable,
gentle, willing to yield, full of mercy
and good fruits, without partiality and
without hypocrisy.

JUDE 1:25.1 COR 1:30.JOB 11:7-8.1 COR 2:7.EPH
3:9-10.JAMES 1:5.JAMES 3:17

Cast your burden on the Lord, and He shall sustain you; He shall never permit the righteous to be moved. ◊ I will trust and not be afraid; for YAH, the Lord, is my strength and my song; He also has become my salvation.

Why are you fearful, O you of little faith? ◊ Be anxious for nothing, but in everything by prayer and supplication, with thanksgiving, let your requests be made known to God; and the peace of God, which surpasses all understanding, will guard your hearts and minds through Christ Jesus. ◊ In quietness and confidence shall be your strength.

The work of righteousness will be peace, and the effect of righteousness, quietness and assurance forever. ◊ Peace I leave with you, My peace I give to you; not as the world gives do I give to you. Let not your heart be troubled, neither let it be afraid. ◊ Peace from Him who is and who was and who is to come.

IS 26:3.PS 55:22.IS 12:2.MATT 8:26.PHIL 4:6-7.IS 30:15.IS 32:17.JOHN 14:27.REV 1:4

You will keep him in perfect peace, whose mind is stayed on You, because he trusts in You.

## January 14

**My Father is greater than I.**

When you pray, say: Our Father in heaven. ◊ My Father and your Father, and . . . My God and your God.

As the Father gave Me commandment, so I do. ◊ The words that I speak to you I do not speak on My own authority; but the Father who dwells in Me does the works.

The Father loves the Son, and has given all things into His hand. ◊ You have given Him authority over all flesh, that He should give eternal life to as many as You have given Him.

"Lord, show us the Father, and it is sufficient for us." Jesus said to him, "Have I been with you so long, and yet you have not known Me, Philip? He who has seen Me has seen the Father; so how can you say, 'Show us the Father'?" ◊ I and My Father are one. ◊ As the Father loved Me, I also have loved you; abide in My love. If you keep My commandments, you will abide in My love, just as I have kept My Father's commandments and abide in His love.

JOHN 14:28.LUKE 11:2.JOHN 20:17.JOHN 14:31.JOHN 14:10.JOHN 3:35.JOHN 17:2.JOHN 14:8-9.JOHN 10:30.JOHN 15:9-10

If then you were raised with Christ, seek those things which are above, where Christ is, sitting at the right hand of God. Set your mind on things above, not on things on the earth. For . . . your life is hidden with Christ in God. ◊ For our citizenship is in heaven, from which we also eagerly wait for the Savior, the Lord Jesus Christ, who will transform our lowly body that it may be conformed to His glorious body, according to the working by which He is able even to subdue all things to Himself.

The flesh lusts against the Spirit, and the Spirit against the flesh; and these are contrary to one another, so that you do not do the things that you wish. ◊ Brethren, we are debtors—not to the flesh, to live according to the flesh. For if you live according to the flesh you will die; but if by the Spirit you put to death the deeds of the body, you will live. ◊ Beloved, I beg you as sojourners and pilgrims, abstain from fleshly lusts which war against the soul.

PS 119:25.COL 3:1-3.PHIL 3:20-21.GAL 5:17.ROM 8:12-13.1 PET 2:11

My soul clings to the dust; revive me according to Your word.

## January 16

It pleased the Father that in Him all the fullness should dwell.

The Father loves the Son, and has given all things into His hand. ◊ God also has highly exalted Him and given Him the name which is above every name, that at the name of Jesus every knee should bow, . . . and that every tongue should confess that Jesus Christ is Lord, to the glory of God the Father. ◊ [He is] far above all principality and power and might and dominion, and every name that is named, not only in this age but also in that which is to come. ◊ By Him all things were created that are in heaven and that are on earth, visible and invisible, whether thrones or dominions or principalities or powers. All things were created through Him and for Him.

Christ died and rose and lived again, that He might be Lord of both the dead and the living. ◊ And you are complete in Him, who is the head of all principality and power. ◊ Of His fullness we have all received.

COL 1:19.JOHN 3:35.PHIL 2:9-11.EPH 1:21.COL 1:16.ROM 14:9.COL 2:10.JOHN 1:16

God has sent His only begotten Son into the world, that we might live through Him. In this is love, not that we loved God, but that He loved us and sent His Son to be the propitiation for our sins.

Who is a God like You, pardoning iniquity and passing over the transgression of the remnant of His heritage? He does not retain His anger forever, because He delights in mercy. He will again have compassion on us, and will subdue our iniquities. You will cast all our sins into the depths of the sea. ◊ O Lord my God, I cried out to You, and You have healed me. O Lord, You have brought my soul up from the grave; You have kept me alive, that I should not go down to the pit. ◊ When my soul fainted within me, I remembered the Lord; and my prayer went up to You, into Your holy temple. ◊ I waited patiently for the Lord. . . . He . . . brought me up out of a horrible pit, out of the miry clay, and set my feet upon a rock, and established my steps.

IS 38:17.1 JOHN 4:9-10.MIC 7:18-19.PS 30:2-3.JON 2:7.PS 40:1-2

But You have lovingly delivered my soul from the pit of corruption.

## January 18

Jesus . . . was made a little lower than the angels, for the suffering of death . . . that He, by the grace of God, might taste death for everyone. ◊ One died for all. ◊ As by one man's disobedience many were made sinners, so also by one Man's obedience many will be made righteous.

The first man Adam became a living being. The last Adam became a life-giving spirit. However, the spiritual is not first, but the natural, and afterward the spiritual. ◊ God said, "Let Us make man in Our image, according to Our likeness." . . . So God created man in His own image; in the image of God He created him. ◊ God . . . has in these last days spoken to us by His Son, . . . the brightness of His glory and the express image of His person. ◊ You have given Him authority over all flesh.

The first man was of the earth, made of dust; the second Man is the Lord from heaven. As was the man of dust, so also are those who are made of dust; and as is the heavenly Man, so also are those who are heavenly.

ROM 5:14.HEB 2:9.2 COR 5:14.ROM 5:19.1 COR 15:45-46.GEN 1:26-27.HEB 1:1-3.JOHN 17:2.1 COR 15:47-48

Whoever desires to become great among you, let him be your servant. And whoever desires to be first among you, let him be your slave—just as the Son of Man did not come to be served, but to serve, and to give His life a ransom for many.

If anyone thinks himself to be something, when he is nothing, he deceives himself. ◊ I say, through the grace given to me, to everyone, . . . not to think of himself more highly than he ought to think, but to think soberly, as God has dealt to each one a measure of faith. ◊ When you have done all those things which you are commanded, say, "We are unprofitable servants. We have done what was our duty to do."

Our boasting is this: . . . we conducted ourselves in the world in simplicity and godly sincerity, not with fleshly wisdom but by the grace of God. ◊ We have this treasure in earthen vessels, that the excellence of the power may be of God and not of us.

ACTS 20:19.MATT 20:26-28.GAL 6:3.ROM 12:3.LUKE 17:10.2 COR 1:12.2 COR 4:7

## January 20

**His name will be called Wonderful.**

The Word became flesh and dwelt among us, and we beheld His glory, the glory as of the only begotten of the Father, full of grace and truth. ◊ For You have magnified Your word above all Your name.

They shall call His name Immanuel, which is translated, "God with us." ◊ Call His name JESUS, for He will save His people from their sins.

All should honor the Son just as they honor the Father. ◊ God . . . has highly exalted Him and given Him the name which is above every name. ◊ Far above all principality and power and might and dominion, and every name that is named, not only in this age but also in that which is to come. And He put all things under His feet. ◊ He has . . . a name written: KING OF KINGS AND LORD OF LORDS.

As for the Almighty, we cannot find Him. ◊ What is His name, and what is His Son's name, if you know?

IS 9:6.JOHN 1:14.PS 138:2.MATT 1:23.MATT 1:21.JOHN 5:23.PHIL 2:9.EPH 1:21-22.REV 19:16.JOB 37:23.PROV 30:4

He is like a refiner's fire and like fuller's soap. He will sit as a refiner and a purifier of silver; He will purify the sons of Levi, and purge them as gold and silver, that they may offer to the Lord an offering in righteousness.

Every branch in Me that does not bear fruit He takes away.

We . . . glory in tribulations, knowing that tribulation produces perseverance; and perseverance, character; and character, hope. Hope does not disappoint, because the love of God has been poured out in our hearts by the Holy Spirit who was given to us. ◊ If you endure chastening, God deals with you as with sons; for what son is there whom a father does not chasten? But if you are without chastening, of which all have become partakers, then you are illegitimate and not sons. ◊ Now no chastening seems to be joyful for the present, but grievous; nevertheless, afterward it yields the peaceable fruit of righteousness to those who have been trained by it. Therefore strengthen the hands which hang down, and the feeble knees.

JOHN 15:2.MAL 3:2-3.ROM 5:3-5.HEB 12:7-8.HEB 12:11-12

## January 22

For this is God, our God forever and ever; He will be our guide even to death.

O Lord, You are my God. I will exalt You, I will praise Your name, for You have done wonderful things; Your counsels of old are faithfulness and truth. ◊ You, O Lord, are the portion of my inheritance and my cup.

He restores my soul; He leads me in the paths of righteousness for His name's sake. Yea, though I walk through the valley of the shadow of death, I will fear no evil; for You are with me; Your rod and Your staff, they comfort me. ◊ You hold me by my right hand. You will guide me with Your counsel, and afterward receive me to glory. Whom have I in heaven but You? And there is none upon earth that I desire besides You. My flesh and my heart fail; but God is the strength of my heart and my portion forever. ◊ Our heart shall rejoice in Him, because we have trusted in His holy name. ◊ The Lord will perfect that which concerns me; Your mercy, O Lord, endures forever; do not forsake the works of Your hands.

PS 48:14.IS 25:1.PS 16:5.PS 23:3-4.PS 73:23-26.PS 33:21.PS 138:8

**Hope does not disappoint.**

They shall not be ashamed who wait for Me. ◊ Blessed is the man who trusts in the Lord, and whose hope is the Lord. ◊ You will keep him in perfect peace, whose mind is stayed on You, because he trusts in You. Trust in the Lord forever, for in YAH, the Lord, is everlasting strength. ◊ My soul, wait silently for God alone, for my expectation is from Him. He only is my rock and my salvation; He is my defense; I shall not be moved. ◊ I am not ashamed, for I know whom I have believed.

God, determining to show more abundantly to the heirs of promise the immutability of His counsel, confirmed it by an oath, that by two immutable things, in which it is impossible for God to lie, we might have strong consolation, who have fled for refuge to lay hold of the hope set before us. This hope we have as an anchor of the soul, both sure and steadfast, and which enters the Presence behind the veil, where the forerunner has entered for us, even Jesus.

ROM 5:5.IS 49:23.JER 17:7.IS 26:3-4.PS 62:5-6.2 TIM 1:12.HEB 6:17-20

## January 24

**The Lord is at hand.**

The Lord Himself will descend from heaven with a shout, with the voice of an archangel, and with the trumpet of God. And the dead in Christ will rise first. We who are alive and remain shall be caught up together with them in the clouds to meet the Lord in the air. And thus we shall always be with the Lord. Therefore comfort one another with these words. ◊ He who testifies to these things says, "Surely I am coming quickly." Amen. Even so, come, Lord Jesus!

Therefore, beloved, looking forward to these things, be diligent to be found by Him in peace, without spot and blameless. ◊ Abstain from every form of evil. May the God of peace Himself sanctify you completely; and may your whole spirit, soul, and body be preserved blameless at the coming of our Lord Jesus Christ. He who calls you is faithful, who also will do it.

You also be patient. Establish your hearts, for the coming of the Lord is at hand.

PHIL 4:5.1 THESS 4:16-18.REV 22:20.2 PET 3:14.1 THESS 5:22-24.JAMES 5:8

He made Him who knew no sin to be sin for us, that we might become the righteousness of God in Him. ◊ Christ has redeemed us from the curse of the law, having become a curse for us. ◊ Christ Jesus . . . became for us wisdom from God—and righteousness and sanctification and redemption. ◊ Not by works of righteousness which we have done, but according to His mercy He saved us, through the washing of regeneration and renewing of the Holy Spirit, whom He poured out on us abundantly through Jesus Christ our Savior.

I also count all things loss for the excellence of the knowledge of Christ Jesus my Lord, for whom I have suffered the loss of all things, and count them as rubbish, that I may gain Christ and be found in Him, not having my own righteousness, which is from the law, but that which is through faith in Christ, the righteousness which is from God by faith.

ROM 3:22.2 COR 5:21.GAL 3:13.1 COR 1:30.TITUS 3:5-6.PHIL 3:8-9

## January 25

The righteousness of God . . . is through faith in Jesus Christ to all and on all who believe.

## January 26

Therefore let us go forth to Him, outside the camp, bearing His reproach. For here we have no continuing city, but we seek the one to come.

Beloved, do not think it strange concerning the fiery trial which is to try you, as though some strange thing happened to you; but rejoice to the extent that you partake of Christ's sufferings, that when His glory is revealed, you may also be glad with exceeding joy. ◊ As you are partakers of the sufferings, so also you will partake of the consolation.

If you are reproached for the name of Christ, blessed are you, for the Spirit of glory and of God rests upon you. On their part He is blasphemed, but on your part He is glorified.

So they departed from the presence of the council, rejoicing that they were counted worthy to suffer shame for His name. ◊ Choosing rather to suffer affliction with the people of God than to enjoy the passing pleasures of sin, esteeming the reproach of Christ greater riches than the treasures in Egypt; for he looked to the reward.

HEB 13:13-14.1 PET 4:12-13.2 COR 1:7.1 PET 4:14.ACTS 5:41.HEB 11:25-26

God . . . has in these last days spoken to us by His Son, . . . who being the brightness of His glory and the express image of His person, and upholding all things by the word of His power, when He had by Himself purged our sins, sat down at the right hand of the Majesty on high. ◊ He made Him who knew no sin to be sin for us.

Conduct yourselves throughout the time of your sojourning here in fear; knowing that you were not redeemed with corruptible things, like silver or gold, . . . but with the precious blood of Christ, as of a lamb without blemish and without spot. He indeed was foreordained before the foundation of the world, but was manifest in these last times for you. ◊ The love of Christ constrains us, because we judge thus: that if One died for all, then all died; and He died for all, that those who live should live no longer for themselves, but for Him who died for them and rose again.

1 JOHN 3:5.HEB 1:1-3.2 COR 5:21.1 PET 1:17-20.2 COR 5:14-15

You know that He was manifested to take away our sins, and in Him there is no sin.

## January 28

*As your days, so shall your strength be.*

When they arrest you and deliver you up, do not worry beforehand, or premeditate what you will speak. But whatever is given you in that hour, speak that; for it is not you who speak, but the Holy Spirit. ◊ Do not worry about tomorrow, for tomorrow will worry about its own things. Sufficient for the day is its own trouble.

The God of Israel is He who gives strength and power to His people. Blessed be God! ◊ He gives power to the weak, and to those who have no might He increases strength.

My grace is sufficient for you, for My strength is made perfect in weakness. Therefore most gladly I will rather boast in my infirmities, that the power of Christ may rest upon me. Therefore I take pleasure in infirmities, in reproaches, in needs, in persecutions, in distresses, for Christ's sake. For when I am weak, then I am strong. I can do all things through Christ who strengthens me. ◊ O my soul, march on in strength!

DEUT 33:25.MARK 13:11.MATT 6:34.PS 68:35.IS 40:29. 2 COR 12:9-10.PHIL 4:13.JUDG 5:21

O Lord, You have searched me and known me. You know my sitting down and my rising up; You understand my thought afar off. You comprehend my path and my lying down, and are acquainted with all my ways. For there is not a word on my tongue, but behold, O Lord, You know it altogether . . . . Such knowledge is too wonderful for me; it is high, I cannot attain it.

The eyes of the Lord are in every place, keeping watch on the evil and the good. ◊ The ways of man are before the eyes of the Lord, and He ponders all his paths. ◊ God knows your hearts. For what is highly esteemed among men is an abomination in the sight of God. ◊ The eyes of the Lord run to and fro throughout the whole earth, to show Himself strong on behalf of those whose heart is loyal to Him.

Jesus . . . knew all men, and had no need that anyone should testify of man, for He knew what was in man. ◊ Lord, You know all things; You know that I love You.

You-Are-the-God-Who-Sees.

GEN 16:13.PS 139:1-4,6.PROV 15:3.PROV 5:21.LUKE 16:15.2 CHR 16:9.JOHN 2:24-25.JOHN 21:17

## January 30

Let us run with endurance the race that is set before us, looking unto Jesus, the author and finisher of our faith.

If anyone desires to come after Me, let him deny himself, and take up his cross daily, and follow Me. ◊ Whoever of you does not forsake all that he has cannot be My disciple. ◊ Therefore let us cast off the works of darkness.

Everyone who competes for the prize is temperate in all things. Now they do it to obtain a perishable crown, but we for an imperishable crown. Therefore I run thus: not with uncertainty. Thus I fight: not as one who beats the air. But I discipline my body and bring it into subjection, lest, when I have preached to others, I myself should become disqualified. ◊ Brethren, I do not count myself to have apprehended; but one thing I do, forgetting those things which are behind and reaching forward to those things which are ahead, I press toward the goal for the prize of the upward call of God in Christ Jesus. ◊ Let us know, let us pursue the knowledge of the Lord.

HEB 12:1-2.LUKE 9:23.LUKE 14:33.ROM 13:12.1 COR 9:25-27.PHIL 3:13-14.HOS 6:3

Fight the good fight of faith. ◊ For the weapons of our warfare are not carnal but mighty in God for pulling down strongholds, casting down arguments and . . . bringing every thought into captivity to the obedience of Christ.

Brethren, we are debtors—not to the flesh, to live according to the flesh. For if you live according to the flesh you will die; but if by the Spirit you put to death the deeds of the body, you will live.

For the flesh lusts against the Spirit, and the Spirit against the flesh; and these are contrary to one another, so that you do not do the things that you wish. ◊ I see another law in my members, warring against the law of my mind, and bringing me into captivity to the law of sin which is in my members. ◊ We are more than conquerors through Him who loved us.

NUM 33:55.1 TIM 6:12.2 COR 10:4-5.ROM 8:12-13.GAL 5:17.ROM 7:23.ROM 8:37

## January 31

If you do not drive out the inhabitants of the land from before you, then it shall be that those whom you let remain shall be irritants in your eyes and thorns in your sides, and they shall harass you in the land where you dwell.

## February 1

**Whom having not seen you love.**

We walk by faith, not by sight. ◊ We love Him because He first loved us. ◊ And we have known and believed the love that God has for us. God is love, and he who abides in love abides in God, and God in him. ◊ In Him you also trusted, after you heard the word of truth, the gospel of your salvation; in whom also, having believed, you were sealed with the Holy Spirit of promise. ◊ To them God willed to make known what are the riches of the glory of this mystery among the Gentiles: which is Christ in you, the hope of glory.

If someone says, "I love God," and hates his brother, he is a liar; for he who does not love his brother whom he has seen, how can he love God whom he has not seen?

Jesus said to him, "Thomas, because you have seen Me, you have believed. Blessed are those who have not seen and yet have believed." ◊ Blessed are all those who put their trust in Him.

1 PET 1:8.2 COR 5:7.1 JOHN 4:19.1 JOHN 4:16.EPH 1:13.COL 1:27.1 JOHN 4:20.JOHN 20:29.PS 2:12

Why do you sleep? Rise and pray, lest you enter into temptation. ◊ The spirit indeed is willing, but the flesh is weak.

Two things I request of You (deprive me not before I die): remove falsehood and lies far from me; give me neither poverty nor riches—feed me with the food You prescribe for me; lest I be full and deny You, and say, "Who is the ·Lord?" Or lest I be poor and steal, and profane the name of my God.

The Lord shall preserve you from all evil; He shall preserve your soul. ◊ I will deliver you from the hand of the wicked, and I will redeem you from the grip of the terrible. ◊ Whoever is born of God does not sin; but he who has been born of God keeps himself, and the wicked one does not touch him.

Because you have kept My command to persevere, I also will keep you from the hour of trial which shall come upon the whole world, to test those who dwell on the earth. ◊ The Lord knows how to deliver the godly out of temptations.

1 CHR 4:10.LUKE 22:46.MATT 26:41.PROV 30:7-9.PS 121:7.JER 15:21.1 JOHN 5:18.REV 3:10.2 PET 2:9

Oh, . . . that You would keep me from evil.

## February 3

"Be strong . . . and work; for I am with you," says the LORD of hosts.

I am the vine, you are the branches. He who abides in Me, and I in him, bears much fruit; for without Me you can do nothing. ◇ I can do all things through Christ who strengthens me. ◇ [Be] strong in the Lord and in the power of His might. ◇ The joy of the Lord is your strength.

Thus says the Lord of hosts: "Let your hands be strong, you who have been hearing in these days these words by the mouth of the prophets." ◇ Strengthen the weak hands, and make firm the feeble knees. Say to those who are fearful-hearted, "Be strong, do not fear!" ◇ The Lord turned to him and said, "Go in this might of yours."

If God is for us, who can be against us? ◇ Therefore, since we have this ministry, as we have received mercy, we do not lose heart.

Let us not grow weary while doing good, for in due season we shall reap if we do not lose heart. ◇ Thanks be to God, who gives us the victory through our Lord Jesus Christ.

HAG 2:4.JOHN 15:5.PHIL 4:13.EPH 6:10.NEH 8:10.ZECH 8:9.IS 35:3-4.JUDG 6:14.ROM 8:31.2 COR 4:1 GAL 6:9.1 COR 15:57

The LORD has said to you, "You shall not return that way again."

Truly if they had called to mind that country from which they had come out, they would have had opportunity to return. But now they desire a better, that is, a heavenly country. By faith Moses . . . [chose] rather to suffer affliction with the people of God than to enjoy the passing pleasures of sin, esteeming the reproach of Christ greater riches than the treasures in Egypt. ◊ The just shall live by faith; but if anyone draws back, my soul has no pleasure in him. ◊ No one, having put his hand to the plow, and looking back, is fit for the kingdom of God.

God forbid that I should glory except in the cross of our Lord Jesus Christ, by whom the world has been crucified to me, and I to the world. ◊ Come out from among them and be separate, says the Lord, . . . and I will receive you.

He who has begun a good work in you will complete it until the day of Jesus Christ.

DEUT 17:16.HEB 11:15-16.HEB 11:24-26.HEB 10:38.LUKE 9:62.GAL 6:14.2 COR 6:17.PHIL 1:6

## February 5

God commanded the man, . . . "In the day that you eat of it you shall surely die." ◊ She took of its fruit and ate. She also gave to her husband with her, and he ate.

The wages of sin is death, but the gift of God is eternal life in Christ Jesus our Lord. ◊ If by the one man's offense death reigned through the one, much more those who receive abundance of grace and of the gift of righteousness will reign in life through the One, Jesus Christ. ◊ Since by man came death, by Man also came the resurrection of the dead. For as in Adam all die, even so in Christ all shall be made alive. ◊ Our Savior Jesus Christ . . . has abolished death and brought life and immortality to light through the gospel.

God has given us eternal life, and this life is in His Son. He who does not have the Son of God does not have life. ◊ For God did not send His Son into the world to condemn the world, but that the world through Him might be saved.

JOHN 10:10.GEN 2:16-17.GEN 3:6.ROM 6:23.ROM.5:17.1 COR 15:21-22.2 TIM 1:10.1 JOHN 5:11-12.JOHN 3:17

You know the grace of our Lord Jesus Christ, that though He was rich, yet for your sakes He became poor, that you through His poverty might become rich. ◊ Where sin abounded, grace abounded much more.

That in the ages to come He might show the exceeding riches of His grace in His kindness toward us in Christ Jesus. For by grace you have been saved through faith, and that not of yourselves; it is the gift of God, not of works, lest anyone should boast. ◊ Knowing that a man is not justified by the works of the law but by faith in Jesus Christ, even we have believed in Christ Jesus, that we might be justified by faith in Christ and not by the works of the law; for by the works of the law no flesh shall be justified. ◊ According to His mercy He saved us, through the washing of regeneration and renewing of the Holy Spirit, whom He poured out on us abundantly through Jesus Christ our Savior.

1 TIM 1:14.2 COR 8:9.ROM 5:20.EPH 2:7-9.GAL 2:16.TITUS 3:5-6

## February 6

The grace of our Lord was exceedingly abundant, with faith and love which are in Christ Jesus.

## February 7

When you have eaten and are full, . . . you shall bless the LORD your God for the good land which He has given you.

Beware that you do not forget the Lord your God. ◊ One of them, when he saw that he was healed, returned, and with a loud voice glorified God, and fell down on his face at His feet, giving Him thanks. And he was a Samaritan. So Jesus answered and said, "Were there not ten cleansed? But where are the nine? Were there not any found who returned to give glory to God except this foreigner?"

Every creature of God is good, and nothing is to be refused if it is received with thanksgiving; for it is sanctified by the word of God and prayer. ◊ He who eats, eats to the Lord, for he gives God thanks. ◊ The blessing of the Lord makes one rich, and He adds no sorrow with it.

Bless the Lord, O my soul; and all that is within me, bless His holy name! Bless the Lord, O my soul, . . . who forgives all your iniquities, . . . who crowns you with lovingkindness and tender mercies.

DEUT 8:10.DEUT 8:11.LUKE 17:15-18.1 TIM 4:4-5.ROM 14:6.PROV 10:22.PS 103:1-4

The Lord said, "Shall I hide from Abraham what I am doing?" ◊ It has been given to you to know the mysteries of the kingdom of heaven. ◊ But God has revealed them to us through His Spirit. For the Spirit searches all things, yes, the deep things of God. ◊ The hidden wisdom which God ordained before the ages for our glory.

Blessed is the man whom You choose, and cause to approach You, that he may dwell in Your courts. We shall be satisfied with the goodness of Your house, of Your holy temple. ◊ The secret of the Lord is with those who fear Him, and He will show them His covenant. ◊ I have given to them the words which You have given Me; and they have received them, and have known surely that I came forth from You; and they have believed that You sent Me. ◊ You are My friends if you do whatever I command you.

JOHN 15:15.GEN 18:17.MATT 13:11.1 COR 2:10.1 COR 2:7 PS 65:4.PS 25:14.JOHN 17:8.JOHN 15:14

## February 8

No longer do I call you servants, for a servant does not know what his master is doing; but I have called you friends.

## February 9

**Now he is comforted.**

Your sun shall no longer go down, nor shall your moon withdraw itself; for the Lord will be your everlasting light, and the days of your mourning shall be ended. ◊ He will swallow up death forever, and the Lord God will wipe away tears from all faces; the rebuke of His people He will take away from all the earth. ◊ These are the ones who come out of the great tribulation, and washed their robes and made them white in the blood of the Lamb. Therefore they are before the throne of God, and serve Him day and night in His temple. And He who sits on the throne will dwell among them. They shall neither hunger anymore nor thirst anymore; the sun shall not strike them, nor any heat; for the Lamb who is in the midst of the throne will shepherd them and lead them to living fountains of waters. ◊ And God will wipe away every tear from their eyes; there shall be no more death, nor sorrow, nor crying; and there shall be no more pain, for the former things have passed away.

LUKE 16:25.IS 60:20.IS 25:8.REV 7:14-17 REV 21:4

The natural man does not receive the things of the Spirit of God, . . . nor can he know them, because they are spiritually discerned. ◊ Open my eyes, that I may see wondrous things from Your law.

I am the light of the world. He who follows Me shall not walk in darkness. ◊ We all, with unveiled face, beholding as in a mirror the glory of the Lord, are being transformed into the same image . . . just as by the Spirit of the Lord. ◊ It is the God who commanded light to shine out of darkness who has shone in our hearts to give the light of the knowledge of the glory of God in the face of Jesus Christ.

The God of our Lord Jesus Christ, the Father of glory, . . . give to you the spirit of wisdom and revelation in the knowledge of Him, . . . that you may know what is the hope of His calling, what are the riches of the glory of His inheritance in the saints.

LUKE 11:34.1 COR 2:14.PS 119:18.JOHN 8:12.2 COR 3:18.2 COR 4:6.EPH 1:17-18

## February 10

The lamp of the body is the eye. Therefore, when your eye is good, your whole body also is full of light.

## February 11

Then those who feared the LORD spoke to one another, and the LORD listened and heard them; so a book of remembrance was written before Him for those who fear the LORD and who meditate on His name.

So it was, while they conversed and reasoned, that Jesus Himself drew near and went with them. ◊ Where two or three are gathered together in My name, I am there in the midst of them. ◊ My fellow workers, whose names are in the Book of Life.

Let the word of Christ dwell in you richly in all wisdom, teaching and admonishing one another in psalms and hymns and spiritual songs, singing with grace in your hearts to the Lord. ◊ Exhort one another daily, while it is called "Today," lest any of you be hardened through the deceitfulness of sin.

Every idle word men may speak, they will give account of it in the day of judgment. For by your words you will be justified, and by your words you will be condemned.

MAL 3:16.LUKE 24:15.MATT 18:20.PHIL 4:3.COL 3:16.HEB 3:13.MATT 12:36-37

I have manifested Your name to the men whom You have given Me out of the world. They were Yours, You gave them to Me, and they have kept Your word. . . . I pray for them. I do not pray for the world but for those whom You have given Me, for they are Yours. And all Mine are Yours, and Yours are Mine, and I am glorified in them. ◊ Father, I desire that they also whom You gave Me may be with Me where I am, that they may behold My glory which You have given Me; for You loved Me before the foundation of the world.

I will come again and receive you to Myself. ◊ He comes, in that Day, to be glorified in His saints and to be admired among all those who believe. ◊ Then we who are alive and remain shall be caught up together with them in the clouds to meet the Lord in the air. And thus we shall always be with the Lord. ◊ You shall also be a crown of glory in the hand of the Lord, and a royal diadem in the hand of your God.

MAL 3:17.JOHN 17:6,9-10.JOHN 17:24.JOHN 14:3. 2 THESS 1:10.1THESS 4:17.IS 62:3

## February 12

"They shall be Mine," says the LORD of hosts, "or the day that I make them My jewels."

## February 13

The Man Christ Jesus. ◊ [Jesus came] . . . in the likeness of men. [He was] found in appearance as a man. ◊ Inasmuch then as the children have partaken of flesh and blood, He Himself likewise shared in the same, that through death He might destroy him who had the power of death.

I am He who lives, and was dead, and behold, I am alive forevermore. ◊ Christ, having been raised from the dead- dies no more. Death no longer has dominion over Him. For the death that He died, He died to sin once for all; but the life that He lives, He lives to God. ◊ What then if you should see the Son of Man ascend where He was before? ◊ He raised Him from the dead and seated Him at His right hand in the heavenly places. ◊ In Him dwells all the fullness of the Godhead bodily. ◊ Though He was crucified in weakness, yet He lives by the power of God. For we also are weak in Him, but we shall live with Him by the power of God toward you.

EZEK 1:26.1 TIM 2:5.PHIL 2:7-8.HEB 2:14.REV 1:18.ROM 6:9-10.JOHN 6:62.EPH 1:20.COL 2:9.2 COR 13:4

I delight to do Your will, O my God, and Your law is within my heart.

Do not think that I came to destroy the Law or the Prophets. I did not come to destroy but to fulfill. For assuredly, I say to you, till heaven and earth pass away, one jot or one tittle will by no means pass from the law till all is fulfilled. ◊ The Lord is well pleased for His righteousness' sake; He will magnify the law and make it honorable. ◊ Unless your righteousness exceeds the righteousness of the scribes and Pharisees, you will by no means enter the kingdom of heaven.

What the law could not do in that it was weak through the flesh, God did by sending His own Son in the likeness of sinful flesh, on account of sin: He condemned sin in the flesh, that the righteous requirement of the law might be fulfilled in us who do not walk according to the flesh but according to the Spirit. ◊ Christ is the end of the law for righteousness to everyone who believes.

MATT 3:15.PS 40:8.MATT 5:17-18.IS 42:21.MATT 5:20.ROM 8:3-4.ROM 10:4

Permit it to be so now, for thus it is fitting for us to fulfill all righteousness.

**Who can say, "I have made my heart clean"?**

The Lord looks down from heaven upon the children of men, to see if there are any who understand, who seek God. They have all turned aside, they have together become corrupt; there is none who does good, no, not one. ◊ Those who are in the flesh cannot please God.

To will is present with me, but how to perform what is good I do not find. For the good that I will to do, I do not do; but the evil I will not to do, that I practice. ◊ We are all like an unclean thing, and all our righteousnesses are like filthy rags; we all fade as a leaf, and our iniquities, like the wind, have taken us away.

The Scripture has confined all under sin, that the promise by faith in Jesus Christ might be given to those who believe. ◊ God was in Christ reconciling the world to Himself, not imputing their trespasses to them. ◊ If we say that we have no sin, we deceive ourselves, and the truth is not in us. If we confess our sins, He is faithful and just to forgive us our sins and to cleanse us from all unrighteousness.

PROV 20:9.PS 14:2-3.ROM 8:8.ROM 7:18-19.IS 64:6.GAL 3:22.2 COR 5:19.1 JOHN 1:8-9

Your name is ointment poured forth.

Christ . . . has loved us and given Himself for us, an offering and a sacrifice to God for a sweet-smelling aroma. ◊ Therefore, to you who believe, He is precious. ◊ God also has highly exalted Him and given Him the name which is above every name, that at the name of Jesus every knee should bow. ◊ In Him dwells all the fullness of the Godhead bodily.

The love of God has been poured out in our hearts by the Holy Spirit who was given to us. ◊ The house was filled with the fragrance of the oil. ◊ They saw the boldness of Peter and John . . . and they realized that they had been with Jesus.

O Lord, our Lord, how excellent is Your name in all the earth, You who set Your glory above the heavens! ◊ Immanuel, . . . God with us. ◊ His name will be called Wonderful, Counselor, Mighty God, Everlasting Father, Prince of Peace. ◊ The name of the Lord is a strong tower; the righteous run to it and are safe.

SONG 1:3.EPH 5:2.1 PET 2:7.PHIL 2:9-10.COL 2:9.ROM 5:5.JOHN 12:3.ACTS 4:13.PS 8:1.MATT 1:23.IS 9:6.PROV 18:10

## February 17

The whole bull he shall carry outside the camp to a clean place, where the ashes are poured out, and burn it on wood with fire.

They took Jesus and led Him away. And He, bearing His cross, went out to a place called the Place of a Skull, which is called in Hebrew, Golgotha, where they crucified Him. ◊ The bodies of those beasts, whose blood is brought into the sanctuary by the high priest for sin, are burned outside the camp. Therefore Jesus also, that He might sanctify the people with His own blood, suffered outside the gate. Therefore let us go forth to Him, outside the camp, bearing His reproach. ◊ I have suffered the loss of all things . . . that I may know . . . the fellowship of His sufferings.

But rejoice to the extent that you partake of Christ's sufferings, that when His glory is revealed, you may also be glad with exceeding joy. ◊ Our light affliction, which is but for a moment, is working for us a far more exceeding and eternal weight of glory.

LEV 4:12.JOHN 19:16-18.HEB 13:11-13.PHIL 3:8-10.
1 PET 4:13.2 COR 4:17

There are many who say, "Who will show us any good?" Lord, lift up the light of Your countenance upon us. ◊ But I will sing of Your power; yes, I will sing aloud of Your mercy in the morning; for You have been my defense and refuge in the day of my trouble.

In my prosperity I said, "I shall never be moved." . . . You hid Your face, and I was troubled. I cried out to You, O Lord; and to the Lord I made supplication: "What profit is there in my blood, when I go down to the pit? Will the dust praise You? Will it declare Your truth? Hear, O Lord, and have mercy on me; Lord, be my helper!"

"For a mere moment I have forsaken you, but with great mercies I will gather you. With a little wrath I hid My face from you for a moment; but with everlasting kindness I will have mercy on you," says the Lord, your Redeemer. ◊ Sorrow will be turned into joy. ◊ Weeping may endure for a night, but joy comes in the morning.

JER 17:17.PS 4:6.PS 59:16.PS 30:6-10.IS 54:7-8.JOHN 16:20.PS 30:5

## February 18

You are my hope in the day of doom.

## February 19

The LORD gives wisdom; from His mouth come knowledge and understanding.

Trust in the Lord with all your heart, and lean not on your own understanding. ◊ If any of you lacks wisdom, let him ask of God, who gives to all liberally and without reproach, and it will be given to him. ◊ The foolishness of God is wiser than men, and the weakness of God is stronger than men. ◊ I will give you a mouth and wisdom which all your adversaries will not be able to contradict or resist. ◊ But God has chosen the foolish things of the world to put to shame the wise.

The entrance of Your words gives light; it gives understanding to the simple. ◊ Your word I have hidden in my heart, that I might not sin against You.

All bore witness to Him, and marveled at the gracious words which proceeded out of His mouth. ◊ No man ever spoke like this Man! ◊ Christ Jesus . . . who became for us wisdom from God—and righteousness and sanctification and redemption.

PROV 2:6.PROV 3:5.JAMES 1:5.1 COR 1:25.LUKE 21:15.1 COR 1:27.PS 119:130.PS 119:11.LUKE 4:22.JOHN 7:46.1 COR 1:30

Jesus . . . said, "It is finished!" And bowing His head, He gave up His spirit. ◊ He made Him who knew no sin to be sin for us, that we might become the righteousness of God in Him.

To the intent that now the manifold wisdom of God might be made known by the church to the principalities and powers in the heavenly places, according to the eternal purpose which He accomplished in Christ Jesus our Lord. ◊ That in the ages to come He might show the exceeding riches of His grace in His kindness toward us in Christ Jesus.

Having believed, you were sealed with the Holy Spirit of promise, who is the guarantee of our inheritance until the redemption of the purchased possession. ◊ You are a chosen generation, a royal priesthood, a holy nation, His own special people, that you may proclaim the praises of Him who called you out of darkness into His marvelous light.

IS 53:11.JOHN 19:30.2 COR 5:21.EPH 3:10-11.EPH 2:7.EPH 1:13-14.1 PET 2:9

He shall see the travail of His soul, and be satisfied.

## February 21

I am the LORD who sanctifies you.

I am the Lord your God, who has separated you from the peoples. . . . You shall be holy to Me, for I the Lord am holy, and have separated you from the peoples, that you should be Mine.

Sanctified by God the Father. ◊ Sanctify them by Your truth. Your word is truth. ◊ May the God of peace Himself sanctify you completely; and may your whole spirit, soul, and body be preserved blameless at the coming of our Lord Jesus Christ. ◊ Jesus . . . that He might sanctify the people with His own blood, suffered outside the gate.

Our . . . Savior Jesus Christ, . . . gave Himself for us, that He might redeem us from every lawless deed and purify for Himself His own special people, zealous for good works. ◊ Both He who sanctifies and those who are being sanctified are all of one, for which reason He is not ashamed to call them brethren. ◊ For their sakes I sanctify Myself, that they also may be sanctified by the truth. ◊ In sanctification of the Spirit, for obedience and sprinkling of the blood of Jesus Christ.

LEV 20:8.LEV 20:24,26.JUDE 1:1.JOHN 17:17.1 THESS 5:23.HEB 13:12.TITUS 2:13-14.HEB 2:11.JOHN 17:19. 1 PET 1:2

The lamp of the body is the eye. If therefore your eye is good, your whole body will be full of light.

Your word is a lamp to my feet and a light to my path. ◊ Your ears shall hear a word behind you, saying, "This is the way, walk in it," whenever you turn to the right hand or whenever you turn to the left. ◊ I will instruct you and teach you in the way you should go; I will guide you with My eye. Do not be like the horse or like the mule, which have no understanding, which must be harnessed with bit and bridle, else they will not come near you. Many sorrows shall be to the wicked; but he who trusts in the Lord, mercy shall surround him. Be glad in the Lord and rejoice, you righteous; and shout for joy, all you upright in heart!

O Lord, I know the way of man is not in himself; it is not in man who walks to direct his own steps.

PS 25:12.MATT 6:22.PS 119:105.IS 30:21.PS 32:8-11.JER 10:23

## February 22

Who is the man that fears the LORD? Him shall He teach in the way He chooses.

## February 23

Behold! The Lamb of God who takes away the sin of the world! ◊ The Lamb slain from the foundation of the world. ◊ For it is not possible that the blood of bulls and goats could take away sins. Therefore, when He came into the world, He said: "Sacrifice and offering You did not desire, but a body You have prepared for Me." ◊ By that will we have been sanctified through the offering of the body of Jesus Christ once for all.

Abel . . . brought of the firstlings of his flock and of their fat. And the Lord respected Abel and his offering. ◊ Christ . . . has loved us and given Himself for us, an offering and a sacrifice to God for a sweet-smelling aroma.

Let us draw near with a true heart in full assurance of faith, having our hearts sprinkled from an evil conscience and our bodies washed with pure water. ◊ [Have] boldness to enter the Holiest by the blood of Jesus.

HEB 12:24.JOHN 1:29.REV 13:8.HEB 10:4-5.HEB 10:10.GEN 4:4.EPH 5:2.HEB 10:22.HEB 10:19

You do not have because you do not ask.

Ask, and it will be given to you; seek, and you will find; knock, and it will be opened to you. For everyone who asks receives, and he who seeks finds, and to him who knocks it will be opened. ◊ This is the confidence that we have in Him, that if we ask anything according to His will, He hears us. And if we know that He hears us, whatever we ask, we know that we have the petitions that we have asked of Him. ◊ If any of you lacks wisdom, let him ask of God, who gives to all liberally and without reproach, and it will be given to him. ◊ Open your mouth wide, and I will fill it. ◊ Men always ought to pray and not lose heart.

The eyes of the Lord are on the righteous, and His ears are open to their cry. . . . The Lord hears, and delivers them out of all their troubles. ◊ You will ask in My name, and I do not say to you that I shall pray the Father for you; for the Father Himself loves you, because you have loved Me.

## February 24

Thus says the Lord GOD: "I will also let the house of Israel inquire of Me to do this for them."

EZEK 36:37.JAMES 4:2.MATT 7:7-8.1 JOHN 5:14-15.JAMES 1:5.PS 81:10.LUKE 18:1.PS 34:15,17.JOHN 16:26-27

## February 25

When the enemy comes in like a flood, the Spirit of the Lord will lift up a standard against him. ◊ "Away with you, Satan! For it is written, 'You shall worship the Lord your God, and Him only you shall serve.'" Then the devil left Him, and behold, angels came and ministered to Him.

Be strong in the Lord and in the power of His might. Put on the whole armor of God, that you may be able to stand against the wiles of the devil. ◊ And have no fellowship with the unfruitful works of darkness, but rather expose them. ◊ Lest Satan should take advantage of us; for we are not ignorant of his devices. ◊ Be sober, be vigilant; because your adversary the devil walks about like a roaring lion, seeking whom he may devour. Resist him, steadfast in the faith, knowing that the same sufferings are experienced by your brotherhood in the world. ◊ Who shall bring a charge against God's elect? It is God who justifies.

JAMES 4:7.IS 59:19.MATT 4:10-11.EPH 6:10-11.EPH 5:11.2 COR 2:11.1 PET 5:8-9.ROM 8:33

Examine me, O Lord, and prove me; try my mind and my heart. ◊ Behold, You desire truth in the inward parts, and in the hidden part You will make me to know wisdom. ◊ I thought about my ways, and turned my feet to Your testimonies. ◊ I made haste, and did not delay to keep Your commandments. ◊ Let a man examine himself, and so let him eat of that bread and drink of that cup. ◊ If we confess our sins, He is faithful and just to forgive us our sins and to cleanse us from all unrighteousness. ◊ We have an Advocate with the Father, Jesus Christ the righteous. ◊ Therefore, brethren, having boldness to enter the Holiest by the blood of Jesus, by a new and living way which He consecrated for us, through the veil, that is, His flesh, and having a High Priest over the house of God, let us draw near with a true heart in full assurance of faith, having our hearts sprinkled from an evil conscience and our bodies washed with pure water.

LAM 3:40.PS 26:2.PS 51:6.PS 119:59-60.1 COR 11:28.
1 JOHN 1:9.1 JOHN 2:1.HEB 10:19-22

## February 26

Let us search out and examine our ways, and turn back to the LORD.

## February 27

Reckon yourselves to be dead indeed to sin, but alive to God in Christ Jesus our Lord.

He who hears My word and believes in Him who sent Me has everlasting life, and shall not come into judgment, but has passed from death into life. ◊ For I through the law died to the law that I might live to God. I have been crucified with Christ; it is no longer I who live, but Christ lives in me; and the life which I now live in the flesh I live by faith in the Son of God, who loved me and gave Himself for me.

Because I live, you will live also. ◊ And I give them eternal life, and they shall never perish; neither shall anyone snatch them out of My hand. My Father, who has given them to Me, is greater than all; and no one is able to snatch them out of My Father's hand. I and My Father are one.

If then you were raised with Christ, seek those things which are above, where Christ is, sitting at the right hand of God. . . . For you died, and your life is hidden with Christ in God.

ROM 6:11.JOHN 5:24.GAL 2:19-20.JOHN 14:19.JOHN 10:28-30.COL 3:1-3

God, . . . has reconciled us to Himself through Jesus Christ, and has given us the ministry of reconciliation, that is, that God was in Christ reconciling the world to Himself, not imputing their trespasses to them, and has committed to us the word of reconciliation. Therefore we are ambassadors for Christ, as though God were pleading through us: we implore you on Christ's behalf, be reconciled to God. For He made Him who knew no sin to be sin for us, that we might become the righteousness of God in Him. ◊ God is love. In this the love of God was manifested toward us, that God has sent His only begotten Son into the world, that we might live through Him. In this is love, not that we loved God, but that He loved us and sent His Son to be the propitiation for our sins. Beloved, if God so loved us, we also ought to love one another.

JOHN 3:16.2 COR 5:18-21.1 JOHN 4:8-11

For God so loved the world that He gave His only begotten Son, that whoever believes in Him should not perish but have everlasting life.

# February 29

Do not boast about tomorrow, for you do not know what a day may bring forth.

Behold, now is the accepted time; behold, now is the day of salvation. ◊ A little while longer the light is with you. Walk while you have the light, lest darkness overtake you; he who walks in darkness does not know where he is going. While you have the light, believe in the light, that you may become sons of light.

Whatever your hand finds to do, do it with your might; for there is no work or device or knowledge or wisdom in the grave where you are going.

"Soul, you have many goods laid up for many years; take your ease; eat, drink, and be merry." . . . You fool! This night your soul will be required of you; then whose will those things be which you have provided? So is he who lays up treasure for himself, and is not rich toward God.

The world is passing away, and the lust of it; but he who does the will of God abides forever.

PROV 27:1.2 COR 6:2.JOHN 12:35-36.ECCL 9:10.LUKE 12:19-21.1 JOHN 2:17

God is love, and he who abides in love abides in God, and God in him. ◊ The love of God has been poured out in our hearts by the Holy Spirit who was given to us. ◊ To you who believe, He is precious. ◊ We love Him because He first loved us. ◊ The love of Christ constrains us, because we judge thus: that if One died for all, then all died; and He died for all, that those who live should live no longer for themselves, but for Him who died for them and rose again.

You yourselves are taught by God to love one another. ◊ This is My commandment, that you love one another as I have loved you. ◊ Above all things have fervent love for one another, for love will cover a multitude of sins. ◊ Walk in love, as Christ also has loved us and given Himself for us, an offering and a sacrifice to God for a sweet-smelling aroma.

GAL 5:22.1 JOHN 4:16.ROM 5:5.1 PET 2:7.1 JOHN 4:19.2 COR 5:14-15.1 THESS 4:9.JOHN 15:12.1 PET 4:8.EPH 5:2

## March 1

The fruit of the Spirit is love.

## March 2

God has caused me to be fruitful in the land of my affliction.

Blessed be the God and Father of our Lord Jesus Christ, the Father of mercies and God of all comfort, who comforts us in all our tribulation, that we may be able to comfort those who are in any trouble, with the comfort with which we ourselves are comforted by God. For as the sufferings of Christ abound in us, so our consolation also abounds through Christ.

He will sit as a refiner and a purifier of silver; He will purify the sons of Levi. ◊ Now for a little while, if need be, you have been grieved by various trials, that the genuineness of your faith, being much more precious than gold that perishes, though it is tested by fire, may be found to praise, honor, and glory at the revelation of Jesus Christ. ◊ The Lord stood with me and strengthened me.

Let those who suffer according to the will of God commit their souls to Him in doing good, as to a faithful Creator.

GEN 41:52.2 COR 1:3-5.MAL 3:3.1 PET 1:6-7.2 TIM 4:17.1 PET 4:19

Trust in Him at all times, you people; pour out your heart before Him; God is a refuge for us.

O our God, will You not judge them? For we have no power against this great multitude that is coming against us; nor do we know what to do, but our eyes are upon You. ◊ I will lift up my eyes to the hills—from whence comes my help? My help comes from the Lord, who made heaven and earth. ◊ But my eyes are upon You, O God the Lord; in You I take refuge; do not leave my soul destitute.

If Your Presence does not go with us, do not bring us up from here. For how then will it be known that Your people and I have found grace in Your sight, except You go with us? So we shall be separate, Your people and I, from all the people who are upon the face of the earth.

PROV 3:5-6.PS 62:8.2 CHR 20:12.PS 121:1-2.PS 141:8.EX 33:15-16

## March 3

Trust in the Lord with all your heart, and lean not on your own understanding; in all your ways acknowledge Him, and He shall direct your paths.

# March 4

Do not love the world or the things in the world. If anyone loves the world, the love of the Father is not in him. ◊ Do not lay up for yourselves treasures on earth, where moth and rust destroy and where thieves break in and steal; but lay up for yourselves treasures in heaven, where neither moth nor rust destroys and where thieves do not break in and steal. For where your treasure is, there your heart will be also.

We walk by faith, not by sight. ◊ We do not lose heart. Even though our outward man is perishing, yet the inward man is being renewed day by day. For our light affliction, which is but for a moment, is working for us a far more exceeding and eternal weight of glory, while we do not look at the things which are seen, but at the things which are not seen. For the things which are seen are temporary, but the things which are not seen are eternal. ◊ An inheritance incorruptible and undefiled and that does not fade away [is] reserved in heaven for you.

COL 3:2.1 JOHN 2:15.MATT 6:19-21.2 COR 5:7.2 COR 4:16-18.1 PET 1:4

Unto You I lift up my eyes, O You who dwell in the heavens. Behold, as the eyes of servants look to the hand of their masters, as the eyes of a maid to the hand of her mistress, so our eyes look to the Lord our God. ◊ Hear my cry, O God; attend to my prayer. From the end of the earth I will cry to You, when my heart is overwhelmed; lead me to the rock that is higher than I. For You have been a shelter for me, and a strong tower from the enemy. I will abide in Your tabernacle forever; I will trust in the shelter of Your wings. ◊ You have been a strength to the poor, a strength to the needy in his distress, a refuge from the storm.

Christ . . . suffered for us, leaving us an example, that you should follow His steps: who committed no sin, nor was guile found in His mouth; who, when He was reviled, did not revile in return; when He suffered, He did not threaten, but committed Himself to Him who judges righteously.

IS 38:14.PS 123:1-2.PS 61:1-4.IS 25:4.1 PET 2:21-23

## March 5

O LORD, I am oppressed; undertake for me!

## March 6

The Lord your God, . . . went in the way before you to search out a place for you to pitch your tents, to show you the way you should go, in the fire by night and in the cloud by day. ◊ As an eagle stirs up its nest, hovers over its young, spreading out its wings, taking them up, carrying them on its wings, so the Lord alone led him. ◊ The steps of a good man are ordered by the Lord, and He delights in his way. Though he fall, he shall not be utterly cast down; for the Lord upholds him with His hand. ◊ Many are the afflictions of the righteous, but the Lord delivers him out of them all. ◊ For the Lord knows the way of the righteous, but the way of the ungodly shall perish. ◊ We know that all things work together for good to those who love God, to those who are the called according to His purpose. ◊ With us is the Lord our God, to help us and to fight our battles.

The Lord your God in your midst, the Mighty One, will save; He will rejoice over you with gladness.

PROV 2:8.DEUT 1:32-33.DEUT 32:11-12.PS 37:23-24.PS 34:19.PS 1:6.ROM 8:28.2 CHR 32:8.ZEPH 3:17

This is a great mystery, but I speak concerning Christ and the church.

You shall no longer be termed Forsaken, . . . but you shall be called Hephzibah [My Delight in Her], . . . for the Lord delights in you. . . . As the bridegroom rejoices over the bride, so shall your God rejoice over you. ◊ He has sent Me . . . to comfort all who mourn, . . . to console those who mourn in Zion, to give them beauty for ashes, the oil of joy for mourning, the garment of praise for the spirit of heaviness.

I will greatly rejoice in the Lord, my soul shall be joyful in my God; for He has clothed me with the garments of salvation, He has covered me with the robe of righteousness, as a bridegroom decks himself with ornaments, and as a bride adorns herself with her jewels.

I will betroth you to Me forever; yes, I will betroth you to Me in righteousness and justice, in lovingkindness and mercy.

Who shall separate us from the love of Christ?

Your Maker is your husband, the LORD of hosts is His name.

IS 54:5.EPH 5:32.IS 62:4-5.IS 61:1-3.IS 61:10.HOS 2:19.ROM 8:35

## March 8

**You have cast all my sins behind Your back.**

Who is a God like You, pardoning iniquity and passing over the transgression of the remnant of His heritage? He does not retain His anger forever, because He delights in mercy. He will again have compassion on us, and will subdue our iniquities. You will cast all our sins into the depths of the sea.

I will forgive their iniquity, and their sin I will remember no more. ◊ "For a mere moment I have forsaken you, but with great mercies I will gather you. With a little wrath I hid My face from you for a moment; but with everlasting kindness I will have mercy on you," says the Lord, your Redeemer.

Blessed is he whose transgression is forgiven, whose sin is covered. Blessed is the man to whom the Lord does not impute iniquity, and in whose spirit there is no guile. ◊ The blood of Jesus Christ His Son cleanses us from all sin.

IS 38:17.MIC 7:18-19.JER 31:34.IS 54:7-8.PS 32:1-2.1 JOHN 1:7

Beware that you do not forget the Lord your God by not keeping His commandments, His judgments, and His statutes which I command you today, lest—when you have eaten and are full, and have built beautiful houses and dwell in them; . . . when your heart is lifted up, and you forget the Lord your God. . . . For it is He who gives you power to get wealth.

Unless the Lord builds the house, they labor in vain who build it; unless the Lord guards the city, the watchman stays awake in vain. It is vain for you to rise up early, to sit up late, to eat the bread of sorrows; for so He gives His beloved sleep. ◊ They did not gain possession of the land by their own sword, nor did their own arm save them; but it was Your right hand, Your arm, and the light of Your countenance, because You favored them. ◊ There are many who say, "Who will show us any good?" Lord, lift up the light of Your countenance upon us.

1 TIM 6:17.DEUT 8:11-12,14,18.PS 127:1-2.PS 44:3.PS 4:6

## March 9

The living God, who gives us richly all things to enjoy.

## March 10

**The-Lord-Will-Provide.**

God will provide for Himself the lamb for a burnt offering.

Behold, the Lord's hand is not shortened, that it cannot save; nor His ear heavy, that it cannot hear. ◊ The Deliverer will come out of Zion, and He will turn away ungodliness from Jacob.

Happy is he who has the God of Jacob for his help, whose hope is in the Lord his God. ◊ Behold, the eye of the Lord is on those who fear Him, on those who hope in His mercy, to deliver their soul from death.

My God shall supply all your need according to His riches in glory by Christ Jesus. ◊ He Himself has said, "I will never leave you nor forsake you." So we may boldly say: "The Lord is my helper; I will not fear. What can man do to me?" ◊ The Lord is my strength and my shield; my heart trusted in Him, and I am helped; therefore my heart greatly rejoices, and with my song I will praise Him.

GEN 22:14.GEN 22:8.IS 59:1.ROM 11:26.PS 146:5.PS 33:18-19.PHIL 4:19.HEB 13:5-6.PS 28:7

The blessing of the Lord makes one rich, and He adds no sorrow with it. ◊ You, O Lord, will bless the righteous; with favor You will surround him as with a shield.

He will not allow your foot to be moved; He who keeps you will not slumber. Behold, He who keeps Israel shall neither slumber nor sleep. The Lord is your keeper; the Lord is your shade at your right hand. . . . The Lord shall preserve you from all evil; He shall preserve your soul. The Lord shall preserve your going out and your coming in from this time forth, and even forevermore. ◊ I, the Lord, keep it, I water it every moment; lest any hurt it, I keep it night and day.

Holy Father, keep through Your name those whom You have given Me. . . . While I was with them in the world, I kept them in Your name. ◊ Those whom You gave Me I have kept.

The Lord will deliver me from every evil work and preserve me for His heavenly kingdom. To Him be glory forever and ever. Amen!

## March 11

The Lord bless you and keep you.

NUM 6:24.PROV 10:22.PS 5:12.PS 121:3-5.PS 121:7-8.IS 27:3.JOHN 17:11-12.2 TIM 4:18

## March 12

No one has seen God at any time. The only begotten Son, who is in the bosom of the Father, He has declared Him. ◊ [Jesus is] the brightness of His glory and the express image of His person. ◊ The god of this age has blinded [their minds], who do not believe, lest the light of the gospel of the glory of Christ, who is the image of God, should shine on them.

Make Your face shine upon Your servant; save me for Your mercies' sake. Do not let me be ashamed, O Lord, for I have called upon You. ◊ Lord, by Your favor You have made my mountain stand strong; You hid Your face, and I was troubled. ◊ Blessed are the people who know the joyful sound! They walk, O Lord, in the light of Your countenance.

The Lord will give strength to His people; the Lord will bless His people with peace. ◊ Be of good cheer! It is I; do not be afraid.

NUM 6:25-26.JOHN 1:18.HEB 1:3.2 COR 4:4.PS 31:16-17.PS 30:7.PS 89:15.PS 29:11.MATT 14:27

Inasmuch . . . as the children have partaken of flesh and blood, He Himself likewise shared in the same.

Look to Me, and be saved, all you ends of the earth! For I am God, and there is no other.

We have an Advocate with the Father, Jesus Christ the righteous. ◊ In Christ Jesus you who once were far off have been made near by the blood of Christ. For He Himself is our peace.

With His own blood He entered the Most Holy Place once for all, having obtained eternal redemption. . . . And for this reason He is the Mediator of the new covenant, by means of death, for the redemption of the transgressions under the first covenant, that those who are called may receive the promise of the eternal inheritance. ◊ He is also able to save to the uttermost those who come to God through Him, since He ever lives to make intercession for them.

1 TIM 2:5.HEB 2:14.IS 45:22.1 JOHN 2:1.EPH 2:13-14.HEB 9:12,15.HEB 7:25

## March 13

For there is one God and one Mediator between God and men, the Man Christ Jesus.

## March 14

Let your conduct be worthy of the gospel of Christ. ◊ If you are reproached for the name of Christ, blessed are you. . . . But let none of you suffer as a murderer, a thief, an evildoer, or as a busybody in other people's matters. ◊ Become blameless and harmless, children of God without fault in the midst of a crooked and perverse generation, among whom you shine as lights in the world. ◊ Let your light so shine before men, that they may see your good works and glorify your Father in heaven.

Bind [mercy and truth] around your neck, write them on the tablet of your heart, and so find favor and high esteem in the sight of God and man. ◊ Whatever things are true, whatever things are noble, whatever things are just, whatever things are pure, whatever things are lovely, whatever things are of good report, if there is any virtue and if there is anything praiseworthy meditate on these things.

TITUS 2:10.PHIL 1:27.1 PET 4:14-15.PHIL 2:15.MATT 5:16.PROV 3:3-4. PHIL 4:8

"My soul is exceedingly sorrowful, even to death. Stay here and watch with Me." He went a little farther and fell on His face, and prayed, saying, "O My Father, if it is possible, let this cup pass from Me; nevertheless, not as I will, but as You will." ◊ And being in agony, He prayed more earnestly. And His sweat became like great drops of blood falling down to the ground.

The pains of death encompassed me, and the pangs of Sheol laid hold of me; I found trouble and sorrow. ◊ Reproach has broken my heart, and I am full of heaviness; I looked for someone to take pity, but there was none; and for comforters, but I found none. ◊ Look on my right hand and see, for there is no one who acknowledges me; refuge has failed me; no one cares for my soul.

He is despised and rejected by men, a man of sorrows and acquainted with grief. And we hid, as it were, our faces from Him; He was despised, and we did not esteem Him.

HEB 2:10.MATT 26:38-39.LUKE 22:44.PS 116:3.PS 69:20.PS 142:4.IS 53:3

Perfect through sufferings.

## March 16

What is your life? It is even a vapor that appears for a little time and then vanishes away.

Now my days are swifter than a runner; they flee away, they see no good. They pass by like swift ships, like an eagle swooping on its prey. ◊ You carry them away like a flood; they are like a sleep. In the morning they are like grass which grows up: in the morning it flourishes and grows up; in the evening it is cut down and withers. ◊ Man who is born of woman is of few days and full of trouble. He comes forth like a flower and fades away.

The world is passing away, and the lust of it; but he who does the will of God abides forever. ◊ They will perish, but You will endure; yes, all of them will grow old like a garment; like a cloak You will change them, and they will be changed. But You are the same, and Your years will have no end. ◊ Jesus Christ is the same yesterday, today, and forever.

JAMES 4:14.JOB 9:25-26.PS 90:5-6.JOB 14:1-2.1 JOHN 2:17.PS 102:26-27.HEB 13:8

You were not redeemed with corruptible things, like silver or gold, . . . but with the precious blood of Christ, as of a lamb without blemish and without spot. ◊ [He] Himself bore our sins in His own body. ◊ He has made us accepted in the Beloved.

You also, as living stones, are being built up a spiritual house, a holy priesthood, to offer up spiritual sacrifices acceptable to God through Jesus Christ. ◊ I beseech you therefore, brethren, by the mercies of God, that you present your bodies a living sacrifice, holy, acceptable to God, which is your reasonable service.

Now to Him who is able to keep you from stumbling, and to present you faultless before the presence of His glory with exceeding joy, to God our Savior, who alone is wise, be glory and majesty, dominion and power, both now and forever.

LEV 1:4.1 PET 1:18-19.1 PET 2:24.EPH 1:6.1 PET 2:5.ROM 12:1.JUDE 1:24-25

## March 17

He shall put his hand on the head of the burnt offering, and it will be accepted on his behalf to make atonement for him.

## March 18

**My eyes fail from looking upward.**

Have mercy on me, O Lord, for I am weak; O Lord, heal me, for my bones are troubled. My soul also is greatly troubled; but You, O Lord—how long? Return, O Lord, deliver me! Oh, save me for Your mercies' sake! ◊ Fearfulness and trembling have come upon me, and horror has overwhelmed me. And I said, "Oh, that I had wings like a dove! For then I would fly away and be at rest."

You have need of endurance.

While they looked steadfastly toward heaven as He went up, behold, two men stood by them in white apparel, who also said, "Men of Galilee, why do you stand gazing up into heaven? This same Jesus, who was taken up from you into heaven, will so come in like manner as you saw Him go into heaven." ◊ Our citizenship is in heaven, from which we also eagerly wait for the Savior, the Lord Jesus Christ. ◊ We should . . . [be] looking for the blessed hope and glorious appearing of our great God and Savior Jesus Christ.

IS 38:14.PS 6:2-4.PS 55:5-6.HEB 10:36.ACTS 1:10-11.PHIL 3:20.TITUS 2:12-13

Blessed be the God and Father of our Lord Jesus Christ, who according to His abundant mercy has begotten us again to a living hope through the resurrection of Jesus Christ from the dead.

Our great God and Savior Jesus Christ, . . . gave Himself for us, that He might redeem us from every lawless deed and purify for Himself His own special people, zealous for good works. ◊ But as He who called you is holy, you also be holy in all your conduct, because it is written, "Be holy, for I am holy."

The God and Father of our Lord Jesus Christ, . . . has blessed us with every spiritual blessing in the heavenly places in Christ. ◊ In Him dwells all the fullness of the Godhead bodily; and you are complete in Him. ◊ Of His fullness we have all received, and grace for grace.

He who did not spare His own Son, but delivered Him up for us all, how shall He not with Him also freely give us all things?

## March 19

God, having raised up His Servant Jesus, sent Him to bless you, in turning away every one of you from your iniquities.

ACTS 3:26.1 PET 1:3.TITUS 2:13-14.1 PET 1:15-16.EPH 1:3.COL 2:9-10.JOHN 1:16.ROM 8:32

## March 20

The entrance of Your words gives light.

This is the message which we have heard from Him and declare to you, that God is light and in Him is no darkness at all. ◊ God who commanded light to shine out of darkness who has shone in our hearts to give the light of the knowledge of the glory of God in the face of Jesus Christ. ◊ The Word was with God. ◊ In Him was life, and the life was the light of men. ◊ If we walk in the light as He is in the light, we have fellowship with one another, and the blood of Jesus Christ His Son cleanses us from all sin.

Your word I have hidden in my heart, that I might not sin against You. ◊ You are already clean because of the word which I have spoken to you.

You were once darkness, but now you are light in the Lord. Walk as children of light. ◊ You are a chosen generation, a royal priesthood, a holy nation, His own special people, that you may proclaim the praises of Him who called you out of darkness into His marvelous light.

PS 119:130.1 JOHN 1:5.2 COR 4:6.JOHN 1:1.JOHN 1:4. 1 JOHN 1:7.PS 119:11.JOHN 15:3.EPH 5:8.1 PET 2:9

The end of all things is at hand; therefore be serious and watchful in your prayers. ◊ Be sober, be vigilant; because your adversary the devil walks about like a roaring lion, seeking whom he may devour. ◊ Take heed to yourself, and diligently keep yourself, lest you forget the things your eyes have seen, and lest they depart from your heart all the days of your life. ◊ The just shall live by faith; but if anyone draws back, my soul has no pleasure in him. But we are not of those who draw back to perdition, but of those who believe to the saving of the soul.

What I say to you, I say to all: Watch!

Fear not, for I am with you; be not dismayed, for I am your God. I will strengthen you, yes, I will help you, I will uphold you with My righteous right hand. . . . I, the Lord your God, will hold your right hand.

## March 21

Be watchful, and strengthen the things which remain, that are ready to die.

REV 3:2.1 PET 4:7.1 PET 5:8.DEUT 4:9.HEB 10:38-39.MARK 13:37.IS 41:10,13

## March 22

Lot lifted his eyes and saw all the plain of Jordan, that it was well watered everywhere . . . like the garden of the LORD. . . . Then Lot chose for himself all the plain of Jordan.

Righteous Lot, . . . dwelling among them, tormented his righteous soul . . . by seeing and hearing their lawless deeds.

Do not be deceived, God is not mocked; for whatever a man sows, that he will also reap. ◊ Remember Lot's wife.

Do not be unequally yoked together with unbelievers. For what fellowship has righteousness with lawlessness? And what communion has light with darkness? ◊ Therefore "Come out from among them and be separate," says the Lord. "Do not touch what is unclean." ◊ Do not be partakers with them. For you were once darkness, but now you are light in the Lord. Walk as children of light . . . proving what is acceptable to the Lord. And have no fellowship with the unfruitful works of darkness, but rather expose them.

GEN 13:10-11.2 PET 2:7-8.GAL 6:7.LUKE 17:32.2 COR 6:14.2 COR 6:17.EPH 5:7-8,10-11

Holy, holy, holy,
Lord God
Almighty.

But You are holy, who inhabit the praises of Israel. ◊ [God] said, "Do not draw near this place. Take your sandals off your feet, for the place where you stand is holy ground." Moreover He said, "I am the God of your father—the God of Abraham, the God of Isaac, and the God of Jacob." And Moses hid his face, for he was afraid to look upon God. ◊ "To whom then will you liken Me, or to whom shall I be equal?" says the Holy One. ◊ I am the Lord your God, the Holy One of Israel, your Savior. ◊ I, even I, am the Lord, and besides Me there is no savior.

As He who called you is holy, you also be holy in all your conduct, because it is written, "Be holy, for I am holy." ◊ Do you not know that your body is the temple of the Holy Spirit who is in you, whom you have from God, and you are not your own? ◊ You are the temple of the living God. As God has said: "I will dwell in them and walk among them. I will be their God, and they shall be My people." ◊ Can two walk together, unless they are agreed?

REV 4:8.PS 22:3.EX 3:5-6.IS 40:25.IS 43:3.IS 43:11.1 PET 1:15-16.1 COR 6:19.2 COR 6:16.AMOS 3:3

## March 24

He did not waver at the promise of God through unbelief, but was strengthened in faith, giving glory to God, and being fully convinced that what He had promised He was also able to perform. And therefore "it was accounted to him for righteousness." Now it was not written for his sake alone that it was imputed to him, but also for us. It shall be imputed to us who believe in Him who raised up Jesus our Lord from the dead.

The promise that he would be the heir of the world was not to Abraham or to his seed through the law, but through the righteousness of faith. ◊ The just shall live by faith. ◊ Let us hold fast the confession of our hope without wavering, for He who promised is faithful. ◊ Our God is in heaven; He does whatever He pleases. ◊ With God nothing will be impossible. ◊ Blessed is she who believed, for there will be a fulfillment of those things which were told her from the Lord.

GEN 15:6.ROM 4:20-24.ROM 4:13.ROM 1:17.HEB 10:23.PS 115:3.LUKE 1:37.LUKE 1:45

So we may boldly say: "The Lord is my helper; I will not fear. What can man do to me?"

Behold, I am with you and will keep you wherever you go, and will bring you back to this land; for I will not leave you until I have done what I have spoken to you. ◇ Be strong and of good courage, do not fear nor be afraid of them; for the Lord your God, He is the One who goes with you. He will not leave you nor forsake you.

Demas has forsaken me, having loved this present world. . . . At my first defense no one stood with me, but all forsook me. . . . But the Lord stood with me and strengthened me. ◇ When my father and my mother forsake me, then the Lord will take care of me.

Lo, I am with you always, even to the end of the age. ◇ I am He who lives, and was dead, and behold, I am alive forevermore. ◇ I will not leave you orphans; I will come to you.

HEB 13:5.HEB 13:6.GEN 28:15.DEUT 31:6.2 TIM 4:10,16-17.PS 27:10.MATT 28:20.REV 1:18.JOHN 14:18

I will never leave you nor forsake you.

## March 26

The kingdom of heaven is like a man traveling to a far country, who called his own servants and delivered his goods to them. . . . He gave . . . to each according to his own ability.

Do you not know that to whom you present yourselves slaves to obey, you are that one's slaves whom you obey?

One and the same Spirit works all these things, distributing to each one individually as He wills. ◊ The manifestation of the Spirit is given to each one for the profit of all. ◊ As each one has received a gift, minister it to one another, as good stewards of the manifold grace of God. ◊ It is required in stewards that one be found faithful. ◊ For everyone to whom much is given, from him much will be required; and to whom much has been committed, of him they will ask the more.

Who is sufficient for these things? ◊ I can do all things through Christ who strengthens me.

MATT 25:14-15.ROM 6:16.1 COR 12:11.1 COR 12:7. 1 PET 4:10.1 COR.4:2.LUKE 12:48.2 COR 2:16.PHIL 4:13

After a long time the lord of those servants came and settled accounts with them. So he who had received five talents came and brought five other talents, saying, "Lord, you delivered to me five talents; look, I have gained five more talents besides them." His lord said to him, "Well done, good and faithful servant; you were faithful over a few things, I will make you ruler over many things. Enter into the joy of your lord."

We must all appear before the judgment seat of Christ, that each one may receive the things done in the body, according to what he has done, whether good or bad.

I have fought the good fight, I have finished the race, I have kept the faith. Finally, there is laid up for me the crown of righteousness, which the Lord, the righteous Judge, will give to me on that Day.

Behold, I come quickly! Hold fast what you have, that no one may take your crown.

PROV 11:18.MATT 25:19-21.2 COR 5:10.2 TIM 4:7-8.REV 3:11

## March 27

To him who sows righteousness will be a sure reward.

## March 28

**Be strong and of good courage.**

The Lord is my light and my salvation; whom shall I fear? The Lord is the strength of my life; of whom shall I be afraid? ◊ He gives power to the weak, and to those who have no might He increases strength. Even the youths shall faint and be weary, and the young men shall utterly fall, but those who wait on the Lord shall renew their strength; they shall mount up with wings like eagles, they shall run and not be weary, they shall walk and not faint. ◊ My flesh and my heart fail; but God is the strength of my heart and my portion forever.

If God is for us, who can be against us? ◊ The Lord is on my side; I will not fear. What can man do to me? ◊ Through You we will push down our enemies; through Your name we will trample those who rise up against us. ◊ We are more than conquerors through Him who loved us.

Arise and begin working, and the Lord be with you.

JOSH 1:18.PS 27:1.IS 40:29-31.PS 73:26.ROM 8:31.PS 118:6.PS 44:5.ROM 8:37.1 CHR 22:16

Do not fear, little flock, for it is your Father's good pleasure to give you the kingdom. ◊ Has God not chosen the poor of this world to be rich in faith and heirs of the kingdom which He promised to those who love Him? ◊ Heirs of God and joint heirs with Christ, if indeed we suffer with Him, that we may also be glorified together.

The Father Himself loves you, because you have loved Me. ◊ God is not ashamed to be called their God, for He has prepared a city for them.

He who overcomes shall inherit all things, and I will be his God and he shall be My son. ◊ There is laid up for me the crown of righteousness, which the Lord, the righteous Judge, will give to me on that Day, and not to me only but also to all who have loved His appearing. ◊ He who has begun a good work in you will complete it until the day of Jesus Christ.

MATT 25:34.LUKE 12:32.JAMES 2:5.ROM 8:17.JOHN 16:27.HEB 11:16.REV 21:7.2 TIM 4:8.PHIL 1:6

## March 29

Come, you blessed of My Father, inherit the kingdom prepared for you from the foundation of the world.

## March 30

Isaac went out to
meditate in the
field in the
evening.

Let the words of my mouth and the
meditation of my heart be acceptable in
Your sight, O Lord, my strength and
my redeemer.

When I consider Your heavens, the
work of Your fingers, the moon and the
stars, which You have ordained, what is
man that You are mindful of him, and
the son of man that You visit him? ◊
The works of the Lord are great, studied
by all who have pleasure in them.

Blessed is the man who walks not in
the counsel of the ungodly, nor stands
in the path of sinners, nor sits in the
seat of the scornful; but his delight is in
the law of the Lord, and in His law he
meditates day and night. ◊ This Book
of the Law shall not depart from your
mouth, but you shall meditate in it day
and night. ◊ My soul shall be satisfied
as with marrow and fatness, and my
mouth shall praise You with joyful lips.
When I remember You on my bed, I
meditate on You in the night watches.

GEN 24:63.PS 19:14.PS 8:3-4.PS 111:2.PS 1:1-2.JOSH
1:8.PS 63:5-6

Seek first the kingdom of God and His righteousness, and all . . . things shall be added to you. ◊ He who did not spare His own Son, but delivered Him up for us all, how shall He not with Him also freely give us all things? ◊ All things are yours: whether Paul or Apollos or Cephas, or the world or life or death, or things present or things to come—all are yours. And you are Christ's, and Christ is God's. ◊ We commend ourselves as ministers of God: . . . as having nothing, and yet possessing all things.

The Lord is my shepherd; I shall not want. ◊ The Lord God is a sun and shield; the Lord will give grace and glory; no good thing will He withhold from those who walk uprightly. ◊ The living God . . . gives us richly all things to enjoy. ◊ God is able to make all grace abound toward you, that you, always having all sufficiency in all things, have an abundance for every good work.

## March 31

My God shall supply all your need according to His riches in glory by Christ Jesus.

PHIL 4:19.MATT 6:33.ROM 8:32.1 COR 3:21-23.2 COR 6:4,10.PS 23:1.PS 84:11.1 TIM 6:17.2 COR 9:8.

The kingdom of God is . . . joy in the Holy Spirit. ◊ Believing, you rejoice with joy inexpressible and full of glory.

We commend ourselves . . . as sorrowful, yet always rejoicing. ◊ I am exceedingly joyful in all our tribulation.

Jesus, the author and finisher of our faith, . . . for the joy that was set before Him endured the cross, despising the shame. ◊ These things I have spoken to you, that My joy may remain in you, and that your joy may be full. ◊ As the sufferings of Christ abound in us, so our consolation also abounds through Christ.

Rejoice in the Lord always. Again I will say, rejoice! ◊ The joy of the Lord is your strength.

In Your presence is fullness of joy; at Your right hand are pleasures forevermore. ◊ For the Lamb who is in the midst of the throne will shepherd them and lead them to living fountains of waters. And God will wipe away every tear from their eyes.

GAL 5:22.ROM 14:17.1 PET 1:8.2 COR 6:4,10.2 COR 7:4.HEB 12:2.JOHN 15:11.2 COR 1:5.PHIL 4:4.NEH 8:10.PS 16:11.REV 7:17

Little children, keep yourselves from idols. ◊ Therefore "Come out from among them and be separate, says the Lord. Do not touch what is unclean, and I will receive you. I will be a Father to you, and you shall be My sons and daughters, says the Lord Almighty." ◊ You cannot serve God and mammon.

You shall worship no other god, for the Lord, whose name is Jealous, is a jealous God. ◊ Serve Him with a loyal heart and with a willing mind; for the Lord searches all hearts and understands all the intent of the thoughts.

For man looks at the outward appearance, but the Lord looks at the heart. ◊ Beloved, if our heart does not condemn us, we have confidence toward God.

1 SAM 7:3.1 JOHN 5:21.2 COR 6:17-18.MATT 6:24.EX 34:14.1 CHR 28:9.1 SAM 16:7.1 JOHN 3:21

## April 2

If you return to the LORD with all your hearts, then put away the foreign gods and the Ashtoreths from among you, and prepare your hearts for the Lord, and serve Him only.

## April 3

Beloved, do not forget this one thing, that with the Lord one day is as a thousand years, and a thousand years as one day. The Lord is not slack concerning His promise, as some count slackness.

"For My thoughts are not your thoughts, nor are your ways My ways," says the Lord. "For as the heavens are higher than the earth, so are My ways higher than your ways, and My thoughts than your thoughts. For as the rain comes down, and the snow from heaven, and do not return there, but water the earth, . . . so shall My word be that goes forth from My mouth; it shall not return to Me void, but it shall accomplish what I please, and it shall prosper in the thing for which I sent it."

For God has committed them all to disobedience, that He might have mercy on all. Oh, the depth of the riches both of the wisdom and knowledge of God! How unsearchable are His judgments and His ways past finding out!

2 PET 3:8-9.IS 55:8-11.ROM 11:32-33

You have not come to the mountain that may be touched and that burned with fire, and to blackness and darkness and tempest, . . . but you have come to Mount Zion to God the Judge of all, to the spirits of just men made perfect, . . . to Jesus the Mediator of the new covenant. ◊ Jesus, the author and finisher of our faith. ◊ We do not have a High Priest who cannot sympathize with our weaknesses, but was in all points tempted as we are, yet without sin. Let us therefore come boldly to the throne of grace, that we may obtain mercy and find grace to help in time of need.

Thus says the Lord, the King of Israel, and his Redeemer, the Lord of hosts: "I am the First and I am the Last; besides Me there is no God." ◊ Mighty God, Everlasting Father, Prince of Peace.

Are You not from everlasting, O Lord my God, my Holy One? ◊ Who is God, except the Lord? And who is a rock, except our God?

REV 1:17.HEB 12:18,22-24.HEB 12:2.HEB 4:15-16.IS 44:6.IS 9:6.HAB 1:12.2 SAM 22:32

## April 4

Do not be afraid; I am the First and the Last.

## April 5

**I will not let You go unless You bless me!**

Or let him take hold of My strength, that he may make peace with Me; and he shall make peace with Me.

O woman, great is your faith! Let it be to you as you desire. ◊ According to your faith let it be to you. ◊ Let him ask in faith, with no doubting, for he who doubts is like a wave of the sea driven and tossed by the wind. For let not that man suppose that he will receive anything from the Lord.

They drew near to the village where they were going, and He indicated that He would have gone farther. But they constrained Him, saying, "Abide with us." . . . He vanished from their sight. And they said to one another, "Did not our heart burn within us while He talked with us on the road, and while He opened the Scriptures to us?" ◊ I pray, if I have found grace in Your sight, show me now Your way, that I may know You and that I may find grace in Your sight. ◊ My Presence will go with you, and I will give you rest.

GEN 32:26.IS 27:5.MATT 15:28.MATT 9:29.JAMES 1:6-7.LUKE 24:28-29,31-32.EX 33:13-14

Who is he who condemns? It is Christ who died, . . . who also makes intercession for us. ◊ Christ has not entered the holy places made with hands, which are copies of the true, but into heaven itself, now to appear in the presence of God for us.

If anyone sins, we have an Advocate with the Father, Jesus Christ the righteous. ◊ There is one God and one Mediator between God and men, the Man Christ Jesus.

Let us hold fast our confession. For we do not have a High Priest who cannot sympathize with our weaknesses, but was in all points tempted as we are, yet without sin. Let us therefore come boldly to the throne of grace, that we may obtain mercy and find grace to help in time of need.

Through Him we . . . have access by one Spirit to the Father.

Heb 7:25.ROM 8:34.HEB 9:24.1 JOHN 2:1.1 TIM 2:5.HEB 4:14-16.EPH 2:18.

He ever lives to make intercession.

## April 7

We commend
ourselves . . . as
sorrowful, yet
always rejoicing;
as poor, yet
making many
rich; as having
nothing, and yet
possessing all
things.

We . . . rejoice in hope of the glory of
God. And not only that, but we also
glory in tribulations. ◊ Believing, you
rejoice with joy inexpressible.

In a great trial of affliction the
abundance of their joy and their deep
poverty abounded in the riches of their
liberality. ◊ To me, who am less than
the least of all the saints, this grace was
given, that I should preach among the
Gentiles the unsearchable riches of
Christ, and to make all people see what
is the fellowship of the mystery, which
from the beginning of the ages has been
hidden in God who created all things
through Jesus Christ.

Has God not chosen the poor of this
world to be rich in faith and heirs of the
kingdom which He promised to those
who love Him? ◊ God is able to make
all grace abound toward you, that you,
always having all sufficiency in all
things, have an abundance for every
good work.

2 COR 6:4,10.ROM 5:2-3.2 COR 7:4.1 PET 1:8.2 COR
8:2.EPH 3:8-9.JAMES 2:5.2 COR 9:8

When we were still without strength, in due time Christ died for the ungodly. ◊ He who did not spare His own Son, but delivered Him up for us all, how shall He not with Him also freely give us all things?

For in Him dwells all the fullness of the Godhead bodily; and you are complete in Him, who is the head of all principality and power.

Abide in Me, and I in you. As the branch cannot bear fruit of itself, unless it abides in the vine, neither can you, unless you abide in Me. I am the vine, you are the branches. He who abides in Me, and I in him, bears much fruit; for without Me you can do nothing. ◊ To will is present with me, but how to perform what is good I do not find. ◊ To each one of us grace was given according to the measure of Christ's gift.

If you abide in Me, and My words abide in you, you will ask what you desire, and it shall be done for you. ◊ Let the word of Christ dwell in you richly in all wisdom.

1 COR 1:5.ROM 5:6.ROM 8:32.COL 2:9-10.JOHN 15:4-5.ROM 7:18.EPH 4:7.JOHN 15:7.COL 3:16

**You were enriched in everything by Him.**

## April 9

**Fear not, for I have redeemed you.**

Do not fear, for you will not be ashamed; nor be disgraced, for you will not be put to shame; for you will forget the shame of your youth, and will not remember the reproach of your widowhood anymore. For your Maker is your husband, the Lord of hosts is His name; and your Redeemer is the Holy One of Israel; He is called the God of the whole earth. ◊ I have blotted out, like a thick cloud, your transgressions, and like a cloud, your sins. Return to Me, for I have redeemed you. ◊ You were . . . redeemed . . . with the precious blood of Christ, as of a lamb without blemish and without spot.

Their Redeemer is strong; the Lord of hosts is His name. He will thoroughly plead their case. ◊ My Father, who has given them to Me, is greater than all; and no one is able to snatch them out of My Father's hand.

Grace to you and peace from God the Father and our Lord Jesus Christ, who gave Himself for our sins, that He might deliver us from this present evil age, according to the will of our God and Father, to whom be glory forever and ever. Amen.

IS 43:1.IS 54:4-5.IS 44:22.1 PET 1:18-19.JER 50:34.JOHN 10:29.GAL 1:3-5

I am dark, but lovely.

Behold, I was brought forth in iniquity, and in sin my mother conceived me. ◊ "Your fame went out among the nations because of your beauty, for it was perfect through My splendor which I had bestowed on you," says the Lord God.

I am a sinful man, O Lord! ◊ Behold, you are fair, my love! Behold, you are fair!

"I abhor myself, and repent in dust and ashes." ◊ You are all fair, my love, and there is no spot in you.

I find then a law, that evil is present with me, the one who wills to do good. ◊ Be of good cheer; your sins are forgiven you.

I know that in me (that is, in my flesh) nothing good dwells. ◊ You are complete in Him. ◊ Perfect in Christ Jesus.

You were washed, . . . you were sanctified, . . . you were justified in the name of the Lord Jesus and by the Spirit of our God. ◊ Proclaim the praises of Him who called you out of darkness into His marvelous light.

SONG 1:5.PS 51:5.EZEK 16:14.LUKE 5:8.SONG 4:1.JOB 42:6.SONG 4:7.ROM 7:21.MATT 9:2.ROM 7:18.COL 2:10.COL 1:28.1 COR 6:11.1 PET 2:9

## April 11

My beloved brethren, let every man be swift to hear, slow to speak, slow to wrath. ◊ He who is slow to anger is better than the mighty, and he who rules his spirit than he who takes a city. ◊ If anyone does not stumble in word, he is a perfect man, able also to bridle the whole body. ◊ For by your words you will be justified, and by your words you will be condemned. ◊ Set a guard, O Lord, over my mouth; keep watch over the door of my lips.

Christ . . . suffered for us, leaving us an example, that you should follow His steps: who committed no sin, nor was guile found in His mouth; who, when He was reviled, did not revile in return; when He suffered, He did not threaten, but committed Himself to Him who judges righteously. ◊ Consider Him who endured such hostility from sinners against Himself, lest you become weary and discouraged in your souls.

In their mouth was found no guile, for they are without fault before the throne of God.

PROV 10:19.JAMES 1:19.PROV 16:32.JAMES 3:2.MATT 12:37.PS 141:3.1 PET 2:21-23.HEB 12:3.REV 14:5

The law, having a shadow of the good things to come, and not the very image of the things, can never with these same sacrifices, which they offer continually year by year, make those who approach perfect. For then would they not have ceased to be offered? ◊ By Him everyone who believes is justified from all things from which you could not be justified by the law of Moses.

Inasmuch . . . as the children have partaken of flesh and blood, He Himself likewise shared in the same, that through death He might destroy him who had the power of death, that is, the devil, and release those who through fear of death were all their lifetime subject to bondage. For indeed He does not give aid to angels, but He does give aid to the seed of Abraham. Therefore, in all things He had to be made like His brethren.

ROM 8:3.HEB 10:1-2.ACTS 13:39.HEB 2:14-17

## April 12

What the law could not do in that it was weak through the flesh, God did by sending His own Son in the likeness of sinful flesh, on account of sin: He condemned sin in the flesh.

## April 13

He who sows sparingly will also reap sparingly, and he who sows bountifully will also reap bountifully. ◊ On the first day of the week let each one of you lay something aside, storing up as he may prosper.

God is not unjust to forget your work and labor of love which you have shown toward His name, in that you have ministered to the saints, and do minister.

I beseech you . . . brethren, by the mercies of God, that you present your bodies a living sacrifice, holy, acceptable to God, which is your reasonable service. ◊ The love of Christ constrains us, because we judge thus: that if One died for all, then all died; and He died for all, that those who live should live no longer for themselves, but for Him who died for them and rose again. ◊ Whether you eat or drink, or whatever you do, do all to the glory of God.

PROV 3:9.2 COR 9:6.1 COR 16:2.HEB 6:10.ROM 12:1.2 COR 5:14-15.1 COR 10:31

How precious . . . are Your thoughts to me, O God! How great is the sum of them! If I should count them, they would be more in number than the sand; when I awake, I am still with You. ◊ How sweet are Your words to my taste, sweeter than honey to my mouth! ◊ Whom have I in heaven but You? And there is none upon earth that I desire besides You.

Like an apple tree among the trees of the woods, so is my beloved among the sons. I sat down in his shade with great delight, and his fruit was sweet to my taste. He brought me to the banqueting house, and his banner over me was love. ◊ His countenance is like Lebanon, excellent as the cedars. His mouth is most sweet, yes, he is altogether lovely. This is my beloved, and this is my friend.

PS 63:5-6.PS 139:17-18.PS 119:103.PS 73:25.SONG 2:3-4.SONG 5:15-16

## April 14

My soul shall be satisfied as with marrow and fatness, and my mouth shall praise You with joyful lips. When I remember You on my bed, I meditate on You in the night watches.

## April 15

**Their Redeemer is strong.**

For I know your manifold transgressions and your mighty sins. ◊ I have given help to one who is mighty. ◊ I, the Lord, am your Savior, and your Redeemer, the Mighty One of Jacob. ◊ I [am] mighty to save. ◊ [He] is able to keep you from stumbling. ◊ Where sin abounded, grace abounded much more.

He who believes in Him is not condemned; but he who does not believe is condemned already, because he has not believed in the name of the only begotten Son of God. ◊ He is also able to save to the uttermost those who come to God through Him.

Is My hand shortened at all that it cannot redeem?

Who shall separate us from the love of Christ? . . . For I am persuaded that neither death nor life, nor angels nor principalities nor powers, nor things present nor things to come, nor height nor depth, nor any other created thing, shall be able to separate us from the love of God which is in Christ Jesus our Lord.

JER 50:34. AMOS 5:12. PS 89:19. IS 49:26. IS 63:1. JUDE 1:24. ROM 5:20. JOHN 3:18. HEB 7:25. IS 50:2. ROM 8:35,38-39

I sink in deep mire, where there is no standing; I have come into deep waters, where the floods overflow me. ◊ Waters flowed over my head; I said, "I am cut off!" I called on Your name, O Lord, from the lowest pit. You have heard my voice: "Do not hide Your ear from my sighing, from my cry for help." You drew near on the day I called on You, and said, "Do not fear!"

Will the Lord cast off forever? And will He be favorable no more? Has His mercy ceased forever? Has His promise failed forevermore? Has God forgotten to be gracious? . . . And I said, "This is my anguish; but I will remember the years of the right hand of the Most High." I will remember the works of the Lord; surely I will remember Your wonders of old. ◊ I would have lost heart, unless I had believed that I would see the goodness of the Lord in the land of the living.

PS 31:22.PS 69:2.LAM 3:54-57.PS 77:7-11.PS 27:13

I said in my haste, "I am cut off from before Your eyes"; nevertheless You heard the voice of my supplications when I cried out to You.

## April 17

Let the word of Christ dwell in you richly in all wisdom, teaching and admonishing one another in psalms and hymns and spiritual songs, singing with grace in your hearts to the Lord. And whatever you do in word or deed, do all in the name of the Lord Jesus, giving thanks to God the Father through Him. ◊ Glorify God in your body and in your spirit, which are God's.

You are . . . a royal priesthood, . . . that you may proclaim the praises of Him who called you out of darkness into His marvelous light. ◊ You . . . as living stones, are being built up a spiritual house, a holy priesthood, to offer up spiritual sacrifices acceptable to God through Jesus Christ. ◊ By Him let us continually offer the sacrifice of praise to God.

My soul shall make its boast in the Lord; the humble shall hear of it and be glad. Oh, magnify the Lord with me, and let us exalt His name together.

PS 50:23.COL 3:16-17.1 COR 6:20.1 PET 2:9.1 PET
2:5.HEB 13:15.PS 34:2-3

I [Moses] stood between the Lord and you at that time, to declare to you the word of the Lord; for you were afraid. ◊ There is one God and one Mediator between God and men, the Man Christ Jesus. ◊ (Now the man Moses was very humble, more than all men who were on the face of the earth.) ◊ Take My yoke upon you and learn from Me, for I am gentle and lowly in heart, and you will find rest for your souls. ◊ Christ Jesus, . . . being in the form of God, did not consider it robbery to be equal with God, but made Himself of no reputation, taking the form of a servant, and coming in the likeness of men.

Moses indeed was faithful in all His house as a servant, for a testimony of those things which would be spoken afterward, but Christ as a Son over His own house, whose house we are if we hold fast the confidence and the rejoicing of the hope firm to the end.

**I will raise up for them a Prophet like you from among their brethren.**

DEUT 18:18.DEUT 5:5.1 TIM 2:5.NUM 12:3.MATT 11:29.PHIL 2:5-7.HEB 3:5-6

## April 19

Most assuredly, I say to you, I am the door of the sheep.

The veil of the temple was torn in two from top to bottom. ◊ Christ also suffered once for sins, the just for the unjust, that He might bring us to God. ◊ The Holy Spirit indicating this, that the way into the Holiest of All was not yet made manifest while the first tabernacle was still standing.

I am the door. If anyone enters by Me, he will be saved, and will go in and out and find pasture. ◊ No one comes to the Father except through Me. ◊ Through Him we . . . have access by one Spirit to the Father. Now, therefore, you are no longer strangers and foreigners, but fellow citizens with the saints and members of the household of God. ◊ [Have] boldness to enter the Holiest by the blood of Jesus, by a new and living way which He consecrated for us, through the veil, that is, His flesh. ◊ We have peace with God through our Lord Jesus Christ, through whom also we have access by faith into this grace in which we stand.

JOHN 10:7.MATT 27:51.1 PET 3:18.HEB 9:8.JOHN 10:9.JOHN 14:6.EPH 2:18-19.HEB 10:19-20.ROM 5:1-2

Come out from among them and be separate, says the Lord. Do not touch what is unclean. ◊ Beloved, I beg you as sojourners and pilgrims, abstain from fleshly lusts which war against the soul. ◊ [Hate] even the garment defiled by the flesh.

None of the accursed things shall remain in your hand.

Beloved, now we are children of God; and it has not yet been revealed what we shall be, but we know that when He is revealed, we shall be like Him, for we shall see Him as He is. And everyone who has this hope in Him purifies himself, just as He is pure. ◊ For the grace of God that brings salvation has appeared to all men, teaching us that, denying ungodliness and worldly lusts, we should live soberly, righteously, and godly in the present age, looking for the blessed hope and glorious appearing of our great God and Savior Jesus Christ, who gave Himself for us, that He might redeem us from every lawless deed and purify for Himself His own special people, zealous for good works.

DEUT 13:17.2 COR 6:17.1 PET 2:11.JUDE 1:23.1 JOHN 3:2-3.TITUS 2:11-14

## April 21

My foot has held fast to His steps; I have kept His way and not turned aside.

The Lord loves justice, and does not forsake His saints; they are preserved forever. ◊ The Lord shall preserve you from all evil; He shall preserve your soul.

The just shall live by faith; but if anyone draws back, my soul has no pleasure in him. But we are not of those who draw back to perdition, but of those who believe to the saving of the soul. ◊ They went out from us, but they were not of us; for if they had been of us, they would have continued with us; but they went out that they might be made manifest, that none of them were of us.

If you abide in My word, you are My disciples indeed. ◊ He who endures to the end shall be saved. ◊ Watch, stand fast in the faith, be brave, be strong. ◊ Hold fast what you have, that no one may take your crown. ◊ He who overcomes shall be clothed in white garments, and I will not blot out his name from the Book of Life.

PHIL 4:1.JOB 23:11.PS 37:28.PS 121:7.HEB 10:38-39.
1 JOHN 2:19.JOHN 8:31.MATT 24:13.1 COR 16:13.REV 3:11.REV 3:5

God will provide for Himself the lamb for a burnt offering. ◊ Behold! The Lamb of God who takes away the sin of the world! ◊ We have been sanctified through the offering of the body of Jesus Christ once for all. ◊ The Son of Man . . . [gave] his life, a ransom for many.

No one takes it from Me, but I lay it down of Myself. I have power to lay it down, and I have power to take it again. ◊ I will love them freely. ◊ The Son of God . . . loved me and gave Himself for me.

He made Him who knew no sin to be sin for us, that we might become the righteousness of God in Him. ◊ He has made us accepted in the Beloved.

LEV 1:3-4.GEN 22:8.JOHN 1:29.HEB 10:10.MATT 20:28.JOHN 10:18.HOS 14:4.GAL 2:20.2 COR 5:21.EPH 1:6

## April 22

If his offering is a burnt sacrifice of the herd, let him offer a male without blemish; he shall offer it of his own free will. . . . Then he shall put his hand on the head of the burnt offering, and it will be accepted on his behalf to make atonement for him.

## April 23

**The Lord was my support.**

Truly, in vain is salvation hoped for from the hills, and from the multitude of mountains; truly, in the Lord our God is the salvation of Israel. ◊ The Lord is my rock and my fortress and my deliverer; my God, my strength, in whom I will trust; my shield and the horn of my salvation, my stronghold. ◊ Cry out and shout, O inhabitant of Zion, for great is the Holy One of Israel in your midst!

The angel of the Lord encamps all around those who fear Him, and delivers them. . . . The righteous cry out, and the Lord hears, and delivers them out of all their troubles. ◊ The eternal God is your refuge, and underneath are the everlasting arms. ◊ So we may boldly say: "The Lord is my helper; I will not fear. What can man do to me?" ◊ For who is God, except the Lord? And who is a rock, except our God? It is God who arms me with strength, and makes my way perfect.

By the grace of God I am what I am.

PS 18:18.JER 3:23.PS 18:2.IS 12:6.PS 34:7,17.DEUT 33:27.HEB 13:6.PS 18:31-32.1 COR 15:10

Trust in Him at all times, you people; pour out your heart before Him; God is a refuge for us. ◊ David strengthened himself in the Lord his God. ◊ God will surely visit you, and bring you out of this land to the land of which He swore to Abraham, to Isaac, and to Jacob. ◊ "I have certainly seen the oppression of my people who are in Egypt; I have heard their groaning and have come down to deliver them." . . . He brought them out, after he had shown wonders and signs in the land of Egypt, and in the Red Sea, and in the wilderness forty years. ◊ Not a word failed of any good thing which the Lord had spoken. . . . All came to pass.

He who promised is faithful. ◊ Has He said, and will He not do it? Or has He spoken, and will He not make it good? ◊ Heaven and earth will pass away, but My words will by no means pass away. ◊ The grass withers, the flower fades, but the word of our God stands forever.

GEN 21:1.PS 62:8.1 SAM 30:6.GEN 50:24.ACTS 7:34,36.JOSH 21:45.HEB 10:23.NUM 23:19.MATT 24:35.IS 40:8

## April 24

The LORD visited Sarah as He had said, and the LORD did for Sarah as He had spoken.

## April 25

You know that He was manifested to take away our sins. ◊ That we, having died to sins, might live for righteousness. ◊ He is also able to save to the uttermost those who come to God through Him.

He was wounded for our transgressions, He was bruised for our iniquities; the chastisement for our peace was upon Him, and by His stripes we are healed. The Lord has laid on Him the iniquity of us all. ◊ Thus it was necessary for the Christ to suffer . . . that repentance and remission of sins should be preached in His name to all nations. ◊ He has appeared to put away sin by the sacrifice of Himself.

Him God has exalted to His right hand to be Prince and Savior, to give repentance. ◊ Through this Man is preached to you the forgiveness of sins; and by Him everyone who believes is justified from all things from which you could not be justified by the law of Moses. ◊ Your sins are forgiven you for His name's sake.

MATT 1:21.1 JOHN 3:5.1 PET 2:24.HEB 7:25.IS 53:5-6.LUKE 24:46-47.HEB 9:26.ACTS 5:31 ACTS 13:38-39 1 JOHN 2:12

Underneath are the everlasting arms.
◊ When he saw that the wind was boisterous, he was afraid; and beginning to sink he cried out, saying, "Lord, save me!" And immediately Jesus stretched out His hand and caught him, and said to him, "O you of little faith, why did you doubt?" ◊ The steps of a good man are ordered by the Lord, and He delights in his way. Though he fall, he shall not be utterly cast down; for the Lord upholds him with His hand.

The beloved of the Lord shall dwell in safety by Him, who shelters him all the day long; and he shall dwell between His shoulders. ◊ [Cast] all your care upon Him, for He cares for you. ◊ He who touches you touches the apple of His eye.

They shall never perish; neither shall anyone snatch them out of My hand. My Father, who has given them to Me, is greater than all.

SONG 2:6.DEUT 33:27.MATT 14:30,31.PS 37:23-24.DEUT 33:12.1 PET 5:7.ZECH 2:8.JOHN 10:28-29

His left hand is under my head, and his right hand embraces me.

## April 27

Brethren, the time is short.

Man who is born of woman is of few days and full of trouble. He comes forth like a flower and fades away; he flees like a shadow and does not continue. ◊ The world is passing away, and the lust of it; but he who does the will of God abides forever. ◊ As in Adam all die, even so in Christ all shall be made alive. . . . Death is swallowed up in victory. ◊ For if we live, we live to the Lord; and if we die, we die to the Lord. Therefore, whether we live or die, we are the Lord's. ◊ To live is Christ, and to die is gain.

Do not cast away your confidence, which has great reward. For you have need of endurance, so that after you have done the will of God, you may receive the promise. . . . "For yet a little while, and He who is coming will come and will not tarry." ◊ The night is far spent, the day is at hand. Therefore let us cast off the works of darkness, and let us put on the armor of light. ◊ The end of all things is at hand; therefore be serious and watchful in your prayers.

1 COR 7:29.JOB 14:1-2.1 JOHN 2:17.1 COR 15:22,54.ROM 14:8.PHIL 1:21.HEB 10:35-37.ROM 13:12. 1 PET 4:7

It is not possible that the blood of bulls and goats could take away sins. Therefore, when He came into the world, He said: "Sacrifice and offering You did not desire, but a body You have prepared for Me. In burnt offerings and sacrifices for sin you had no pleasure. Then I said, 'Behold, I have come—in the volume of the book it is written of Me—to do Your will, O God.' " ◊ He was oppressed and He was afflicted, yet He opened not His mouth; He was led as a lamb to the slaughter, and as a sheep before its shearers is silent, so He opened not his mouth.

You were not redeemed with corruptible things, like silver or gold, . . . but with the precious blood of Christ, as of a lamb without blemish and without spot. He indeed was . . . manifest in these last times for you who through Him believe in God, . . . that your faith and hope are in God.

Worthy is the Lamb who was slain to receive power and riches and wisdom, and strength and honor and glory and blessing!

JOHN 1:29.HEB 10:4-7.IS 53:7.1 PET 1:18-21.REV 5:12

April 28

Behold! The Lamb of God.

## April 29

You shall remember that the Lord your God led you all the way these forty years in the wilderness, to humble you and test you, to know what was in your heart, whether you would keep His commandments or not. . . . So you should know in your heart that as a man chastens his son, so the Lord your God chastens you.

I know, O Lord, that Your judgments are right, and that in faithfulness You have afflicted me. ◊ It is good for me that I have been afflicted, that I may learn Your statutes. ◊ Before I was afflicted I went astray, but now I keep Your word. ◊ The Lord has chastened me severely, but He has not given me over to death. ◊ He has not dealt with us according to our sins, nor punished us according to our iniquities. For as the heavens are high above the earth, so great is His mercy toward those who fear Him. . . . He knows our frame; He remembers that we are dust.

1 SAM 12:24.DEUT 8:2,5.PS 119:75.PS 119:71.PS 119:67.PS 118:18.PS 103:10-11,14

The God of peace who brought up our Lord Jesus from the dead, that great Shepherd of the sheep, through the blood of the everlasting covenant, make you complete in every good work to do His will, working in you what is well pleasing in His sight, through Jesus Christ, to whom be glory forever and ever. Amen.

Now by this we know that we know Him, if we keep His commandments. ◊ If anyone loves Me, he will keep My word; and My Father will love him, and We will come to him and make Our home with him. ◊ Whoever abides in Him does not sin. Whoever sins has neither seen Him nor known Him. Little children, let no one deceive you. He who practices righteousness is righteous, just as He is righteous. ◊ Love has been perfected among us in this: that we may have boldness in the day of judgment; because as He is, so are we in this world.

1 JOHN 2:5.HEB 13:20-21.1 JOHN 2:3.JOHN 14:23.
1 JOHN 3:6-7.1 JOHN 4:17

Whoever keeps His word, truly the love of God is perfected in him.

## May 1

To be spiritually minded is life and peace. ◇ God has called us to peace. ◇ Peace I leave with you, My peace I give to you; not as the world gives do I give to you. Let not your heart be troubled, neither let it be afraid. ◇ The God of hope fill you with all joy and peace in believing.

I know whom I have believed and am persuaded that He is able to keep what I have committed to Him until that Day. ◇ You will keep him in perfect peace, whose mind is stayed on You, because he trusts in You.

The work of righteousness will be peace, and the effect of righteousness, quietness and assurance forever. My people will dwell in a peaceful habitation, in secure dwellings, and in quiet resting places. ◇ Whoever listens to me will dwell safely, and will be secure, without fear of evil. ◇ Great peace have those who love Your law.

GAL 5:22.ROM 8:6.1 COR 7:15.JOHN 14:27.ROM 15:13.2 TIM 1:12.IS 26:3.IS 32:17-18.PROV 1:33.PS 119:165

Where two or three are gathered together in My name, I am there in the midst of them. ◊ Lo, I am with you always, even to the end of the age. ◊ My Presence will go with you, and I will give you rest.

Where can I go from Your Spirit? Or where can I flee from Your presence? If I ascend into heaven, You are there; if I make my bed in hell, behold, You are there. ◊ "Am I a God near at hand," says the Lord, "and not a God afar off? Can anyone hide himself in secret places, so I shall not see him?" says the Lord; "do I not fill heaven and earth?" says the Lord.

Behold, heaven and the heaven of heavens cannot contain You. How much less this temple which I have built! ◊ Thus says the High and Lofty One who inhabits eternity, whose name is Holy: "I dwell in the high and holy place, with him who has a contrite and humble spirit, to revive the spirit of the humble, and to revive the heart of the contrite ones."

Surely the LORD is in this place, and I did not know it.

GEN 28:16.MATT 18:10.MATT 28:20.EX 33:14.PS 139:7-8.JER 23:23-24.1 KIN 8:27.IS 57:15

## May 3

You shall be perfect, just as your Father in heaven is perfect.

I am Almighty God; walk before Me and be blameless. ◊ You shall be holy to Me, for I the Lord am holy, and have separated you from the peoples, that you should be Mine. ◊ You were bought at a price; therefore glorify God in your body and in your spirit, which are God's.

You are complete in Him, who is the head of all principality and power. ◊ Who gave Himself for us, that He might redeem us from every lawless deed. ◊ Be diligent to be found by Him in peace, without spot and blameless.

Blessed are the undefiled in the way, who walk in the law of the Lord! ◊ He who looks into the perfect law of liberty and continues in it, and is not a forgetful hearer but a doer of the work, this one will be blessed in what he does. ◊ Search me, O God, and know my heart; try me, and know my anxieties; and see if there is any wicked way in me, and lead me in the way everlasting.

MATT 5:48.GEN 17:1.LEV 20:26.1 COR 6:20.COL 2:10.TITUS 2:14.2 PET 3:14.PS 119:1.JAMES 1:25.PS 139:23-24

In the day when I cried out, You answered me, and made me bold with strength in my soul. ◊ While I was speaking in prayer, the man Gabriel, whom I had seen in the vision at the beginning, being caused to fly swiftly, reached me about the time of the evening offering.

Do not hide Your face from me; do not turn Your servant away in anger; You have been my help; do not leave me nor forsake me, O God of my salvation. ◊ But You, O Lord, do not be far from Me; O My Strength, hasten to help Me!

Ah, Lord God! Behold, You have made the heavens and the earth by Your great power and outstretched arm. There is nothing too hard for You. ◊ [He] delivered us from so great a death, and does deliver us; in whom we trust that He will still deliver us. ◊ Shall God not avenge His own elect who cry out day and night to Him, though He bears long with them? I tell you that He will avenge them speedily.

IS 59:1.PS 138:3.DAN 9:21.PS 27:9.PS 22:19.JER 32:17
2 COR 1:10.LUKE 18:7-8

## May 4

Behold, the Lord's hand is not shortened, that it cannot save; nor His ear heavy, that it cannot hear.

## May 5

*Therefore do not worry, saying, "What shall we eat?" or "What shall we drink?" or "What shall we wear?" For your heavenly Father knows that you need all these things.*

Oh, fear the Lord, you His saints! There is no want to those who fear Him. The young lions lack and suffer hunger; but those who seek the Lord shall not lack any good thing. ◊ No good thing will He withhold from those who walk uprightly. O Lord of hosts, blessed is the man who trusts in You!

I want you to be without care. ◊ Be anxious for nothing, but in everything by prayer and supplication, with thanksgiving, let your requests be made known to God.

Are not two sparrows sold for a copper coin? And not one of them falls to the ground apart from your Father's will. But the very hairs of your head are all numbered. Do not fear therefore; you are of more value than many sparrows. ◊ Why are you so fearful? How is it that you have no faith? ◊ Have faith in God.

MATT 6:31-32.PS 34:9-10.PS 84:11-12.1 COR 7:32.PHIL 4:6.MATT 10:29-31.MARK 4:40.MARK 11:22

[I am] a just God and a Savior.
The Lord is well pleased for His righteousness' sake; He will magnify the law and make it honorable.

God was in Christ reconciling the world to Himself, not imputing their trespasses to them. ◊ God set [Him] forth to be a propitiation by His blood, through faith, to demonstrate His righteousness, because in His forbearance God had passed over the sins that were previously committed, to demonstrate at the present time His righteousness, that He might be just and the justifier of the one who has faith in Jesus. ◊ He was wounded for our transgressions, He was bruised for our iniquities; the chastisement for our peace was upon Him, and by His stripes we are healed. ◊ Who shall bring a charge against God's elect? It is God who justifies. ◊ To him who does not work but believes on Him who justifies the ungodly, his faith is accounted for righteousness.

PS 85:10.IS 45:21.IS 42:21.2 COR 5:19.ROM 3:25-26.IS 53:5.ROM 8:33.ROM 4:5

Mercy and truth have met together; righteousness and peace have kissed each other.

## May 7

God is our refuge and strength, a very present help in trouble. Therefore we will not fear, though the earth be removed, and though the mountains be carried into the midst of the sea. ◊ Come, my people, enter your chambers, and shut your doors behind you; hide yourself, as it were, for a little moment, until the indignation is past. For behold, the Lord comes out of His place to punish the inhabitants of the earth for their iniquity. ◊ In the shadow of Your wings I will make my refuge, until these calamities have passed by. ◊ Your life is hidden with Christ in God.

He will not be afraid of evil tidings; his heart is steadfast, trusting in the Lord.

These things I have spoken to you, that in Me you may have peace. In the world you will have tribulation; but be of good cheer, I have overcome the world.

MATT 24:6.PS 46:1-2.IS 26:20-21.PS 57:1.COL 3:3.PS 112:7.JOHN 16:33

"Now My soul is troubled, and what shall I say? 'Father, save Me from this hour'? But for this purpose I came to this hour. Father, glorify Your name." Then a voice came from heaven, saying, "I have both glorified it and will glorify it again." ◊ "Father, if it is Your will, remove this cup from Me; nevertheless not My will, but Yours, be done." Then an angel appeared to Him from heaven, strengthening Him.

Being found in appearance as a man, He humbled Himself and became obedient to the point of death, even the death of the cross. ◊ Therefore My Father loves Me, because I lay down My life that I may take it again. ◊ For I have come down from heaven, not to do My own will, but the will of Him who sent Me. ◊ Shall I not drink the cup which My Father has given Me?

The Father has not left Me alone, for I always do those things that please Him. ◊ This is My beloved Son, in whom I am well pleased.

IS 53:10.JOHN 12:27-28.LUKE 22:42-43.PHIL 2:8.JOHN 10:17.JOHN 6:38.JOHN 18:11.JOHN 8:29.MATT 3:17

## May 8

It pleased the LORD to bruise Him; He has put Him to grief.

## May 9

Faith is the substance of things hoped for, the evidence of things not seen.

If in this life only we have hope in Christ, we are of all men the most pitiable.

Eye has not seen, nor ear heard, nor have entered into the heart of man the things which God has prepared for those who love Him. But God has revealed them to us through His Spirit. ◊ After you . . . believed, you were sealed with the Holy Spirit of promise, who is the guarantee of our inheritance until the redemption of the purchased possession.

Jesus said to him, "Thomas, because you have seen Me, you have believed. Blessed are those who have not seen and yet have believed." ◊ Jesus Christ whom having not seen you love. Though now you do not see Him, yet believing, you rejoice with joy inexpressible and full of glory, receiving the end of your faith—the salvation of your souls.

We walk by faith, not by sight. ◊ Do not cast away your confidence, which has great reward.

HEB 11:1.1 COR 15:19.1 COR 2:9-10.EPH 1:13-14.JOHN 20:29.1 PET 1:7-9.2 COR 5:7.HEB 10:35

For we do not wrestle against flesh and blood, but against principalities, against powers, against the rulers of the darkness of this age, against spiritual hosts of wickedness in the heavenly places. ◊ Inasmuch . . . as the children have partaken of flesh and blood, He Himself likewise shared in the same, that through death He might destroy him who had the power of death, that is, the devil. ◊ Having disarmed principalities and powers, He made a public spectacle of them, triumphing over them in it. ◊ I heard a loud voice saying in heaven, "Now salvation, and strength, and the kingdom of our God, and the power of His Christ have come, for the accuser of our brethren, who accused them before our God day and night, has been cast down. And they overcame him by the blood of the Lamb and by the word of their testimony and they did not love their lives to the death."

Thanks be to God, who gives us the victory through our Lord Jesus Christ.

1 JOHN 3:8.EPH 6:12.HEB 2:14.COL 2:15.REV 12:10-11.1 COR 15:57

## May 10

For this purpose the Son of God was manifested, that He might destroy the works of the devil.

## May 11

**Awake to righteousness, and do not sin.**

You are all sons of light and sons of the day. Therefore let us not sleep, as others do, but let us watch and be sober.

It is high time to awake out of sleep; for now our salvation is nearer than when we first believed. The night is far spent, the day is at hand. Therefore let us cast off the works of darkness, and let us put on the armor of light. ◊ Therefore take up the whole armor of God, that you may be able to withstand in the evil day, and having done all, to stand. ◊ Cast away from you all the transgressions which you have committed, and get yourselves a new heart and a new spirit. ◊ Lay aside all filthiness and overflow of wickedness, and receive with meekness the implanted word, which is able to save your souls. ◊ Little children, abide in Him, that when He appears, we may have confidence and not be ashamed before Him at His coming. If you know that He is righteous, you know that everyone who practices righteousness is born of Him.

1 COR 15:34.1 THESS 5:5-6.ROM 13:11-12.EPH 6:13.EZEK 18:31.JAMES 1:21.1 JOHN 2:28-29

The love of God has been poured out in our hearts by the Holy Spirit who was given to us. ◇ You did not receive the spirit of bondage again to fear, but you received the Spirit of adoption by whom we cry out, "Abba, Father." The Spirit Himself bears witness with our spirit that we are children of God. ◇ He who believes in the Son of God has the witness in himself.

In this the love of God was manifested toward us, that God has sent His only begotten Son into the world, that we might live through Him. ◇ In Him we have redemption through His blood, the forgiveness of sins, according to the riches of His grace. ◇ That in the ages to come He might show the exceeding riches of His grace in His kindness toward us in Christ Jesus.

Beloved, if God so loved us, we also ought to love one another.

1 JOHN 4:7.ROM 5:5.ROM 8:15-16.1 JOHN 5:10.
1 JOHN 4:9.EPH 1:7.EPH 2:7.1 JOHN 4:11

## May 12

Beloved, let us love one another, for love is of God; and everyone who loves is born of God and knows God.

## May 13

Pray everywhere, lifting up holy hands, without wrath and doubting.

The true worshipers will worship the Father in spirit and truth; for the Father is seeking such to worship Him. God is Spirit, and those who worship Him must worship in spirit and truth. ◊ Then you shall call, and the Lord will answer; you shall cry, and He will say, "Here I am." ◊ Whenever you stand praying, if you have anything against anyone, forgive him.

Without faith it is impossible to please Him, for he who comes to God must believe that He is, and that He is a rewarder of those who diligently seek Him. ◊ Let him ask in faith, with no doubting, for he who doubts is like a wave of the sea driven and tossed by the wind. For let not that man suppose that he will receive anything from the Lord.

If I regard iniquity in my heart, the Lord will not hear. ◊ My little children, these things I write to you, that you may not sin. And if anyone sins, we have an Advocate with the Father, Jesus Christ the righteous.

1 TIM 2:8.JOHN 4:23-24.IS 58:9.MARK 11:25.HEB 11:6.JAMES 1:6-7.PS 66:18.1 JOHN 2:1

It is enough for a disciple that he be like his teacher, and a servant like his master.

He is despised and rejected by men, a man of sorrows and acquainted with grief. And we hid, as it were, our faces from Him; He was despised, and we did not esteem Him. ◊ Because you are not of the world, but I chose you out of the world, therefore the world hates you.

I looked for someone to take pity, but there was none. ◊ At my first defense no one stood with me, but all forsook me.

Foxes have holes and birds of the air have nests, but the Son of Man has nowhere to lay His head. ◊ Here we have no continuing city, but we seek the one to come.

Let us run with endurance the race that is set before us, looking unto Jesus, the author and finisher of our faith, who for the joy that was set before Him endured the cross, despising the shame, and has sat down at the right hand of the throne of God.

PHIL 3:10.MATT 10:25.IS 53:3.JOHN 15:19.PS 69:20.
2 TIM 4:16.MATT 8:20.HEB 13:14.HEB 12:1-2

## May 14

I may know Him and . . . the fellowship of His sufferings.

## May 15

God will wipe away every tear . . . there shall be no more death, nor sorrow, . . . for the former things have passed away.

He will swallow up death forever, and the Lord God will wipe away tears from all faces; the rebuke of His people He will take away from all the earth; for the Lord has spoken. ◊ Your sun shall no longer go down, nor shall your moon withdraw itself; for the Lord will be your everlasting light, and the days of your mourning shall be ended. ◊ The inhabitant will not say, "I am sick"; the people who dwell in it will be forgiven their iniquity. ◊ The voice of weeping shall no longer be heard in her, nor the voice of crying. ◊ Sorrow and sighing shall flee away.

I will ransom them from the power of the grave; I will redeem them from death. O Death, I will be your plagues! O Grave, I will be your destruction! ◊ The last enemy that will be destroyed is death. . . . Then shall be brought to pass the saying that is written: "Death is swallowed up in victory."

REV 21:4.IS 25:8.IS 60:20.IS 33:24.IS 65:19.IS 35:10.HOS 13:14.1 COR 15:26,54

You call me Teacher and Lord, and you say well, for so I am. ◊ If anyone serves Me, let him follow Me; and where I am, there My servant will be also. ◊ Take My yoke upon you and learn from Me, for I am gentle and lowly in heart, and you will find rest for your souls. For My yoke is easy and My burden is light.

What things were gain to me, these I have counted loss for Christ. ◊ Having been set free from sin, and having become slaves of God, you have your fruit to holiness, and the end, everlasting life.

No longer do I call you servants, for a servant does not know what his master is doing; but I have called you friends, for all things that I heard from My Father I have made known to you.

Stand fast therefore in the liberty by which Christ has made us free, and do not be entangled again with a yoke of bondage. ◊ For you, brethren, have been called to liberty; only do not use liberty as an opportunity for the flesh.

ROM 1:1.JOHN 13:13.JOHN 12:26.MATT 11:29-30.PHIL 3:7.ROM 6:22.JOHN 15:15.GAL 5:1.GAL 5:13

A servant of Jesus Christ.

## May 17

As He who called you is holy, you also be holy in all your conduct. ◊ He who says he abides in Him ought himself also to walk just as He walked. ◊ If you know that He is righteous, you know that everyone who practices righteousness is born of Him. ◊ Circumcision is nothing and uncircumcision is nothing, but keeping the commandments of God is what matters. ◊ Whoever shall keep the whole law, and yet stumble in one point, he is guilty of all.

Not that we are sufficient . . . to think of anything as being from ourselves, but our sufficiency is from God. ◊ Teach me, O Lord, the way of Your statutes.

Work out your own salvation with fear and trembling; for it is God who works in you both to will and to do for His good pleasure. ◊ The God of peace . . . make you complete in every good work to do His will, working in you what is well pleasing in His sight, through Jesus Christ.

EZEK 20:19.1 PET 1:15.1 JOHN 2:6.1 JOHN 2:29.1 COR 7:19.JAMES 2:10.2 COR 3:5.PS 119:33.PHIL 2:12-13.HEB 13:20-21

Our Savior Jesus Christ . . . has abolished death and brought life and immortality to light through the gospel. ◊ I am the resurrection and the life. ◊ Because I live, you will live also. ◊ We have become partakers of Christ. ◊ Partakers of the Holy Spirit. ◊ Partakers of the divine nature. ◊ The first man Adam became a living being. The last Adam became a life-giving spirit. ◊ Behold, I tell you a mystery: We shall not all sleep, but we shall all be changed—in a moment, in the twinkling of an eye, at the last trumpet. For the trumpet will sound, and the dead will be raised incorruptible, and we shall be changed.

"Holy, holy, holy, Lord God Almighty, who was and is and is to come!" . . . [He] lives forever and ever. ◊ The blessed and only Potentate, the King of kings and Lord of lords, who alone has immortality. ◊ Now to the King eternal . . . be honor and glory forever and ever. Amen.

JOHN 5:26.2 TIM 1:10.JOHN 11:25.JOHN 14:19.HEB 3:14.HEB 6:4.2 PET 1:4.1 COR 15:45.1 COR 15:51-52.REV 4:8-9.1 TIM 6:15-16.1 TIM 1:17

## May 18

As the Father has life in Himself, so He has granted the Son to have life in Himself.

## May 19

**Wash me thoroughly from my iniquity.**

I will cleanse them from all their iniquity by which they have sinned against Me, and I will pardon all their iniquities by which they have sinned and by which they have transgressed against Me. ◊ Then I will sprinkle clean water on you, and you shall be clean; I will cleanse you from all your filthiness and from all your idols.

Unless one is born of water and the Spirit, he cannot enter the kingdom of God. ◊ If the blood of bulls and goats and the ashes of a heifer, sprinkling the unclean, sanctifies for the purifying of the flesh, how much more shall the blood of Christ, who through the eternal Spirit offered Himself without spot to God, purge your conscience from dead works to serve the living God?

He saved them for His name's sake, that He might make His mighty power known. ◊ Not unto us, O Lord, not unto us, but to Your name give glory, because of Your mercy, and because of Your truth. . . . We will bless the Lord from this time forth and forevermore. Praise the Lord!

PS 51:2.JER 33:8.EZEK 36:25.JOHN 3:5.HEB 9:13-14.PS 106:8.PS 115:1,18.

And everyone who competes for the prize is temperate in all things. Now they do it to obtain a perishable crown, but we for an imperishable crown. Therefore I run thus: not with uncertainty. . . . But I discipline my body and bring it into subjection, lest, when I have preached to others, I myself should become disqualified.

Put on the whole armor of God, that you may be able to stand against the wiles of the devil. For we do not wrestle against flesh and blood, but against principalities, against powers, against the rulers of the darkness of this age, against spiritual hosts of wickedness in the heavenly places.

Those who are Christ's have crucified the flesh with its passions and desires. If we live in the Spirit, let us also walk in the Spirit. ◊ For as many as are led by the Spirit of God, these are sons of God. ◊ Meditate on these things; give yourself entirely to them, that your progress may be evident to all.

1 TIM 4:16.1 COR 9:25-27.EPH 6:11-12.GAL 5:24-25.ROM 8:14.1 TIM 4:15

## May 21

My brethren, be strong in the Lord and in the power of His might.

"My grace is sufficient for you, for My strength is made perfect in weakness." Therefore most gladly I will rather boast in my infirmities, that the power of Christ may rest upon me. Therefore I take pleasure in infirmities, in reproaches, in needs, in persecutions, in distresses, for Christ's sake. For when I am weak, then I am strong. ◊ I will go in the strength of the Lord God; I will make mention of Your righteousness, of Yours only. ◊ The gospel of Christ, . . . is the power of God to salvation.

I can do all things through Christ who strengthens me. ◊ I also labor, striving according to His working which works in me mightily. ◊ We have this treasure in earthen vessels, that the excellence of the power may be of God and not of us.

The joy of the Lord is your strength. ◊ Strengthened with all might, according to His glorious power, for all patience and longsuffering with joy.

EPH 6:10.2 COR 12:9 10.PS 71:16.ROM 1:16.PHIL 4:13.COL 1:29.2 COR 4:7.NEH 8:10.COL 1:11

The world is passing away, and the lust of it. ◊ Surely every man walks about like a shadow; surely they busy themselves in vain; he heaps up riches, and does not know who will gather them. ◊ What fruit did you have then in the things of which you are now ashamed? For the end of those things is death.

Martha, Martha, you are worried and troubled about many things. But one thing is needed, and Mary has chosen that good part, which will not be taken away from her.

These things I have spoken to you, that in Me you may have peace. In the world you will have tribulation; but be of good cheer, I have overcome the world. ◊ The Lord of peace Himself give you peace always in every way. ◊ The Lord bless you and keep you; the Lord make His face shine upon you, and be gracious to you; the Lord lift up His countenance upon you, and give you peace.

JOHN 14:27.1 JOHN 2:17.PS 39:6.ROM 6:21.LUKE 10:41-42.JOHN 16:33.2 THESS 3:16.NUM 6:24-26

## May 22

Peace I leave with you, My peace I give to you; not as the world gives do I give to you.

## May 23

He, because He continues forever, has an unchangeable priesthood. Therefore He is also able to save to the uttermost those who come to God through Him, since He ever lives to make intercession for them. ◊ [He] is able to keep you from stumbling, and to present you faultless before the presence of His glory.

Seeing . . . that we have a great High Priest who has passed through the heavens, Jesus the Son of God, let us hold fast our confession. For we do not have a High Priest who cannot sympathize with our weaknesses, but was in all points tempted as we are, yet without sin. Let us therefore come boldly to the throne of grace.

The beloved of the Lord shall dwell in safety by Him, who shelters him all the day long; and he shall dwell between His shoulders.

EX 28:12.HEB 7:24-25.JUDE 1:24.HEB 4:14-16.DEUT 33:12

The love of the Spirit. ◊ The Helper, the Holy Spirit. ◊ In all their affliction He was afflicted, and the Angel of His Presence saved them; in His love and in His pity He redeemed them; and He bore them and carried them all the days of old. But they rebelled and grieved His Holy Spirit; so He turned Himself against them as an enemy, and He fought against them.

We know that we abide in Him, and He in us, because He has given us of His Spirit. ◊ Having believed, you were sealed with the Holy Spirit of promise, who is the guarantee of our inheritance until the redemption of the purchased possession. ◊ I say then: Walk in the Spirit, and you shall not fulfill the lust of the flesh. For the flesh lusts against the Spirit, and the Spirit against the flesh; and these are contrary to one another, so that you do not do the things that you wish.

The Spirit also helps in our weaknesses.

## May 24

Do not grieve the Holy Spirit of God, by whom you were sealed for the day of redemption.

EPH 4:30.ROM 15:30.JOHN 14:26.IS 63:9-10.1 JOHN 4:13.EPH 1:13-14.GAL 5:16-17.ROM 8:26

## May 25

How great is Your goodness, which You have laid up for those who fear You.

Since the beginning of the world men have not heard nor perceived by the ear, nor has the eye seen any God besides You, who acts for the one who waits for Him. ◊ Eye has not seen, nor ear heard, nor have entered into the heart of man the things which God has prepared for those who love Him. But God has revealed them to us through His Spirit. ◊ You will show me the path of life; in Your presence is fullness of joy; at Your right hand are pleasures forevermore.

How precious is Your lovingkindness, O God! Therefore the children of men put their trust under the shadow of Your wings. They are abundantly satisfied with the fullness of Your house, and You give them drink from the river of Your pleasures.

Godliness is profitable for all things, having promise of the life that now is and of that which is to come.

PS 31:19.IS 64:4.1 COR 2:9-10.PS 16:11.PS 36:7-8.1 TIM 4:8

I am the good shepherd; and I know My sheep, and am known by My own. . . . My sheep hear My voice, and I know them, and they follow Me. And I give them eternal life, and they shall never perish; neither shall anyone snatch them out of My hand.

The Lord is my shepherd; I shall not want. He makes me to lie down in green pastures; He leads me beside the still waters. He restores my soul; He leads me in the paths of righteousness for His name's sake.

All we like sheep have gone astray; we have turned, every one, to his own way; and the Lord has laid on Him the iniquity of us all. ◊ I am the good shepherd. The good shepherd gives His life for the sheep. ◊ I will seek what was lost and bring back what was driven away, bind up the broken and strengthen what was sick. ◊ You were like sheep going astray, but have now returned to the Shepherd and Overseer of your souls.

HEB 13:20.JOHN 10:14,27-28.PS 23:1-3.IS 53:6.JOHN 10:11.EZEK 34:16.1 PET 2:25

## May 26

Our Lord Jesus . . . that great Shepherd of the sheep.

## May 27

The LORD is good, a stronghold in the day of trouble; and He knows those who trust in Him.

Praise the Lord of hosts, for the Lord is good, for His mercy endures forever. ◊ God is our refuge and strength, a very present help in trouble. ◊ I will say of the Lord, "He is my refuge and my fortress; my God, in Him I will trust." ◊ Who is like you, a people saved by the Lord, the shield of your help and the sword of your majesty! ◊ As for God, His way is perfect; the word of the Lord is proven; he is a shield to all who trust in Him. For who is God, except the Lord? ◊ And who is a rock, except our God?

If anyone loves God, this one is known by Him. ◊ The solid foundation of God stands, having this seal: "The Lord knows those who are His," and, "Let everyone who names the name of Christ depart from iniquity." ◊ The Lord knows the way of the righteous, but the way of the ungodly shall perish. ◊ You have found grace in My sight, and I know you by name.

NAH 1:7.JER 33:11.PS 46:1.PS 91:2.DEUT 33:29.2 SAM 22:31-32.1 COR 8:3.2 TIM 2:19.PS 1:6.EX 33:17

The grace of God that brings salvation has appeared to all men, teaching us that, denying ungodliness and worldly lusts, we should live soberly, righteously, and godly in the present age, looking for the blessed hope and glorious appearing of our great God and Savior Jesus Christ, who gave Himself for us, that He might redeem us from every lawless deed and purify for Himself His own special people, zealous for good works. ◊ We, according to His promise, look for new heavens and a new earth in which righteousness dwells. Therefore, beloved, looking forward to these things, be diligent to be found by Him in peace, without spot and blameless.

Christ was offered once to bear the sins of many. To those who eagerly wait for Him He will appear a second time, apart from sin, for salvation. ◊ And it will be said in that day: "Behold, this is our God; we have waited for Him, and He will save us. This is the Lord; we have waited for Him; we will be glad and rejoice in His salvation."

PHIL 3:20.TITUS 2:11-14.2 PET 3:13-14.HEB 9:28.IS 25:9

**We also eagerly wait for the Savior.**

## May 29

The life of the flesh is in the blood, and I have given it to you upon the altar to make atonement for your souls; for it is the blood that makes atonement for the soul.

Behold! The Lamb of God who takes away the sin of the world! ◊ The blood of the Lamb. ◊ The precious blood of Christ, as of a lamb without blemish and without spot. ◊ Without shedding of blood there is no remission. ◊ The blood of Jesus Christ His Son cleanses us from all sin.

With His own blood He entered the Most Holy Place once for all, having obtained eternal redemption. ◊ Therefore, brethren, having boldness to enter the Holiest by the blood of Jesus, by a new and living way which He consecrated for us, through the veil, that is, His flesh, . . . let us draw near with a true heart in full assurance of faith.

You were bought at a price; therefore glorify God in your body and in your spirit, which are God's.

LEV 17:11.JOHN 1:29.REV 7:14.1 PET 1:19.HEB 9:22. 1 JOHN 1:7.HEB 9:12.HEB 10:19-20,22.1 COR 6:20

Enter by the narrow gate; for wide is the gate and broad is the way that leads to destruction. . . . Narrow is the gate and difficult is the way which leads to life, and there are few who find it. ◊ The kingdom of heaven suffers violence, and the violent take it by force. ◊ Do not labor for the food which perishes, but for the food which endures to everlasting life, which the Son of Man will give you. ◊ Be even more diligent to make your calling and election sure, . . . for so an entrance will be supplied to you abundantly into the everlasting kingdom of our Lord and Savior Jesus Christ.

Run in such a way that you may obtain it. And everyone who competes for the prize is temperate in all things. Now they do it to obtain a perishable crown, but we for an imperishable crown.

For he who has entered His rest has himself also ceased from his works as God did from His. ◊ The Lord will be to you an everlasting light, and your God your glory.

HEB 4:11.MATT 7:13-14.MATT 11:12.JOHN 6:27.2 PET 1:10-11.1 COR 9:24-25.HEB 4:10.IS 60:19

Let us therefore be diligent to enter that rest.

## May 31

Your name shall . . . be called . . . Israel; for you have struggled with God and with men, and have prevailed.

, In his strength he struggled with God. Yes he struggled with the Angel and prevailed; he wept, and sought favor from Him. ◊ [Abraham] did not waver at the promise of God through unbelief, but was strengthened in faith, giving glory to God.

Have faith in God. For assuredly, I say to you, whoever says to this mountain, "Be removed and be cast into the sea," and does not doubt in his heart, but believes that those things he says will come to pass, he will have whatever he says. Therefore I say to you, whatever things you ask when you pray, believe that you receive them, and you will have them. ◊ If you can believe, all things are possible to him who believes. ◊ Blessed is she who believed, for there will be a fulfillment of those things which were told her from the Lord.

Lord, increase our faith.

GEN 32:28.HOS 12:3-4.ROM 4:20.MARK 11:22-24.MARK 9:23.LUKE 1:45.LUKE 17:5

The Lord, the Lord God, merciful and gracious, longsuffering, and abounding in goodness and truth.

Walk worthy of the calling with which you were called, with all lowliness and gentleness, with longsuffering, bearing with one another in love. ◊ Be kind to one another, tenderhearted, forgiving one another, just as God in Christ also forgave you. ◊ The wisdom that is from above is first pure, then peaceable, gentle, willing to yield, full of mercy and good fruits. ◊ Love suffers long and is kind.

In due season we shall reap if we do not lose heart. ◊ Therefore be patient, brethren, until the coming of the Lord. See how the farmer waits for the precious fruit of the earth, waiting patiently for it until it receives the early and latter rain. You also be patient. Establish your hearts, for the coming of the Lord is at hand.

GAL 5:22.EX 34:6.EPH 4:1-2.EPH 4:32.JAMES 3:17.
1 COR 13:4.GAL 6:9.JAMES 5:7-8

## June 1

The fruit of the Spirit is love, joy, peace, longsuffering, kindness, goodness, faithfulness.

## June 2

Thus you shall eat it: with a belt on your waist. . . . So you shall eat it in haste. It is the LORD's Passover.

Arise and depart, for this is not your rest. ◊ Here we have no continuing city, but we seek the one to come. ◊ There remains therefore a rest for the people of God.

Let your waist be girded and your lamps burning; and you yourselves be like men who wait for their master, when he will return from the wedding, that when he comes and knocks they may open to him immediately. Blessed are those servants whom the master, when he comes, will find watching. ◊ Gird up the loins of your mind, be sober, and rest your hope fully upon the grace that is to be brought to you at the revelation of Jesus Christ. ◊ One thing I do, forgetting those things which are behind . . . I press toward the goal for the prize of the upward call of God in Christ Jesus. Therefore let us, as many as are mature, have this mind.

EX 12:11.MIC 2:10.HEB 13:14.HEB 4:9.LUKE 12:35-37. 1 PET 1:13.PHIL 3:13-15

Take heed to yourselves, lest your hearts be weighed down with carousing, drunkenness, and cares of this life, and that Day come on you unexpectedly. For it will come as a snare on all those who dwell on the face of the whole earth. Watch therefore, and pray always that you may be counted worthy to escape all these things that will come to pass, and to stand before the Son of Man.

The day of the Lord so comes as a thief in the night. For when they say, "Peace and safety!" then sudden destruction comes upon them, as labor pains upon a pregnant woman. And they shall not escape. But you, brethren, are not in darkness, so that this Day should overtake you as a thief. You are all sons of light and sons of the day. We are not of the night nor of darkness. Therefore let us not sleep, as others do, but let us watch and be sober.

MATT 25:13.LUKE 21:34-36.1 THESS 5:2-6

Watch therefore, for you know neither the day nor the hour in which the Son of Man is coming.

## June 4

The house that is to be built for the Lord must be exceedingly magnificent, famous and glorious throughout all countries. ◊ The glory of the Lord . . . filled the Lord's house.

"Destroy this temple, and in three days I will raise it up." . . . He was speaking of the temple of His body. ◊ What was made glorious had no glory in this respect, because of the glory that excels. ◊ The Word became flesh and dwelt among us, and we beheld His glory, the glory as of the only begotten of the Father, full of grace and truth. ◊ God . . . has in these last days spoken to us by His Son, whom He has appointed heir of all things, through whom also He made the worlds.

Glory to God in the highest, and on earth peace, good will toward men! ◊ Prince of Peace. ◊ He Himself is our peace. ◊ The peace of God, which surpasses all understanding, will guard your hearts and minds through Christ Jesus.

HAG 2:9.1 CHR 22:5.2 CHR 7:2.JOHN 2:19,21.2 COR 3:10.JOHN 1:14.HEB 1:1-2.LUKE 2:14.IS 9:6.EPH 2:14.PHIL 4:7

Where is boasting then? It is excluded. By what law? Of works? No, but by the law of faith. ◊ What do you have that you did not receive? Now if you did indeed receive it, why do you glory as if you had not received it? ◊ For by grace you have been saved through faith, and that not of yourselves; it is the gift of God, not of works, lest anyone should boast. For we are His workmanship, created in Christ Jesus for good works, which God prepared beforehand that we should walk in them.

By the grace of God I am what I am, and His grace toward me was not in vain; but I labored more abundantly than they all, yet not I, but the grace of God which was with me. ◊ For of Him and through Him and to Him are all things. ◊ Of Your own we have given You.

Do not enter into judgment with Your servant, for in Your sight no one living is righteous.

LUKE 17:10.ROM 3:27.1 COR 4:7.EPH 2:8-10.1 COR 15:10.ROM 11:36.1 CHR 29:14.PS 143:2

## June 5

When you have done all those things which you are commanded, say, "We are unprofitable servants."

## June 6

**He will quiet you in His love.**

The Lord did not set His love on you nor choose you because you were more in number than any other people, for you were the least of all peoples; but because the Lord loves you. ◊ We love Him because He first loved us. ◊ You . . . He has reconciled in the body of His flesh through death, to present you holy, and blameless, and irreproachable in His sight.

In this is love, not that we loved God, but that He loved us and sent His Son to be the propitiation for our sins. ◊ God demonstrates His own love toward us, in that while we were still sinners, Christ died for us.

Suddenly a voice came from heaven, saying, "This is My beloved Son, in whom I am well pleased." ◊ Therefore My Father loves Me, because I lay down My life that I may take it again. ◊ His Son . . . who being the brightness of His glory and the express image of His person, and upholding all things by the word of His power, when He had by Himself purged our sins, sat down at the right hand of the Majesty on high.

ZEPH 3:17.DEUT 7:7-8.1 JOHN 4:19.COL 1:21-22.
1 JOHN 4:10.ROM 5:8.MATT 3:17.JOHN 10:17.HEB 1:2-3

Which of you shall have a friend, and go to him at midnight and say to him, "Friend, lend me three loaves; for a friend of mine has come to me on his journey, and I have nothing to set before him"; and he will answer from within and say, "Do not trouble me; the door is now shut, and my children are with me in bed; I cannot rise and give to you"? I say to you, though he will not rise and give to him because he is his friend, yet because of his persistence he will rise and give him as many as he needs. ◊ [Pray] always with all prayer and supplication in the Spirit, being watchful to this end with all perseverance and supplication for all the saints.

"I will not let You go unless You bless me!" . . . "You have struggled with God and with men, and have prevailed." ◊ Continue earnestly in prayer, being vigilant in it with thanksgiving.

[Jesus] went out to the mountain to pray, and continued all night in prayer to God.

LUKE 18:1.LUKE 11:5-8.EPH 6:18.GEN 32:26,28.COL
4:2.LUKE 6:12

## June 7

Men always ought to pray and not lose heart.

## June 8

Blessed is every one who fears the Lord, who walks in His ways. When you eat the labor of your hands, you shall be happy, and it shall be well with you. ◊ Trust in the Lord, and do good; dwell in the land, and feed on His faithfulness. Delight yourself also in the Lord, and He shall give you the desires of your heart. ◊ Do not be afraid, nor be dismayed, for the Lord your God is with you wherever you go.

Seek first the kingdom of God and His righteousness, and all these things shall be added to you.

As long as he sought the Lord, God made him prosper. ◊ Beware that you do not forget the Lord your God by not keeping His commandments, His judgments, and His statutes which I command you today, . . . then you say in your heart, "My power and the might of my hand have gained me this wealth." ◊ Is not the Lord your God with you? And has He not given you rest on every side?

GEN 39:3.PS 128:1-2.PS 37:3-4.JOSH 1:9.MATT 6:33. 2 CHR 26:5.DEUT 8:11,17.1 CHR 22:18

You are fairer than the sons of men; grace is poured upon Your lips; therefore God has blessed You forever. ◇ The Lord God has given Me the tongue of the learned, that I should know how to speak a word in season to him who is weary. ◇ His mouth is most sweet, yes, he is altogether lovely. This is my beloved, and this is my friend.

All bore witness to Him, and marveled at the gracious words which proceeded out of His mouth. ◇ He taught them as one having authority, and not as the scribes.

Let the word of Christ dwell in you richly in all wisdom. ◇ The sword of the Spirit . . . is the word of God. ◇ The word of God is living and powerful, and sharper than any two-edged sword. ◇ The weapons of our warfare are not carnal but mighty in God for pulling down strongholds, casting down arguments and every high thing that exalts itself against the knowledge of God, bringing every thought into captivity to the obedience of Christ.

JOHN 7:46.PS 45:2.IS 50:4.SONG 5:16.LUKE 4:22.MATT 7:29.COL 3:16.EPH 6:17.HEB 4:12.2 COR 10:4-5

## June 10

*The younger son . . . journeyed to a far country, and there wasted his possessions with prodigal living.*

Such were some of you. But you were washed, but you were sanctified, but you were justified in the name of the Lord Jesus and by the Spirit of our God. ◊ We . . . were by nature children of wrath, just as the others. But God, who is rich in mercy, because of His great love with which He loved us, even when we were dead in trespasses, made us alive together with Christ (by grace you have been saved), and raised us up together, and made us sit together in the heavenly places in Christ Jesus.

In this is love, not that we loved God, but that He loved us and sent His Son to be the propitiation for our sins.

God demonstrates His own love toward us, in that while we were still sinners, Christ died for us. . . . If when we were enemies we were reconciled to God through the death of His Son, much more, having been reconciled, we shall be saved by His life.

LUKE 15:13.1 COR 6:11.EPH 2:3-6.1 JOHN 4:10.ROM 5:8,10

The Lord is merciful and gracious, slow to anger, and abounding in mercy. He will not always strive with us, nor will He keep His anger forever. He has not dealt with us according to our sins, nor punished us according to our iniquities. For as the heavens are high above the earth, so great is His mercy toward those who fear Him; as far as the east is from the west, so far has He removed our transgressions from us. As a father pities his children, so the Lord pities those who fear Him.

You received the Spirit of adoption by whom we cry out, "Abba, Father." The Spirit Himself bears witness with our spirit that we are children of God. ◊ You who once were far off have been made near by the blood of Christ. . . . Now, therefore, you are no longer strangers and foreigners, but fellow citizens with the saints and members of the household of God.

LUKE 15:20.PS 103:8-13.ROM 8:15-16.EPH 2:13,19

## June 11

He arose and came to his father. But when he was still a great way off, his father saw him and had compassion, and ran and fell on his neck and kissed him.

## June 12

Everything that can endure fire, you shall put through the fire, and it shall be clean.

The Lord your God is testing you to know whether you love the Lord your God with all your heart and with all your soul. ◊ He will sit as a refiner and a purifier of silver; He will purify the sons of Levi, and purge them as gold and silver, that they may offer to the Lord an offering in righteousness. ◊ Each one's work will become manifest; for the Day will declare it, because it will be revealed by fire; and the fire will test each one's work, of what sort it is.

I will turn My hand against you, and thoroughly purge away your dross, and take away all your alloy. ◊ I will refine them and try them.

You, O God, have proved us; You have refined us as silver is refined. . . . We went through fire and through water; but You brought us out to rich fulfillment.

When you walk through the fire, you shall not be burned, nor shall the flame scorch you.

NUM 31:23.DEUT 13:3.MAL 3:3.1 COR 3:13.IS 1:25.JER 9:7.PS 66:10,12.IS 43:2

I have been crucified with Christ; it is no longer I who live, but Christ lives in me; and the life which I now live in the flesh I live by faith in the Son of God, who loved me and gave Himself for me.

For I know that in me (that is, in my flesh) nothing good dwells; for to will is present with me, but how to perform what is good I do not find. . . . O wretched man that I am! Who will deliver me from this body of death? I thank God—through Jesus Christ our Lord! ◊ If Christ is in you, the body is dead because of sin, but the Spirit is life because of righteousness. ◊ Indeed you continue in the faith, grounded and steadfast, and are not moved away from the hope of the gospel which you heard.

Little children, abide in Him, that when He appears, we may have confidence and not be ashamed before Him at His coming. ◊ He who says he abides in Him ought himself also to walk just as He walked.

JOHN 15:4.GAL 2:20.ROM 7:18,24-25.ROM 8:10.COL 1:23.1 JOHN 2:28.1 JOHN 2:6

Abide in Me, and I in you.

## June 14

As the sufferings of Christ abound in us, so our consolation also abounds through Christ.

I have suffered the loss of all things . . . that I may know . . . the fellowship of His sufferings. ◊ Rejoice to the extent that you partake of Christ's sufferings, that when His glory is revealed, you may also be glad with exceeding joy. ◊ For if we died with Him, we shall also live with Him. ◊ If children, then heirs—heirs of God and joint heirs with Christ, if indeed we suffer with Him, that we may also be glorified together.

God, determining to show more abundantly to the heirs of promise the immutability of His counsel, confirmed it by an oath, that by two immutable things, in which it is impossible for God to lie, we might have strong consolation, who have fled for refuge to lay hold of the hope set before us. ◊ Our Lord Jesus Christ Himself, and our God and Father, who has loved us and given us everlasting consolation and good hope by grace, comfort your hearts and establish you in every good word and work.

2 COR 1:5.PHIL 3:8,10.1 PET 4:13.2 TIM 2:11.ROM 8:17.HEB 6:17-18.2 THESS 2:16-17

Lord, my heart is not haughty, nor my eyes lofty. Neither do I concern myself with great matters, nor with things too profound for me. Surely I have calmed and quieted my soul, like a weaned child with his mother; like a weaned child is my soul within me.

The secret of the Lord is with those who fear Him, and He will show them His covenant. ◊ There is a God in heaven who reveals secrets. ◊ Indeed these are the mere edges of His ways, and how small a whisper we hear of Him!

No longer do I call you servants, for a servant does not know what his master is doing; but I have called you friends, for all things that I heard from My Father I have made known to you. ◊ If you love Me, keep My commandments. And I will pray the Father, and He will give you another Helper, that He may abide with you forever, even the Spirit of truth.

DEUT 29:29.PS 131:1-2.PS 25:14.DAN 2:28.JOB 26:14.JOHN 15:15.JOHN 14:15-17

## June 16

See then that
you walk
circumspectly, not
as fools but as
wise, redeeming
the time, because
the days are evil.

Take diligent heed to do the
commandment and the law, . . . to love
the Lord your God, to walk in all His
ways, to keep His commandments, to
hold fast to Him, and to serve Him with
all your heart and with all your soul. ◊
Walk in wisdom toward those who are
outside, redeeming the time. Let your
speech always be with grace, seasoned
with salt, that you may know how you
ought to answer each one. ◊ Abstain
from every form of evil.

While the bridegroom was delayed,
they all slumbered and slept. And at
midnight a cry was heard: "Behold, the
bridegroom is coming; go out to meet
him!" ◊ Watch therefore, for you know
neither the day nor the hour in which
the Son of Man is coming.

Brethren, be even more diligent to
make your calling and election sure, for
if you do these things you will never
stumble. ◊ Blessed are those servants
whom the master, when he comes, will
find watching.

EPH 5:15-16.JOSH 22:5.COL 4:5-6.1 THESS 5:22.MATT
25:5-6.MATT 25:13.2 PET 1:10.LUKE 12:37

I love the Lord, because He has heard My voice and my supplications. Because He has inclined His ear to me, therefore I will call upon Him as long as I live.

When you pray, do not use vain repetitions as the heathen do. For they think that they will be heard for their many words. ◊ The Spirit . . . helps in our weaknesses. For we do not know what we should pray for as we ought, but the Spirit Himself makes intercession for us with groanings which cannot be uttered.

Therefore I desire that the men pray everywhere, lifting up holy hands, without wrath and doubting. ◊ Praying always with all prayer and supplication in the Spirit, being watchful to this end with all perseverance and supplication for all the saints.

If two of you agree on earth concerning anything that they ask, it will be done for them by My Father in heaven.

PHIL 4:6.PS 116:1-2.MATT 6:7.ROM 8:26.1 TIM 2:8.EPH 6:18.MATT 18:19

## June 17

In everything by prayer and supplication, with thanksgiving, let your requests be made known to God.

## June 18

You shall put the mercy seat on top of the ark, . . . And there I will meet with you.

The way into the Holiest of All was not yet made manifest. ◊ Jesus, when He had cried out again with a loud voice, yielded up His spirit. And behold, the veil of the temple was torn in two from top to bottom.

Brethren, having boldness to enter the Holiest by the blood of Jesus, by a new and living way which He consecrated for us, through the veil, that is, His flesh, . . . let us draw near with a true heart in full assurance of faith, having our hearts sprinkled from an evil conscience and our bodies washed with pure water. ◊ Let us therefore come boldly to the throne of grace, that we may obtain mercy and find grace to help in time of need.

Christ Jesus, . . . whom God set forth to be a propitiation by His blood, through faith, to demonstrate His righteousness, because in His forbearance God had passed over the sins that were previously committed. ◊ Through Him we . . . have access by one Spirit to the Father.

EX 25:21-22.HEB 9:8.MATT 27:50-51.HEB 10:19-20,22.HEB 4:16.ROM 3:24-25.EPH 2:18

Unless one is born again, he cannot see the kingdom of God. ◊ There shall by no means enter it anything that defiles. ◊ There is no spot in you.

You shall be holy, for I the Lord your God am holy. ◊ As obedient children, not conforming yourselves to the former lusts, as in your ignorance; but as He who called you is holy, you also be holy in all your conduct, because it is written, "Be holy, for I am holy." And if you call on the Father, who without partiality judges according to each one's work, conduct yourselves throughout the time of your sojourning here in fear. ◊ Put off, concerning your former conduct, the old man which grows corrupt according to the deceitful lusts, and be renewed in the spirit of your mind, and . . . put on the new man which was created according to God, in righteousness and true holiness. ◊ He chose us in Him before the foundation of the world, that we should be holy and without blame before Him in love.

HEB 12:14.JOHN 3:3.REV 21:27.SONG 4:7.LEV 19:2.
1 PET 1:14-17.EPH 4:22-24.EPH 1:4

## June 19

Pursue . . . holiness, without which no one will see the Lord.

## June 20

Take this child away and nurse him for me, and I will give you your wages.

Go into the vineyard, and whatever is right I will give you. ◊ Whoever gives you a cup of water to drink in My name, because you belong to Christ, assuredly, I say to you, he will by no means lose his reward. ◊ The generous soul will be made rich, and he who waters will also be watered himself. ◊ God is not unjust to forget your work and labor of love . . . in that you have ministered to the saints, and do minister.

Each one will receive his own reward according to his own labor.

"Lord, when did we see You hungry and feed You, or thirsty and give You drink? When did we see You a stranger and take You in, or naked and clothe You?" And the King will answer and say to them, ". . . inasmuch as you did it to one of the least of these My brethren, you did it to Me." ◊ Come, you blessed of My Father, inherit the kingdom prepared for you from the foundation of the world.

EX 2:9.MATT 20:4.MARK 9:41.PROV 11:25.HEB 6:10.
1 COR 3:8.MATT 25:37-38,40.MATT 25:34

Even the Son of Man did not come to be served, but to serve. ◊ Whoever of you desires to be first shall be slave of all.

Jesus of Nazareth . . . went about doing good. ◊ Bear one another's burdens, and so fulfill the law of Christ.

The meekness and gentleness of Christ. ◊ In lowliness of mind let each esteem others better than himself.

Father, forgive them, for they do not know what they do. ◊ Be kind to one another, tenderhearted, forgiving one another, just as God in Christ also forgave you.

He who says he abides in Him ought himself also to walk just as He walked. ◊ [Look] unto Jesus, the author and finisher of our faith, who for the joy that was set before Him endured the cross, despising the shame, and has sat down at the right hand of the throne of God.

1 PET 2:21.MARK 10:45.MARK 10:44.ACTS 10:38.GAL 6:2.2 COR 10:1.PHIL 2:3.LUKE 23:34.EPH 4:32.1 JOHN 2:6.HEB 12:2

## June 21

Christ also suffered for us, leaving us an example, that you should follow His steps.

## June 22

**You died, and your life is hidden with Christ in God.**

How shall we who died to sin live any longer in it? ◊ I have been crucified with Christ; it is no longer I who live, but Christ lives in me; and the life which I now live in the flesh I live by faith in the Son of God, who loved me and gave Himself for me. ◊ He died for all, that those who live should live no longer for themselves, but for Him who died for them and rose again. ◊ If anyone is in Christ, he is a new creation; old things have passed away; behold, all things have become new.

We are in Him who is true, in His Son Jesus Christ. ◊ They all may be one as You, Father, are in Me, and I in You; that they also may be one in Us. ◊ You are the body of Christ, and members individually. ◊ Because I live, you will live also.

To him who overcomes I will give some of the hidden manna to eat. And I will give him a white stone, and on the stone a new name written which no one knows except him who receives it.

COL 3:3.ROM 6:2.GAL 2:20.2 COR 5:15.2 COR 5:17.
1 JOHN 5:20.JOHN 17:21.1 COR 12:27.JOHN 14:19.REV 2:17

It is to your advantage that I go away; for if I do not go away, the Helper will not come to you; but if I depart, I will send Him to you.

The Spirit Himself bears witness with our spirit that we are children of God. ◊ You did not receive the spirit of bondage again to fear, but you received the Spirit of adoption by whom we cry out, "Abba, Father." ◊ The Spirit . . . helps in our weaknesses. For we do not know what we should pray for as we ought, but the Spirit Himself makes intercession for us with groanings which cannot be uttered.

The God of hope fill you with all joy and peace in believing, that you may abound in hope by the power of the Holy Spirit. ◊ Hope does not disappoint, because the love of God has been poured out in our hearts by the Holy Spirit who was given to us.

By this we know that we abide in Him, and He in us, because He has given us of His Spirit.

JOHN 14:16-17.JOHN 16:7.ROM 8:16.ROM 8:15.ROM 8:26.ROM 15:13.ROM 5:5.1 JOHN 4:13

## June 23

I will pray the Father, and He will give you another Helper, . . . even the Spirit of truth.

## June 24

The ark of the covenant of the LORD went before them . . . to search out a resting place for them.

My times are in Your hand. ◊ He will choose our inheritance for us. ◊ Lead me, O Lord, in Your righteousness, . . . make Your way straight before my face.

Commit your way to the Lord, trust also in Him, and He shall bring it to pass. ◊ In all your ways acknowledge Him, and He shall direct your paths. ◊ Your ears shall hear a word behind you, saying, "This is the way, walk in it," whenever you turn to the right hand or whenever you turn to the left.

The Lord is my shepherd; I shall not want. He makes me to lie down in green pastures; He leads me beside the still waters. ◊ As a father pities his children, so the Lord pities those who fear Him. For He knows our frame; He remembers that we are dust. ◊ Your heavenly Father knows that you need all these things. ◊ [Cast] all your care upon Him, for He cares for you.

NUM 10:33.PS 31:15.PS 47:4.PS 5:8.PS 37:5.PROV 3:6.IS 30:21.PS 23:1-2.PS 103:13-14.MATT 6:32.1 PET 5:7

As many as received Him, to them He gave the right to become children of God, even to those who believe in His name. ◊ By which have been given to us exceedingly great and precious promises, that through these you may be partakers of the divine nature, having escaped the corruption that is in the world through lust.

Since the beginning of the world men have not heard nor perceived by the ear, nor has the eye seen any God besides You, who acts for the one who waits for Him.

Now we see in a mirror, dimly, but then face to face. Now I know in part, but then I shall know just as I also am known. ◊ Christ . . . will transform our lowly body that it may be conformed to His glorious body, according to the working by which He is able even to subdue all things to Himself. ◊ As for me, I will see Your face in righteousness; I shall be satisfied when I awake in Your likeness.

1 JOHN 3:2.JOHN 1:12.2 PET 1:4.IS 64:4.1 COR 13:12.PHIL 3:20-21.PS 17:15

When He is revealed, we shall be like Him, for we shall see Him as He is.

## June 26

"Oh, that You would bless me indeed, . . . and that You would keep me from evil." . . . So God granted him what he requested.

The blessing of the Lord makes one rich, and He adds no sorrow with it. ◊ When He gives quietness, who then can make trouble? And when He hides His face, who then can see Him?

Salvation belongs to the Lord. Your blessing is upon Your people. ◊ How great is Your goodness, which You have laid up for those who fear You, which You have prepared for those who trust in You in the presence of the sons of men! ◊ I do not pray that You should take them out of the world, but that You should keep them from the evil one.

Ask, and it will be given to you; seek, and you will find; knock, and it will be opened to you. For everyone who asks receives, and he who seeks finds, and to him who knocks it will be opened. ◊ The Lord redeems the soul of His servants, and none of those who trust in Him shall be condemned.

1 CHR 4:10.PROV 10:22.JOB 34:29.PS 3:8.PS 31:19.JOHN 17:15.MATT 7:7-8.PS 34:22

But who can endure the day of His coming? And who can stand when He appears? For He is like a refiner's fire and like fuller's soap.

I looked, and behold, a great multitude which no one could number, of all nations, tribes, peoples, and tongues, standing before the throne and before the Lamb, clothed with white robes, with palm branches in their hands. . . . These are the ones who come out of the great tribulation, and washed their robes and made them white in the blood of the Lamb. . . . They shall neither hunger anymore nor thirst anymore; the sun shall not strike them, nor any heat; for the Lamb who is in the midst of the throne will shepherd them and lead them to living fountains of waters. And God will wipe away every tear from their eyes.

There is . . . no condemnation to those who are in Christ Jesus, who do not walk according to the flesh, but according to the Spirit. ◊ Stand fast therefore in the liberty by which Christ has made us free.

REV 6:17.MAL 3:2.REV 7:9,14,16-17.ROM 8:1.GAL 5:1

## June 28

I know that my
Redeemer lives.

If when we were enemies we were reconciled to God through the death of His Son, much more, having been reconciled, we shall be saved by His life. ◊ But He, because He continues forever, has an unchangeable priesthood. Therefore He is also able to save to the uttermost those who come to God through Him, since He ever lives to make intercession for them.

Because I live, you will live also. ◊ If in this life only we have hope in Christ, we are of all men the most pitiable. But now Christ is risen from the dead, and has become the firstfruits of those who have fallen asleep.

"The Redeemer will come to Zion, and to those who turn from transgression in Jacob," says the Lord. ◊ We have redemption through His blood, the forgiveness of sins, according to the riches of His grace. ◊ You were not redeemed with corruptible things, like silver or gold, from your aimless conduct received by tradition from your fathers, but with the precious blood of Christ, as of a lamb without blemish and without spot.

JOB 19:25.ROM 5:10.HEB 7:24-25.JOHN 14:19.1 COR 15:19-20.IS 59:20.EPH 1:7.1 PET 1:18-19

This is the will of Him who sent Me,
that everyone who sees the Son and
believes in Him may have everlasting
life. ◇ Whatever we ask we receive
from Him, because we keep His
commandments and do those things
that are pleasing in His sight.

My yoke is easy and My burden is
light. ◇ If you love Me, keep My
commandments. ◇ He who has My
commandments and keeps them, it is he
who loves Me. And he who loves Me
will be loved by My Father, and I will
love him and manifest Myself to him.

Happy is the man who finds wisdom,
and the man who gains understanding.
. . . Her ways are ways of pleasantness,
and all her paths are peace. ◇ Great
peace have those who love Your law,
and nothing causes them to stumble. ◇
I delight in the law of God according to
the inward man.

This is His commandment: that we
should believe on the name of His Son
Jesus Christ and love one another. ◇
Love does no harm to a neighbor;
therefore love is the fulfillment of the
law.

1 JOHN 5:3.JOHN 6:40.1 JOHN 3:22.MATT 11:30.JOHN
14:15.JOHN 14:21.PROV 3:13,17.PS 119:165.ROM 7:22.
1 JOHN 3:23.ROM 13:10

## June 30

As many as I
love, I rebuke
and chasten.

My son, do not despise the
chastening of the Lord, nor be
discouraged when you are rebuked by
Him; for whom the Lord loves He
chastens, and scourges every son whom
He receives. ◊ Just as a father the son
in whom he delights. ◊ He bruises, but
He binds up; He wounds, but His
hands make whole. ◊ Humble
yourselves under the mighty hand of
God, that He may exalt you in due
time. ◊ I have tested you in the furnace
of affliction.

He does not afflict willingly, nor
grieve the children of men. ◊ He has
not dealt with us according to our sins,
nor punished us according to our
iniquities. For as the heavens are high
above the earth, so great is His mercy
toward those who fear Him; as far as
the east is from the west, so far has He
removed our transgressions from us. As
a father pities his children, so the Lord
pities those who fear Him. For He
knows our frame; He remembers that
we are dust.

REV 3:19.HEB 12:5-6.PROV 3:12.JOB 5:18.1 PET 5:6.IS
48:10.LAM 3:33.PS 103:10-14

Be followers of God as dear children. ◇ Love your enemies, bless those who curse you, do good to those who hate you, and pray for those who spitefully use you and persecute you, that you may be sons of your Father in heaven; for He makes His sun rise on the evil and on the good, and sends rain on the just and on the unjust. ◇ Be merciful, just as your Father also is merciful.

The fruit of the Spirit is in all goodness, righteousness, and truth.

When the kindness and the love of God our Savior toward man appeared, not by works of righteousness which we have done, but according to His mercy He saved us, through the washing of regeneration and renewing of the Holy Spirit, whom He poured out on us abundantly through Jesus Christ our Savior. ◇ The Lord is good to all, and His tender mercies are over all His works. ◇ He who did not spare His own Son, but delivered Him up for us all, how shall He not with Him also freely give us all things?

GAL 5:22.EPH 5:1.MATT 5:44-45.LUKE 6:36.EPH 5:9.TITUS 3:4-6.PS 145:9.ROM 8:32

The fruit of the Spirit is . . . goodness.

## July 2

This is the
ordinance of the
Passover: No
outsider shall eat
it.

We have an altar from which those
who serve the tabernacle have no right
to eat. ◊ Unless one is born again, he
cannot see the kingdom of God. ◊ At
that time you were without Christ,
being aliens from the commonwealth of
Israel and strangers from the covenants
of promise, . . . but now in Christ Jesus
you who once were far off have been
made near by the blood of Christ.

For He Himself is our peace, who has
made both one, . . . having abolished in
His flesh the enmity, that is, the law of
commandments contained in ordinances,
so as to create in Himself one new man
from the two, thus making peace.

Now, therefore, you are no longer
strangers and foreigners, but fellow
citizens with the saints and members of
the household of God.

If anyone hears My voice and opens
the door, I will come in to him and dine
with him, and he with Me.

EX 12:43.HEB 13:10.JOHN 3:3.EPH 2:12-13.EPH
2:14-15.EPH 2:19.REV 3:20

If you are Christ's, then you are Abraham's seed, and heirs according to the promise.

Behold what manner of love the Father has bestowed on us, that we should be called children of God! ◊ Therefore you are no longer a slave but a son, and if a son, then an heir of God through Christ. ◊ [God] predestined us to adoption as sons by Jesus Christ to Himself, according to the good pleasure of His will.

Father, I desire that they also whom You gave Me may be with Me where I am, that they may behold My glory which You have given Me.

And he who overcomes, and keeps My works until the end, to him I will give power over the nations. ◊ To him who overcomes I will grant to sit with Me on My throne, as I also overcame and sat down with My Father on His throne.

ROM 8:17.GAL 3:29.1 JOHN 3:1.GAL 4:7.EPH 1:5.JOHN 17:24.REV 2:26.REV 3:21

## July 3

If children, then heirs—heirs of God and joint heirs with Christ.

## July 4

As one whom his mother comforts, so I will comfort you. ◊ Then they brought young children to Him, that He might touch them. . . . And He took them up in His arms, put His hands on them, and blessed them. ◊ Jesus called His disciples to Him and said, "I have compassion on the multitude, because they have now continued with Me three days and have nothing to eat. And I do not want to send them away hungry, lest they faint on the way." ◊ We . . . have a High Priest . . . tempted as we are. ◊ In His love and in His pity He redeemed them.

I will not leave you orphans; I will come to you. ◊ Can a woman forget her nursing child, and not have compassion on the son of her womb? Surely they may forget, yet I will not forget you.

The Lamb who is in the midst of the throne will shepherd them and lead them to living fountains of waters. And God will wipe away every tear from their eyes.

JOHN 13:23.IS 66:13.MARK 10:13,16.MATT 15:32.HEB 4:15.IS 63:9.JOHN 14:18.IS 49:15.REV 7:17

**We have known and believed the love that God has for us.**

God, who is rich in mercy, because of His great love with which He loved us, even when we were dead in trespasses, made us alive together with Christ (by grace you have been saved), and raised us up together, and made us sit together in the heavenly places in Christ Jesus, that in the ages to come He might show the exceeding riches of His grace in His kindness toward us in Christ Jesus.

God so loved the world that He gave His only begotten Son, that whoever believes in Him should not perish but have everlasting life. ◊ He who did not spare His own Son, but delivered Him up for us all, how shall He not with Him also freely give us all things? ◊ The Lord is good to all, and His tender mercies are over all His works.

We love Him because He first loved us.

Blessed is she who believed, for there will be a fulfillment of those things which were told her from the Lord.

1 JOHN 4:16.EPH 2:4-7.JOHN 3:16.ROM 8:32.PS 145:9.
1 JOHN 4:19.LUKE 1:45

Let your speech always be with grace.

A word fitly spoken is like apples of gold in settings of silver. Like an earring of gold and an ornament of fine gold is a wise reprover to an obedient ear. ◊ Let no corrupt communication proceed out of your mouth, but what is good for necessary edification, that it may impart grace to the hearers. ◊ A good man out of the good treasure of his heart brings forth good things, and an evil man out of the evil treasure brings forth evil things. . . . By your words you will be justified. ◊ The tongue of the wise promotes health.

Those who feared the Lord spoke to one another, and the Lord listened and heard them; so a book of remembrance was written before Him for those who fear the Lord and who meditate on His name.

If you take out the precious from the vile, you shall be as My mouth. ◊ But as you abound in everything in faith, in speech, in knowledge, in all diligence, . . . see that you abound in this grace also.

COL 4:6.PROV 25:11-12.EPH 4:29.MATT 12:35,37.PROV 12:18.MAL 3:16.JER 15:19.2 COR 8:7

In the days of His flesh, when He had offered up prayers and supplications, with vehement cries and tears to Him who was able to save Him from death, and was heard because of His godly fear, though He was a Son, yet He learned obedience by the things which He suffered. And having been perfected, He became the author of eternal salvation to all who obey Him. ◊ We do not have a High Priest who cannot sympathize with our weaknesses, but was in all points tempted as we are, yet without sin.

No temptation has overtaken you except such as is common to man; but God is faithful, who will not allow you to be tempted beyond what you are able, but with the temptation will also make the way of escape, that you may be able to bear it. ◊ My grace is sufficient for you, for My strength is made perfect in weakness.

MATT 4:1.HEB 5:7-9.HEB 4:15.1 COR 10:13.2 COR 12:9

## July 7

**Then Jesus was led up by the Spirit into the wilderness to be tempted by the devil.**

## July 8

If we confess our sins, He is faithful and just to forgive us our sins and to cleanse us from all unrighteousness.

I acknowledge my transgressions, and my sin is ever before me. Against You, You only, have I sinned, and done this evil in Your sight.

And he arose and came to his father. But when he was still a great way off, his father saw him and had compassion, and ran and fell on his neck and kissed him. ◊ I have blotted out, like a thick cloud, your transgressions, and like a cloud, your sins. Return to Me, for I have redeemed you. ◊ Your sins are forgiven you for His name's sake. ◊ God in Christ also forgave you. ◊ That He might be just and the justifier of the one who has faith in Jesus.

Then I will sprinkle clean water on you, and you shall be clean. ◊ They shall walk with Me in white, for they are worthy.

This is He who came by water and blood—Jesus Christ; not only by water, but by water and blood.

1 JOHN 1:9.PS 51:3-4.LUKE 15:20.IS 44:22.1 JOHN 2:12.EPH 4:32.ROM 3:26.EZEK 36:25.REV 3:4.1 JOHN 5:6

I have removed
your iniquity
from you, and I
will clothe you
with rich robes.

Blessed is he whose transgression is forgiven, whose sin is covered. ◊ We are all like an unclean thing. ◊ I know that in me (that is, in my flesh) nothing good dwells; for to will is present with me, but how to perform what is good I do not find.

As many of you as were baptized into Christ have put on Christ. ◊ You have put off the old man with his deeds, and have put on the new man who is renewed in knowledge according to the image of Him who created him. ◊ Not having my own righteousness, which is from the law, but . . . the righteousness which is from God by faith.

Bring out the best robe and put it on him. ◊ The fine linen is the righteous acts of the saints. ◊ I will greatly rejoice in the Lord, my soul shall be joyful in my God; for He has clothed me with the garments of salvation, He has covered me with the robe of righteousness.

ZECH 3:4.PS 32:1.IS 64:6.ROM 7:18.GAL 3:27.COL 3:9-10.PHIL 3:9.LUKE 15:22.REV 19:8.IS 61:10

**A disciple is not above his teacher.**

You call me Teacher and Lord, and you say well, for so I am.

It is enough for a disciple that he be like his teacher, and a servant like his master. ◊ If they persecuted Me, they will also persecute you. If they kept My word, they will keep yours also. ◊ I have given them Your word; and the world has hated them because they are not of the world, just as I am not of the world.

Consider Him who endured such hostility from sinners against Himself, lest you become weary and discouraged in your souls. You have not yet resisted to bloodshed, striving against sin.

Let us run with endurance the race that is set before us, looking unto Jesus, the author and finisher of our faith, who for the joy that was set before Him endured the cross, despising the shame, and has sat down at the right hand of the throne of God. ◊ Therefore, since Christ suffered for us in the flesh, arm yourselves also with the same mind.

MATT 10:24.JOHN 13:13.MATT 10:25.JOHN 15:20.JOHN 17:14.HEB 12:3-4.HEB 12:1-2.1 PET 4:1

Shall the prey be taken from the mighty, or the captives of the righteous be delivered? But thus says the Lord: "Even the captives of the mighty shall be taken away, and the prey of the terrible be delivered; for I will contend with him who contends with you. . . . All flesh shall know that I, the Lord, am your Savior, and your Redeemer, the Mighty One of Jacob." ◊ Fear not, for I am with you; be not dismayed, for I am your God. I will strengthen you, yes, I will help you, I will uphold you with My righteous right hand.

We do not have a High Priest who cannot sympathize with our weaknesses, but was in all points tempted as we are, yet without sin. ◊ In that He Himself has suffered, being tempted, He is able to aid those who are tempted. ◊ The steps of a good man are ordered by the Lord, and He delights in his way. Though he fall, he shall not be utterly cast down; for the Lord upholds him with His hand.

JER 15:20.IS 49:24-26.IS 41:10.HEB 4:15.HEB 2:18.PS 37:23-24

I am with you to save you.

## July 12

My Presence will go with you, and I will give you rest.

Be strong and of good courage, do not fear nor be afraid of them; for the Lord your God, He is the One who goes with you. He will not leave you nor forsake you. . . . The Lord, He is the one who goes before you. He will be with you, He will not leave you nor forsake you; do not fear nor be dismayed. ◊ Have I not commanded you? Be strong and of good courage; do not be afraid, nor be dismayed, for the Lord your God is with you wherever you go. ◊ In all your ways acknowledge Him, and He shall direct your paths.

He Himself has said, "I will never leave you nor forsake you." . . . So we may boldly say: "The Lord is my helper; I will not fear. What can man do to me?" ◊ Our sufficiency is from God.

Do not lead us into temptation. ◊ O Lord, I know the way of man is not in himself; it is not in man who walks to direct his own steps. ◊ My times are in Your hand.

EX 33:14.DEUT 31:6,8.JOSH 1:9.PROV 3:6.HEB 13:5-6. 2 COR 3:5.MATT 6:13.JER 10:23.PS 31:15

I know whom I have believed and am persuaded that He is able to keep what I have committed to Him until that Day. ◊ I am persuaded that neither death nor life, nor angels nor principalities nor powers, nor things present nor things to come, nor height nor depth, nor any other created thing, shall be able to separate us from the love of God which is in Christ Jesus our Lord. ◊ Those whom You gave Me I have kept; and none of them is lost.

The Lord takes pleasure in His people. ◊ My delight was with the sons of men. ◊ His great love with which He loved us. ◊ Greater love has no one than this, than to lay down one's life for his friends.

You were bought at a price; therefore glorify God in your body and in your spirit, which are God's. ◊ If we live, we live to the Lord; and if we die, we die to the Lord. Therefore, whether we live or die, we are the Lord's.

SONG 7:10.2 TIM 1:12.ROM 8:38-39.JOHN 17:12.PS 149:4.PROV 8:31.EPH 2:4.JOHN 15:13.1 COR 6:20.ROM 14:8

## July 13

I am my beloved's, and his desire is toward me.

## July 14

Out of the
abundance of the
heart the mouth
speaks.

Let the word of Christ dwell in you richly in all wisdom.

Keep your heart with all diligence, for out of it spring the issues of life. ◊ Death and life are in the power of the tongue. ◊ The mouth of the righteous speaks wisdom, and his tongue talks of justice. The law of his God is in his heart; none of his steps shall slide. Let no corrupt communication proceed out of your mouth, but what is good for necessary edification, that it may impart grace to the hearers.

For we cannot but speak the things which we have seen and heard. ◊ I believed, therefore I spoke.

Whoever confesses Me before men, him I will also confess before My Father who is in heaven. ◊ With the heart one believes to righteousness, and with the mouth confession is made to salvation.

MATT 12:34.COL 3:16.PROV 4:23.PROV 18:21.PS 37:30-31.EPH 4:29.ACTS 4:20.PS 116:10.MATT 10:32.ROM 10:10

Bless the Lord, you His angels, who excel in strength, who do His word, heeding the voice of His word. Bless the Lord, all you His hosts, you ministers of His, who do His pleasure.

I have come down from heaven, not to do My own will, but the will of Him who sent Me. ◊ I delight to do Your will, O my God, and Your law is within my heart. ◊ O My Father, if this cup cannot pass away from Me unless I drink it, Your will be done.

Not everyone who says to Me, "Lord, Lord," shall enter the kingdom of heaven, but he who does the will of My Father in heaven. ◊ Not the hearers of the law are just in the sight of God, but the doers of the law will be justified. ◊ If you know these things, happy are you if you do them. ◊ To him who knows to do good and does not do it, to him it is sin.

Do not be conformed to this world, but be transformed by the renewing of your mind.

MATT 6:10.PS 103:20-21.JOHN 6:38.PS 40:8.MATT 26:42.MATT 7:21.ROM 2:13.JOHN 13:17.JAMES 4:17.ROM 12:2

## July 16

You shall be to Me a kingdom of priests and a holy nation.

You were slain, and have redeemed us to God by Your blood out of every tribe and tongue and people and nation, and have made us kings and priests to our God. ◊ You are a chosen generation, a royal priesthood, a holy nation, His own special people, that you may proclaim the praises of Him who called you out of darkness into His marvelous light.

You shall be named the Priests of the Lord, men shall call you the Servants of our God. ◊ Priests of God and of Christ.

Therefore, holy brethren, partakers of the heavenly calling, consider the Apostle and High Priest of our confession, Christ Jesus. ◊ Therefore by Him let us continually offer the sacrifice of praise to God, that is, the fruit of our lips, giving thanks to His name.

For we are His workmanship, created in Christ Jesus for good works, which God prepared beforehand that we should walk in them. ◊ The temple of God is holy, which temple you are.

EX 19:6.REV 5:9-10.1 PET 2:9.IS 61:6.REV 20:6.HEB 3:1.HEB 13:15.EPH 2:10.1 COR 3:17

I pray, let the power of my Lord be great, just as You have spoken, saying, "The Lord is longsuffering and abundant in mercy, forgiving iniquity and transgression; but He by no means clears the guilty, visiting the iniquity of the fathers on the children to the third and fourth generation."

Oh, do not remember former iniquities against us! Let Your tender mercies come speedily to meet us. . . . Help us, O God of our salvation, for the glory of Your name; and deliver us, and provide atonement for our sins, for Your name's sake! ◊ O Lord, though our iniquities testify against us, do it for Your name's sake; for our backslidings are many, we have sinned against You. ◊ We acknowledge, O Lord, our wickedness and the iniquity of our fathers, for we have sinned against You.

If You, Lord, should mark iniquities, O Lord, who could stand? But there is forgiveness with You, that You may be feared.

JON 4:2.NUM 14:17-18.PS 79:8-9.JER 14:7.JER 14:20.PS 130:3-4

You are a gracious and merciful God, slow to anger and abundant in lovingkindness, One who relents from doing harm.

## July 18

The solid foundation of God stands, having this seal: "The Lord knows those who are His," and, "Let everyone who names the name of Christ depart from iniquity." ◊ Many will say to Me in that day, "Lord, Lord, have we not prophesied in Your name, cast out demons in Your name, and done many wonders in Your name?" And then I will declare to them, "I never knew you; depart from Me, you who practice lawlessness!" ◊ The Lord knows the way of the righteous, but the way of the ungodly shall perish.

See, I have inscribed you on the palms of My hands; your walls are continually before Me. ◊ Set me as a seal upon your heart, as a seal upon your arm. ◊ The Lord is good, a stronghold in the day of trouble; and He knows those who trust in Him.

I go to prepare a place for you. And if I go and prepare a place for you, I will come again and receive you to Myself; that where I am, there you may be also.

JOHN 10:3.2 TIM 2:19.MATT 7:22-23.PS 1:6.IS 49:16.SONG 8:6.NAH 1:7.JOHN 14:2-3

Who is like You, O Lord, among the gods? Who is like You, glorious in holiness, fearful in praises, doing wonders? ◊ Among the gods there is none like You, O Lord; nor are there any works like Your works. ◊ Who shall not fear You, O Lord, and glorify Your name? For You alone are holy. ◊ Hallowed be Your name.

Blessed is the Lord God of Israel, for He has visited and redeemed His people.

Who is this who comes from Edom, with dyed garments from Bozrah, this One who is glorious in His apparel, traveling in the greatness of His strength? I who speak in righteousness, mighty to save. ◊ I have given help to one who is mighty; I have exalted one chosen from the people.

Now to Him who is able to do exceedingly abundantly above all that we ask or think, according to the power that works in us, . . . be glory.

LUKE 1:49.EX 15:11.PS 86:8.REV 15:4.MATT 6:9.LUKE 1:68.IS 63:1.PS 89:19.EPH 3:20-21

## July 19

He who is mighty has done great things for me, and holy is His name.

## July 20

He is despised and rejected by men, a man of sorrows and acquainted with grief. ◊ In the world you will have tribulation; but be of good cheer, I have overcome the world.

Such a High Priest was fitting for us, who is holy, harmless, undefiled, separate from sinners. ◊ That you may become blameless and harmless, children of God without fault in the midst of a crooked and perverse generation.

Jesus of Nazareth . . . went about doing good and healing all who were oppressed by the devil, for God was with Him. ◊ Therefore, as we have opportunity, let us do good to all, especially to those who are of the household of faith.

That was the true Light which gives light to every man who comes into the world. ◊ You are the light of the world. A city that is set on a hill cannot be hidden. . . . Let your light so shine before men, that they may see your good works and glorify your Father in heaven.

JOHN 17:16.IS 53:3.JOHN 16:33.HEB 7:26.PHIL 2:15.ACTS 10:38.GAL 6:10.JOHN 1:9.MATT 5:14,16

Much in every way! ◊ Circumcise yourselves to the Lord, and take away the foreskins of your hearts. ◊ If their uncircumcised hearts are humbled, and they accept their guilt—then I will remember My covenant with Jacob, and My covenant with Isaac and My covenant with Abraham I will remember.

Jesus Christ has become a servant to the circumcision for the truth of God, to confirm the promises made to the fathers. ◊ In Him you were also circumcised with the circumcision made without hands, by putting off the body of the sins of the flesh, by the circumcision of Christ. ◊ You, being dead in your trespasses and the uncircumcision of your flesh, He has made alive together with Him, having forgiven you all trespasses.

Put off, concerning your former conduct, the old man which grows corrupt according to the deceitful lusts, and be renewed in the spirit of your mind, and . . . put on the new man which was created according to God, in righteousness and true holiness.

ROM 3:1.ROM 3:2.JER 4:4.LEV 26:41-42.ROM 15:8.COL 2:11.COL 2:13.EPH 4:22-24

What is the profit of circumcision?

## July 22

For the death that He died, He died to sin once for all; but the life that He lives, He lives to God.

He was numbered with the transgressors. ◊ Christ was offered once to bear the sins of many. ◊ [He] Himself bore our sins in His own body on the tree, that we, having died to sins, might live for righteousness—by whose stripes you were healed. ◊ By one offering He has perfected forever those who are being sanctified.

But He, because He continues forever, has an unchangeable priesthood. Therefore He is also able to save to the uttermost those who come to God through Him, since He ever lives to make intercession for them. ◊ While we were still sinners, Christ died for us. Much more then, having now been justified by His blood, we shall be saved from wrath through Him.

Therefore, since Christ suffered for us in the flesh, arm yourselves also with the same mind, for he who has suffered in the flesh has ceased from sin, that he no longer should live the rest of his time in the flesh for the lusts of men, but for the will of God.

ROM 6:10.IS 53:12.HEB 9:28.1 PET 2:24.HEB 10:14.HEB 7:24-25.ROM 5:8-9.1 PET 4:1-2

Of that day and hour no one knows, neither the angels in heaven, nor the Son, but only the Father. Take heed, watch and pray; for you do not know when the time is. And what I say to you, I say to all: Watch! ◊ The Lord is not slack concerning His promise, as some count slackness, but is longsuffering toward us, not willing that any should perish but that all should come to repentance. ◊ The coming of the Lord is at hand. . . . The Judge is standing at the door! ◊ Surely I am coming quickly.

Therefore, since all these things will be dissolved, what manner of persons ought you to be in holy conduct and godliness?

The end of all things is at hand; therefore be serious and watchful in your prayers. ◊ Let your waist be girded and your lamps burning; and you yourselves be like men who wait for their master, when he will return from the wedding, that when he comes and knocks they may open to him immediately.

1 COR 15:24.MARK 13:32-33.MARK 13:37.2 PET 3:9.JAMES 5:8-9.REV 22:20.2 PET 3:11.1 PET 4:7.LUKE 12:35-36

Then comes the end.

## July 24

[Be] patient in tribulation.

It is the Lord. Let Him do what seems good to Him. ◊ For though I were righteous, I could not answer Him; I would beg mercy of my Judge. ◊ The Lord gave, and the Lord has taken away; blessed be the name of the Lord. ◊ Shall we indeed accept good from God, and shall we not accept adversity?

Jesus wept. ◊ A man of sorrows and acquainted with grief. . . . Surely He has borne our griefs and carried our sorrows.

Whom the Lord loves He chastens, and scourges every son whom He receives. . . . Now no chastening seems to be joyful for the present, but grievous; nevertheless, afterward it yields the peaceable fruit of righteousness to those who have been trained by it. ◊ [Be] strengthened with all might, according to His glorious power, for all patience and longsuffering with joy. ◊ In the world you will have tribulation; but be of good cheer, I have overcome the world.

ROM 12:12.1 SAM 3:18.JOB 9:15.JOB 1:21.JOB 2:10.JOHN 11:35.IS 53:3-4.HEB 12:6,11.COL 1:11.JOHN 16:33

He who hears My word and believes in Him who sent Me has everlasting life, and shall not come into judgment, but has passed from death into life. ◊ He who has the Son has life; he who does not have the Son of God does not have life.

He who establishes us with you in Christ and has anointed us is God, who also has sealed us and given us the Spirit in our hearts as a deposit. ◊ By this we know that we are of the truth, and shall assure our hearts before Him. . . . Beloved, if our heart does not condemn us, we have confidence toward God. ◊ We know that we are of God, and the whole world lies under the sway of the wicked one.

You He made alive, who were dead in trespasses and sins. ◊ [He] made us alive together with Christ. ◊ He has delivered us from the power of darkness and translated us into the kingdom of the Son of His love.

1 JOHN 3:14.JOHN 5:24.1 JOHN 5:12.2 COR 1:21-22.
1 JOHN 3:19, 21.JOHN 5:19.EPH 2:1.EPH 2:5.COL 1:13

We know that we have passed from death to life.

## July 26

By faith Abraham obeyed when he was called to go out to the place which he would afterward receive as an inheritance.

He will choose our inheritance for us. ◊ He encircled him, He instructed him, He kept him as the apple of His eye. As an eagle stirs up its nest, hovers over its young, spreading out its wings, taking them up, carrying them on its wings, so the Lord alone led him, and there was no foreign god with him.

I am the Lord your God, who teaches you to profit, who leads you by the way you should go. ◊ Who teaches like Him?

We walk by faith, not by sight. ◊ Here we have no continuing city, but we seek the one to come. ◊ Beloved, I beg you as sojourners and pilgrims, abstain from fleshly lusts which war against the soul. ◊ Arise and depart, for this is not your rest; because it is defiled, it shall destroy you, even with utter destruction.

HEB 11:8.PS 47:4.DEUT 32:10-12.IS 48:17.JOB 36:22.
2 COR 5:7.HEB 13:14.1 PET 2:11.MIC 2:10

The glory of the Lord shall be revealed, and all flesh shall see it together. ◊ No one has seen God at any time. The only begotten Son, who is in the bosom of the Father, He has declared Him. ◊ And the Word became flesh and dwelt among us, and we beheld His glory, the glory as of the only begotten of the Father, full of grace and truth. ◊ He who has seen Me has seen the Father. ◊ The brightness of His glory and the express image of His person. ◊ God was manifested in the flesh.

In whom we have redemption through His blood, the forgiveness of sins. He is the image of the invisible God, the firstborn over all creation. ◊ Whom He foreknew, He also predestined to be conformed to the image of His Son, that He might be the firstborn among many brethren.

As we have borne the image of the man of dust, we shall also bear the image of the heavenly Man.

2 COR 4:4.IS 40:5.JOHN 1:18.JOHN 14:9.HEB 1:3.1 TIM 3:16.COL 1:14-15.ROM 8:29.1 COR 15:49

## July 27

**Christ, who is the image of God.**

## July 28

**Walk in love.**

A new commandment I give to you, that you love one another; as I have loved you, that you also love one another. ◊ Above all things have fervent love for one another, for love will cover a multitude of sins. ◊ Love covers all sins.

Whenever you stand praying, if you have anything against anyone, forgive him, that your Father in heaven may also forgive you your trespasses. ◊ Love your enemies, do good, and lend, hoping for nothing in return. ◊ Do not rejoice when your enemy falls, and do not let your heart be glad when he stumbles. ◊ Not returning evil for evil or reviling for reviling, but on the contrary blessing, knowing that you were called to this, that you may inherit a blessing. ◊ If it is possible, as much as depends on you, live peaceably with all men. ◊ Be kind to one another, tenderhearted, forgiving one another, just as God in Christ also forgave you.

My little children, let us not love in word or in tongue, but in deed and in truth.

EPH 5:2.JOHN 13:34.1 PET 4:8.PROV 10:12.MARK 11:25.LUKE 6:35.PROV 24:17.1 PET 3:9.ROM 12:18.EPH 4:32.1 JOHN 3:18

Make haste, my beloved, and be like a gazelle or a young stag on the mountains of spices. ◊ We ourselves groan within ourselves, eagerly waiting for the adoption, the redemption of our body. ◊ Bow down Your heavens, O Lord, and come down; touch the mountains, and they shall smoke.

This same Jesus, who was taken up from you into heaven, will so come in like manner as you saw Him go into heaven. ◊ To those who eagerly wait for Him He will appear a second time, apart from sin, for salvation. ◊ It will be said in that day: "Behold, this is our God; we have waited for Him, and He will save us. This is the Lord; we have waited for Him; we will be glad and rejoice in His salvation."

He who testifies to these things says, "Surely I am coming quickly." Amen. Even so, come, Lord Jesus! ◊ The blessed hope and glorious appearing of our great God and Savior Jesus Christ. ◊ Our citizenship is in heaven.

IS 64:1.SONG 8:14.ROM 8:23.PS 144:5.ACTS 1:11.HEB 9:28.IS 25:9.REV 22:20.TITUS 2:13.PHIL 3:20

## July 29

Oh, that You would rend the heavens! That You would come down!

## July 30

Seek those things which are above, where Christ is, sitting at the right hand of God.

Get wisdom! Get understanding! ◊ The wisdom that is from above. ◊ The deep says, "It is not in me"; and the sea says, "It is not with me." ◊ We were buried with Him through baptism into death, that just as Christ was raised from the dead by the glory of the Father, even so we also should walk in newness of life. For if we have been united together in the likeness of His death, certainly we also shall be in the likeness of His resurrection.

Let us lay aside every weight, and the sin which so easily ensnares us, and let us run with endurance the race that is set before us. ◊ God . . . made us alive together with Christ . . . and raised us up together, and made us sit together in the heavenly places in Christ Jesus.

Those who say such things declare plainly that they seek a homeland. ◊ Seek the Lord, all you meek of the earth, who have upheld His justice. Seek righteousness, seek humility.

COL 3:1.PROV 4:5.JAMES 3:17.JOB 28:14.ROM 6:4-5.HEB 12:1.EPH 2:4-6.HEB 11:14.ZEPH 2:3

I have given him as a witness to the people, a leader and commander for the people. ◇ It was fitting for Him, for whom are all things and by whom are all things, in bringing many sons to glory, to make the author of their salvation perfect through sufferings. ◇ We must through many tribulations enter the kingdom of God.

We do not wrestle against flesh and blood, but against principalities, against powers, against the rulers of the darkness of this age, against spiritual hosts of wickedness in the heavenly places. Therefore take up the whole armor of God. ◇ We do not war according to the flesh. For the weapons of our warfare are not carnal but mighty in God for pulling down strongholds.

May the God of all grace, who called us to His eternal glory by Christ Jesus, after you have suffered a while, perfect, establish, strengthen, and settle you.

2 TIM 2:3.IS 55:4.HEB 2:10.ACTS 14:22.EPH 6:12-13.
2 COR 10:3-4.1 PET 5:10

Endure hardship as a good soldier of Jesus Christ.

## August 1

By grace you have been saved through faith, and that not of yourselves; it is the gift of God. ◊ Without faith it is impossible to please Him. ◊ He who believes in Him is not condemned; but he who does not believe is already, because he has not believed in the name of the only begotten Son of God. ◊ Lord, I believe; help my unbelief!

Whoever keeps His word, truly the love of God is perfected in him. By this we know that we are in Him. ◊ Faith working through love. ◊ Faith without works is dead.

We walk by faith, not by sight. ◊ I have been crucified with Christ; it is no longer I who live, but Christ lives in me; and the life which I now live in the flesh I live by faith in the Son of God, who loved me and gave Himself for me. ◊ Jesus Christ whom having not seen you love. Though now you do not see Him, yet believing, you rejoice with joy inexpressible and full of glory, receiving the end of your faith—the salvation of your souls.

GAL 5:22.EPH 2:8.HEB 11:6.JOHN 3:18.MARK 9:24.
1 JOHN 2:5.GAL 5:6.JAMES 2:20.2 COR 5:7.GAL 2:20.
1 PET 1:7-9

Your lamb shall be without blemish. .
. . Then the whole assembly of the
congregation of Israel shall kill it at
twilight. And they shall take some of
the blood and put it on the two
doorposts and on the lintel of the
houses where they eat it. . . . And
when I see the blood, I will pass over
you. ◊ The blood of sprinkling. ◊
Christ, our Passover, was sacrificed for
us. ◊ Being delivered by the
determined counsel and foreknowledge
of God. ◊ God . . . saved us . . .
according to His own purpose and grace
which was given to us in Christ Jesus
before time began.

We have redemption through His
blood, the forgiveness of sins.

Therefore, since Christ suffered for us
in the flesh, arm yourselves also with
the same mind, for he who has suffered
in the flesh has ceased from sin, that he
no longer should live the rest of his
time in the flesh for the lusts of men,
but for the will of God.

REV 13:8.EX 12:5-7,13.HEB 12:24.1 COR 5:7.ACTS
2:23.2 TIM 1:9.EPH 1:7.1 PET 4:1-2

## August 2

The Lamb slain
from the
foundation of the
world.

## August 3

His mercy is on those who fear Him.

Oh, how great is Your goodness, which You have laid up for those who fear You, which You have prepared for those who trust in You in the presence of the sons of men! You shall hide them in the secret place of Your presence from the plots of man; You shall keep them secretly in a pavilion from the strife of tongues.

If you call on the Father, who without partiality judges according to each one's work, conduct yourselves throughout the time of your sojourning here in fear. ◊ The Lord is near to all who call upon Him . . . in truth. He will fulfill the desire of those who fear Him; He also will hear their cry and save them.

"Because your heart was tender, and you humbled yourself before the Lord . . . and you tore your clothes and wept before Me, I also have heard you," says the Lord. ◊ On this one will I look: on him who is poor and of a contrite spirit, and who trembles at My word. ◊ The Lord is near to those who have a broken heart, and saves such as have a contrite spirit.

LUKE 1:50.PS 31:19-20.1 PET 1:17.PS 145:18-19.2 KIN 22:19.IS 66:2.PS 34:18

Jesus, the author and finisher of our faith. ◊ I have glorified You on the earth. I have finished the work which You have given Me to do. ◊ We have been sanctified through the offering of the body of Jesus Christ once for all. And every priest stands ministering daily and offering repeatedly the same sacrifices, which can never take away sins. But this Man, after He had offered one sacrifice for sins forever, sat down at the right hand of God, from that time waiting till His enemies are made His footstool. For by one offering He has perfected forever those who are being sanctified. ◊ Having wiped out the handwriting of requirements that was against us, which was contrary to us. And He has taken it out of the way, having nailed it to the cross.

I lay down My life that I may take it again. No one takes it from Me, but I lay it down of Myself. I have power to lay it down, and I have power to take it again. ◊ Greater love has no one than this, than to lay down one's life for his friends.

JOHN 19:30.HEB 12:2.JOHN 17:4.HEB 10:10-14.COL 2:14.JOHN 10:17-18.JOHN 15:13

## August 4

"It is finished!" And bowing His head, He gave up His spirit.

## August 5

**Walk in newness of life.**

As you presented your members as slaves of uncleanness, and of lawlessness leading to more lawlessness, so now present your members as slaves of righteousness for holiness. ◊ I beseech you . . . brethren, by the mercies of God, that you present your bodies a living sacrifice, holy, acceptable to God, which is your reasonable service. And do not be conformed to this world, but be transformed by the renewing of your mind.

If anyone is in Christ, he is a new creation; old things have passed away; behold, all things have become new. ◊ In Christ Jesus neither circumcision nor uncircumcision avails anything, but a new creation. And as many as walk according to this rule, peace and mercy be upon them. ◊ This I say, therefore, and testify in the Lord, that you should no longer walk as the rest of the Gentiles walk, in the futility of their mind. ◊ You have not so learned Christ, if indeed you have heard Him and have been taught by Him, as the truth is in Jesus. . . . Put on the new man which was created according to God, in righteousness and true holiness.

ROM 6:4.ROM 6:19.ROM 12:1-2.2 COR 5:17.GAL 6:15-16.EPH 4:17.EPH 4:20-21,24

Now see that I, even I, am He, and there is no God besides Me; I kill and I make alive; I wound and I heal; nor is there any who can deliver from My hand. ◇ I know the thoughts that I think toward you, says the Lord, thoughts of peace and not of evil, to give you a future and a hope. ◇ "My thoughts are not your thoughts, nor are your ways My ways," says the Lord.

I will allure her, will bring her into the wilderness, and speak comfort to her. ◇ As a man chastens his son, so the Lord your God chastens you. ◇ Now no chastening seems to be joyful for the present, but grievous; nevertheless, afterward it yields the peaceable fruit of righteousness to those who have been trained by it. ◇ Humble yourselves under the mighty hand of God, that He may exalt you in due time.

I know, O Lord, that Your judgments are right, and that in faithfulness You have afflicted me.

PROV 3:12.DEUT 32:39.JER 29:11.IS 55:8.HOS 2:14.DEUT 8:5.HEB 12:11.1 PET 5:6.PS 119:75

For whom the LORD loves He corrects.

## August 7

The Helper, the Holy Spirit, whom the Father will send in My name.

If you knew the gift of God, and who it is who says to you, "Give Me a drink," you would have asked Him, and He would have given you living water. ◊ If you . . . being evil, know how to give good gifts to your children, how much more will your heavenly Father give the Holy Spirit to those who ask Him! ◊ Most assuredly, I say to you, whatever you ask the Father in My name He will give you. Until now you have asked nothing in My name. Ask, and you will receive, that your joy may be full. ◊ You do not have because you do not ask.

When . . . the Spirit of truth, has come, He will guide you into all truth; for He will not speak on His own authority, but whatever He hears He will speak; and He will tell you things to come. He will glorify Me, for He will take of what is Mine and declare it to you.

They rebelled and grieved His Holy Spirit; so He turned Himself against them as an enemy, and He fought against them.

JOHN 14:26.JOHN 4:10.LUKE 11:13.JOHN 16:23-24.JAMES 4:2.JOHN 16:13-14.IS 63:10

Not that I have already attained, or am already perfected; but I press on, that I may lay hold of that for which Christ Jesus has also laid hold of me. ◊ Let us know, let us pursue the knowledge of the Lord.

Then the righteous will shine forth as the sun in the kingdom of their Father. ◊ We all, with unveiled face, beholding as in a mirror the glory of the Lord, are being transformed into the same image from glory to glory, just as by the Spirit of the Lord. ◊ When that which is perfect has come, then that which is in part will be done away. . . . For now we see in a mirror, dimly, but then face to face. Now I know in part, but then I shall know just as I also am known. ◊ Beloved, now we are children of God; and it has not yet been revealed what we shall be, but we know that when He is revealed, we shall be like Him, for we shall see Him as He is. And everyone who has this hope in Him purifies himself, just as He is pure.

PROV 4:18.PHIL 3:12.HOS 6:3.MATT 13:43.2 COR 3:18.1 COR 13:10,12.1 JOHN 3:2-3

## August 8

The path of the just is like the shining sun, that shines ever brighter unto the perfect day.

## August 9

You are all fair, my love, and there is no spot in you.

The whole head is sick, and the whole heart faints. From the sole of the foot even to the head, there is no soundness in it, but wounds and bruises and putrefying sores; they have not been closed or bound up, or soothed with ointment. ◊ We are all like an unclean thing, and all our righteousnesses are like filthy rags. ◊ I know that in me (that is, in my flesh) nothing good dwells.

You were washed, . . . you were sanctified, . . . you were justified in the name of the Lord Jesus and by the Spirit of our God. ◊ The royal daughter is all glorious within. ◊ "Your beauty . . . was perfect through My splendor which I had bestowed on you," says the Lord God.

Let the beauty of the Lord our God be upon us.

These are the ones who . . . washed their robes and made them white in the blood of the Lamb. ◊ A glorious church, not having spot or wrinkle or any such thing, but . . . holy and without blemish. ◊ You are complete in Him.

SONG 4:7.IS 1:5-6.IS 64:6.ROM 7:18.1 COR 6:11.PS 45:13.EZEK 16:14.PS 90:17.REV 7:14.EPH 5:27.COL 2:10

Blameless and harmless, children of God without fault in the midst of a crooked and perverse generation, among whom you shine as lights in the world. ◊ You are the salt of the earth; . . . the light of the world. ◊ Let your light so shine before men, that they may see your good works and glorify your Father in heaven.

I also withheld you from sinning against Me.

The Lord is faithful, who will establish you and guard you from the evil one. ◊ I did not do so, because of the fear of God. ◊ [He] gave Himself for our sins, that He might deliver us from this present evil age, according to the will of our God and Father. ◊ Now to Him who is able to keep you from stumbling, and to present you faultless before the presence of His glory with exceeding joy, to God our Savior, who alone is wise, be glory and majesty, dominion and power, both now and forever. Amen.

JOHN 17:15.PHIL 2:15.MATT 5:13-14.MATT 5:16.GEN 20:6.2 THESS 3:3.NEH 5:15.GAL 1:4.JUDE 1:24-25

I do not pray that You should take them out of the world, but that You should keep them from the evil one.

# August 11

**That through death He might destroy him who had the power of death.**

Our Savior Jesus Christ . . . has abolished death and brought life and immortality to light through the gospel. ◊ He will swallow up death forever, and the Lord God will wipe away tears from all faces; the rebuke of His people He will take away from all the earth; for the Lord has spoken. ◊ When this corruptible has put on incorruption, and this mortal has put on immortality, then shall be brought to pass the saying that is written: "Death is swallowed up in victory." "O Death, where is your sting? O Hades, where is your victory?" The sting of death is sin, and the strength of sin is the law. But thanks be to God, who gives us the victory through our Lord Jesus Christ.

God has not given us a spirit of fear, but of power and of love and of a sound mind. ◊ Yea, though I walk through the valley of the shadow of death, I will fear no evil; for You are with me; Your rod and Your staff, they comfort me.

HEB 2:14.2 TIM 1:10.IS 25:8.1 COR 15:54-57.2 TIM 1:7.PS 23:4

"Do not fear, O Jacob My servant,"
. . . says the Lord, "for I am with you;
. . . I will not make a complete end of
you. I will rightly correct you." ◊ "For
a mere moment I have forsaken you,
but with great mercies I will gather you.
With a little wrath I hid My face from
you for a moment; but with everlasting
kindness I will have mercy on you,"
says the Lord, your Redeemer. . . . "For
the mountains shall depart and the hills
be removed, but My kindness shall not
depart from you, nor shall My covenant
of peace be removed," says the Lord,
who has mercy on you. "O you afflicted
one, tossed with tempest, and not
comforted, behold, I will lay your stones
with colorful gems, and lay your
foundations with sapphires."

I will bear the indignation of the
Lord, because I have sinned against
Him, until He pleads my case and
executes justice for me; He will bring
me forth to the light, and I will see His
righteousness.

LAM 3:31-32.JER 46:28.IS 54:7-8,10-11.MIC 7:9

The Lord will not
cast off forever.
Though He causes
grief, yet He will
show compassion.

## August 13

He has prepared a city for them.

If I go and prepare a place for you, I will come again and receive you to Myself; that where I am, there you may be also. ◊ An inheritance incorruptible and undefiled and that does not fade away, reserved in heaven for you. ◊ Here we have no continuing city, but we seek the one to come.

This same Jesus, who was taken up from you into heaven, will so come in like manner as you saw Him go into heaven. ◊ See how the farmer waits for the precious fruit of the earth, waiting patiently for it until it receives the early and latter rain. You also be patient. Establish your hearts, for the coming of the Lord is at hand. ◊ Yet a little while, and He who is coming will come and will not tarry.

We who are alive and remain shall be caught up together with them in the clouds to meet the Lord in the air. And thus we shall always be with the Lord. Therefore comfort one another with these words.

HEB 11:16.JOHN 14:3.1 PET 1:4.HEB 13:14.ACTS 1:11.JAMES 5:7-8.HEB 10:37.1 THESS 4:17-18

Sing, O heavens! Be joyful, O earth! And break out in singing, O mountains! For the Lord has comforted His people, and will have mercy on His afflicted. ◊ Behold, God is my salvation, I will trust and not be afraid; for YAH, the Lord, is my strength and my song; He also has become my salvation. ◊ The Lord is my strength and my shield; my heart trusted in Him, and I am helped; therefore my heart greatly rejoices, and with my song I will praise Him. ◊ My soul shall be joyful in my God; for He has clothed me with the garments of salvation, He has covered me with the robe of righteousness, as a bridegroom decks himself with ornaments, and as a bride adorns herself with her jewels.

Therefore I have reason to glory in Christ Jesus in the things which pertain to God. ◊ We . . . rejoice in God through our Lord Jesus Christ, through whom we have now received the reconciliation. ◊ I will joy in the God of my salvation.

NEH 8:10.IS 49:13.IS 12:2.PS 28:7.IS 61:10.ROM 15:17.ROM 5:11.HAB 3:18

## August 14

The joy of the LORD is your strength.

## August 15

The God of peace . . . make you complete in every good work to do His will.

Become complete. Be of good comfort, be of one mind, live in peace; and the God of love and peace will be with you.

By grace you have been saved through faith, and that not of yourselves; it is the gift of God, not of works, lest anyone should boast. ◊ Every good gift and every perfect gift is from above, and comes down from the Father of lights, with whom there is no variation or shadow of turning.

Work out your own salvation with fear and trembling; for it is God who works in you both to will and to do for His good pleasure. ◊ Be transformed by the renewing of your mind, that you may prove what is that good and acceptable and perfect will of God. ◊ [Be] filled with the fruits of righteousness which are by Jesus Christ, to the glory and praise of God.

Not that we are sufficient of ourselves to think of anything as being from ourselves, but our sufficiency is from God.

HEB 13:20-21.2 COR 13:11.EPH 2:8-9.JAMES 1:17.PHIL 2:12-13.ROM 12:2.PHIL 1:11.2 COR 3:5

You . . . as living stones, are being built up a spiritual house. ◊ Do you not know that you are the temple of God and that the Spirit of God dwells in you? If anyone defiles the temple of God, God will destroy him. For the temple of God is holy, which temple you are. ◊ Your body is the temple of the Holy Spirit who is in you, whom you have from God, and you are not your own. For you were bought at a price; therefore glorify God in your body and in your spirit, which are God's. ◊ What agreement has the temple of God with idols? For you are the temple of the living God. As God has said: "I will dwell in them and walk among them. I will be their God, and they shall be My people." ◊ You . . . having been built on the foundation of the apostles and prophets, Jesus Christ Himself being the chief cornerstone, in whom the whole building, being joined together, grows into a holy temple in the Lord, in whom you also are being built together for a habitation of God in the Spirit.

1 CHR 22:5.1 PET 2:5.1 COR 3:16-17.1 COR 6:19-20.
2 COR 6:16.EPH 2:19-22

The house that is to be built for the LORD must be exceedingly magnificent.

## August 17

Pray for one another, that you may be healed.

Abraham answered and said, "Indeed now, I who am but dust and ashes have taken it upon myself to speak to the Lord: Suppose there were five less than the fifty righteous; would You destroy all of the city for lack of five?" And He said, "If I find there forty-five, I will not destroy it."

Father, forgive them, for they do not know what they do. ◊ Pray for those who spitefully use you and persecute you.

I pray for them. I do not pray for the world but for those whom You have given Me, for they are Yours. . . . I do not pray for these alone, but also for those who will believe in Me through their word. ◊ Bear one another's burdens, and so fulfill the law of Christ.

The effective, fervent prayer of a righteous man avails much. Elijah was a man with a nature like ours, and he prayed earnestly that it would not rain; and it did not rain on the land for three years and six months.

JAMES 5:16.GEN 18:27-28.LUKE 23:34.MATT 5:44.JOHN 17:9,20.GAL 6:2.JAMES 5:16-17

Who in the heavens can be compared to the Lord? Who among the sons of the mighty can be likened to the Lord? . . . O Lord God of hosts, who is mighty like You, O Lord? Your faithfulness also surrounds You. ◊ Among the gods there is none like You, O Lord; nor are there any works like Your works. ◊ For Your word's sake, and according to Your own heart, You have done all these great things, to make Your servant know them. Therefore You are great, O Lord God. For there is none like You, nor is there any God besides You, according to all that we have heard with our ears.

Eye has not seen, nor ear heard, nor have entered into the heart of man the things which God has prepared for those who love Him. But God has revealed them to us through His Spirit. ◊ The secret things belong to the Lord our God, but those things which are revealed belong to us and to our children.

What god is there in heaven or on earth who can do anything like Your works and Your mighty deeds?

DEUT 3:24.PS 89:6,8.PS 86:8.2 SAM 7:21-22.1 COR 2:9-10.DEUT 29:29

## August 19

As He who called you is holy, you also be holy in all your conduct.

You know how we exhorted . . . and charged every one of you, . . . that you would have a walk worthy of God who calls you into His own kingdom and glory. ◇ You may proclaim the praises of Him who called you out of darkness into His marvelous light.

You were once darkness, but now you are light in the Lord. Walk as children of light (for the fruit of the Spirit is in all goodness, righteousness, and truth), proving what is acceptable to the Lord. And have no fellowship with the unfruitful works of darkness, but rather expose them. ◇ Being filled with the fruits of righteousness which are by Jesus Christ, to the glory and praise of God.

Let your light so shine before men, that they may see your good works and glorify your Father in heaven. ◇ Therefore, whether you eat or drink, or whatever you do, do all to the glory of God.

1 PET 1:15.1 THESS 2:11-12.1 PET 2:9.EPH 5:8-11.PHIL 1:11.MATT 5:16.1 COR 10:31

**God is not a man, that He should lie, nor a son of man, that He should repent.**

The Father of lights, with whom there is no variation or shadow of turning. ◊ Jesus Christ is the same yesterday, today, and forever.

His truth shall be your shield and buckler.

God, determining to show more abundantly to the heirs of promise the immutability of His counsel, confirmed it by an oath, that by two immutable things, in which it is impossible for God to lie, we might have strong consolation, who have fled for refuge to lay hold of the hope set before us.

The faithful God . . . keeps covenant and mercy for a thousand generations with those who love Him and keep His commandments. ◊ All the paths of the Lord are mercy and truth, to such as keep His covenant and His testimonies. ◊ Happy is he who has the God of Jacob for his help, whose hope is in the Lord his God, . . . who keeps truth forever.

NUM 23:19.JAMES 1:17.HEB 13:8.PS 91:4.HEB 6:17-18.DEUT 7:9.PS 25:10.PS 146:5-6

## August 21

You are my
portion, O Lord.

All things are yours. . . . And you are Christ's, and Christ is God's. ◊ Our . . . Savior Jesus Christ . . . gave Himself for us. ◊ He . . . gave Him to be head over all things to the church. ◊ Christ . . . loved the church and gave Himself for it, . . . that He might present it to Himself a glorious church, not having spot or wrinkle or any such thing, but that it should be holy and without blemish.

My soul shall make its boast in the Lord. ◊ I will greatly rejoice in the Lord, my soul shall be joyful in my God; for He has clothed me with the garments of salvation, He has covered me with the robe of righteousness.

Whom have I in heaven but You? And there is none upon earth that I desire besides You. My flesh and my heart fail; but God is the strength of my heart and my portion forever. ◊ O my soul, you have said to the Lord, "You are my Lord." . . . You, O Lord, are the portion of my inheritance and my cup; You maintain my lot. The lines have fallen to me in pleasant places; yes, I have a good inheritance.

PS 119:57.1 COR 3:21,23.TITUS 2:13-14.EPH 1:22.EPH 5:25,27.PS 34:2.IS 61:10.PS 73:25-26.PS 16:2,5-6

If we live, we live to the Lord; and if we die, we die to the Lord. Therefore, whether we live or die, we are the Lord's. ◊ Let no one seek his own, but each one the other's well-being. ◊ You were bought at a price; therefore glorify God in your body and in your spirit, which are God's.

Christ will be magnified in my body, whether by life or by death. For to me, to live is Christ, and to die is gain. But if I live on in the flesh, this will mean fruit from my labor; yet what I shall choose I cannot tell. For I am hard pressed between the two, having a desire to depart and be with Christ, which is far better.

I through the law died to the law that I might live to God. I have been crucified with Christ; it is no longer I who live, but Christ lives in me; and the life which I now live in the flesh I live by faith in the Son of God, who loved me and gave Himself for me.

ROM 14:7.ROM 14:8.1 COR 10:24.1 COR 6:20.PHIL 1:20-23.GAL 2:19-20

None of us lives to himself, and no one dies to himself.

## August 23

I have loved you with an everlasting love; therefore with lovingkindness I have drawn you.

We are bound to give thanks to God always for you, brethren beloved by the Lord, because God from the beginning chose you for salvation through sanctification by the Spirit and belief in the truth, to which He called you by our gospel, for the obtaining of the glory of our Lord Jesus Christ. ◊ [God] has saved us and called us with a holy calling, not according to our works, but according to His own purpose and grace which was given to us in Christ Jesus before time began. ◊ Your eyes saw my substance, being yet unformed. And in Your book they all were written, the days fashioned for me, when as yet there were none of them.

God so loved the world that He gave His only begotten Son, that whoever believes in Him should not perish but have everlasting life.

In this is love, not that we loved God, but that He loved us and sent His Son to be the propitiation for our sins.

JER 31:3.2 THESS 2:13-14.2 TIM 1:9.PS 139:16.JOHN 3:16.1 JOHN 4:10

A man of sorrows and acquainted with grief. ◊ Sympathize with our weaknesses.

Himself took our infirmities and bore our sicknesses. ◊ Jesus . . . being wearied from His journey, sat thus by the well.

When Jesus saw her weeping, and the Jews who came with her weeping, He groaned in the spirit and was troubled. . . . Jesus wept. ◊ For in that He Himself has suffered, being tempted, He is able to aid those who are tempted.

He looked down from the height of His sanctuary; from heaven the Lord viewed the earth, to hear the groaning of the prisoner, to loose those appointed to death. ◊ He knows the way that I take; when He has tested me, I shall come forth as gold. ◊ When my spirit was overwhelmed within me, then You knew my path.

He who touches you touches the apple of His eye. ◊ In all their affliction He was afflicted, and the Angel of His Presence saved them.

EX 3:7.IS 53:3.HEB 4:15.MATT 8:17.JOHN 4:6.JOHN 11:33,35.HEB 2:18.PS 102:19-20.JOB 23:10.PS 142:3.ZECH 2:8.IS 63:9

## August 25

Look to the rock
from which you
were hewn, and
to the hole of the
pit from which
you were dug.

Behold, I was brought forth in iniquity. ◊ No eye pitied you, . . . but you were thrown out into the open field, when you yourself were loathed on the day you were born. And when I passed by you and saw you struggling in your own blood, I said to you . . . , "Live!"

He also brought me up out of a horrible pit, out of the miry clay, and set my feet upon a rock, and established my steps. He has put a new song in my mouth—praise to our God.

When we were still without strength, in due time Christ died for the ungodly. For scarcely for a righteous man will one die; yet perhaps for a good man someone would even dare to die. But God demonstrates His own love toward us, in that while we were still sinners, Christ died for us. ◊ God, who is rich in mercy, because of His great love with which He loved us, even when we were dead in trespasses, made us alive together with Christ.

IS 51:1.PS 51:5.EZEK 16:5-6.PS 40:2-3.ROM 5:6-8.EPH 2:4-5

Pursue . . . holiness, without which no one will see the Lord. ◊ God is Spirit, and those who worship Him must worship in spirit and truth. ◊ But we are all like an unclean thing, and all our righteousnesses are like filthy rags. ◊ By those who come near Me I must be regarded as holy; and before all the people I must be glorified.

This is the law of the temple: The whole area surrounding the mountaintop shall be most holy. ◊ Holiness adorns Your house, O Lord, forever.

For their sakes I sanctify Myself, that they also may be sanctified by the truth. ◊ Seeing . . . that we have a great High Priest who has passed through the heavens, Jesus the Son of God, let us . . . come boldly to the throne of grace, that we may obtain mercy and find grace to help in time of need.

EX 28:36.HEB 12:14.JOHN 4:24.IS 64:6.LEV 10:3.EZEK 43:12.PS 93:5.JOHN 17:19.HEB 4:14,16

## August 26

You shall also make a plate of pure gold and engrave on it, like the engraving of a signet:
HOLINESS TO THE LORD.

## August 27

Your word is a
lamp to my feet
and a light to my
path.

By the word of Your lips, I have kept
myself from the paths of the destroyer.
Uphold my steps in Your paths, that my
footsteps may not slip. ◊ When you
roam, they will lead you; when you
sleep, they will keep you; and when
you awake, they will speak with you.
For the commandment is a lamp, and
the law is light. ◊ Your ears shall hear
a word behind you, saying, "This is the
way, walk in it," whenever you turn to
the right hand or whenever you turn to
the left.

I am the light of the world. He who
follows Me shall not walk in darkness,
but have the light of life. ◊ We also
have the prophetic word made more
sure, which you do well to heed as a
light that shines in a dark place. ◊
Now we see in a mirror, dimly, but
then face to face. Now I know in part,
but then I shall know just as I also am
known. ◊ They need no lamp nor light
of the sun, for the Lord God gives them
light. And they shall reign forever and
ever.

PS 119:105.PS 17:4-5.PROV 6:22-23.IS 30:21.JOHN 8:12.
2 PET 1:19.1 COR 13:12.REV 22:5

They overcame him by the blood of the Lamb and by the word of their testimony. ◊ Who shall bring a charge against God's elect? It is God who justifies. Who is he who condemns? It is Christ who died, and furthermore is also risen, who is even at the right hand of God, who also makes intercession for us.

Having disarmed principalities and powers, He made a public spectacle of them. ◊ That through death He might destroy him who had the power of death, that is, the devil, and release those who through fear of death were all their lifetime subject to bondage. ◊ In all these things we are more than conquerors through Him who loved us. ◊ Put on the whole armor of God, that you may be able to stand against the wiles of the devil. . . . And take . . . the sword of the Spirit, which is the word of God. ◊ Thanks be to God, who gives us the victory through our Lord Jesus Christ.

REV 12:10.REV 12:11.ROM 8:33-34.COL 2:15.HEB 2:14-15.ROM 8:37.EPH 6:11,17.1 COR 15:57

## August 28

The accuser of our brethren, who accused them before our God day and night, has been cast down.

## August 29

Whoever trusts in the LORD, happy is he.

[Abraham] did not waver at the promise of God through unbelief, but was strengthened in faith, giving glory to God, and being fully convinced that what He had promised He was also able to perform. ◇ The children of Judah prevailed, because they relied on the Lord God of their fathers.

God is our refuge and strength, a very present help in trouble. Therefore we will not fear, though the earth be removed, and though the mountains be carried into the midst of the sea. ◇ It is better to trust in the Lord than to put confidence in man. It is better to trust in the Lord than to put confidence in princes. ◇ The steps of a good man are ordered by the Lord, and He delights in his way. Though he fall, he shall not be utterly cast down; for the Lord upholds him with His hand.

Oh, taste and see that the Lord is good; blessed is the man who trusts in Him! Oh, fear the Lord, you His saints! There is no want to those who fear Him.

PROV 16:20.ROM 4:20-21.2 CHR 13:18.PS 46:1-2.PS 118:8-9.PS 37:23-24.PS 34:8-9

And it will be that when he cries to Me, I will hear, for I am gracious.

The king held out . . . the golden scepter. . . . Then Esther went near and touched the top of the scepter.

We have known and believed the love that God has for us. God is love, and he who abides in love abides in God, and God in him. Love has been perfected among us in this: that we may have boldness in the day of judgment; because as He is, so are we in this world. There is no fear in love; but perfect love casts out fear, because fear involves torment. But he who fears has not been made perfect in love. We love Him because He first loved us.

Let us draw near with a true heart in full assurance of faith, having our hearts sprinkled from an evil conscience and our bodies washed with pure water. ◊ For through Him we both have access by one Spirit to the Father. ◊ We have boldness and access with confidence through faith in Him. ◊ Let us therefore come boldly to the throne of grace, that we may obtain mercy and find grace to help in time of need.

ESTH 5:2.EX 22:27.1 JOHN 4:16-19.HEB 10:22.EPH 2:18.EPH 3:12.HEB 4:16

## August 31

The free gift which came from many offenses resulted in justification.

Though your sins are like scarlet, they shall be as white as snow; though they are red like crimson, they shall be as wool. ◊ I, even I, am He who blots out your transgressions for My own sake; and I will not remember your sins. Put Me in remembrance; let us contend together; state your case, that you may be acquitted. ◊ I have blotted out, like a thick cloud, your transgressions, and like a cloud, your sins. Return to Me, for I have redeemed you.

God so loved the world that He gave His only begotten Son, that whoever believes in Him should not perish but have everlasting life. ◊ But the free gift is not like the offense. For if by the one man's offense many died, much more the grace of God and the gift by the grace of the one Man, Jesus Christ, abounded to many. ◊ And such were some of you. But you were washed, but you were sanctified, but you were justified in the name of the Lord Jesus and by the Spirit of our God.

ROM 5:16.IS 1:18.IS 43:25-26.IS 44:22.JOHN 3:16.ROM 5:15.1 COR 6:11

The humble . . . shall increase their joy in the Lord, and the poor among men shall rejoice in the Holy One of Israel. ◊ Unless you are converted and become as little children, you will by no means enter the kingdom of heaven. Therefore whoever humbles himself as this little child is the greatest in the kingdom of heaven. ◊ The incorruptible ornament of a gentle and quiet spirit . . . is very precious in the sight of God. ◊ Love does not parade itself, is not puffed up.

Pursue . . . gentleness. ◊ Take My yoke upon you and learn from Me, for I am gentle and lowly in heart. ◊ He was oppressed and He was afflicted, yet He opened not His mouth; He was led as a lamb to the slaughter, and as a sheep before its shearers is silent, so He opened not his mouth. ◊ Christ also suffered for us, leaving us an example, that you should follow His steps: "Who committed no sin, nor was guile found in His mouth"; who, when He was reviled, did not revile in return; . . . but committed Himself to Him who judges righteously.

GAL 5:22.IS 29:19.MATT 18:3-4.1 PET 3:4.1 COR 13:4.
1 TIM 6:11.MATT 11:29.IS 53:7.1 PET 2:21-23

The fruit of the Spirit is . . . kindness.

## September 2

**Wait on the LORD; be of good courage, and He shall strengthen your heart.**

Have you not known? Have you not heard? The everlasting God, the Lord, the Creator of the ends of the earth, neither faints nor is weary. He gives power to the weak, and to those who have no might He increases strength. ◊ Fear not, for I am with you; be not dismayed, for I am your God. I will strengthen you, yes, I will help you, I will uphold you with My righteous right hand. ◊ You have been a strength to the poor, a strength to the needy in his distress, a refuge from the storm, a shade from the heat; for the blast of the terrible ones is as a storm against the wall.

The testing of your faith produces patience. But let patience have its perfect work, that you may be perfect and complete, lacking nothing. ◊ Do not cast away your confidence, which has great reward. For you have need of endurance, so that after you have done the will of God, you may receive the promise.

PS 27:14.IS 40:28-29.IS 41:10.IS 25:4.JAMES 1:3-4.HEB 10:35-36

The fear of the Lord is to hate evil. ◊ Abhor what is evil. ◊ Abstain from every form of evil. ◊ [Look] diligently lest anyone fall short of the grace of God; lest any root of bitterness springing up cause trouble, and by this many become defiled.

If I regard iniquity in my heart, the Lord will not hear.

Do you not know that a little leaven leavens the whole lump? Therefore purge out the old leaven, that you may be a new lump, since you truly are unleavened. For indeed Christ, our Passover, was sacrificed for us. Therefore let us keep the feast, not with old leaven, nor with the leaven of malice and wickedness, but with the unleavened bread of sincerity and truth. ◊ Let a man examine himself, and so let him eat of that bread and drink of that cup.

Let everyone who names the name of Christ depart from iniquity. ◊ Such a High Priest was fitting for us, who is holy, harmless, undefiled, separate from sinners. ◊ In Him there is no sin.

## September 3

Nor shall leaven be seen among you in all your quarters.

EX 13:7.PROV 8:13.ROM 12:9.1 THESS 5:22.HEB 12:15.PS 66:18.1 COR 5:6-8.1 COR 11:28.2 TIM 2:19.HEB 7:26.1 JOHN 3:5

## September 4

**Sit still, my daughter.**

Take heed, and be quiet; do not fear or be fainthearted. ◇ Be still, and know that I am God. ◇ Did I not say to you that if you would believe you would see the glory of God? ◇ The loftiness of man shall be bowed down, and the haughtiness of men shall be brought low; the Lord alone will be exalted in that day.

Mary . . . sat at Jesus' feet and heard His word. ◇ Mary has chosen that good part, which will not be taken away from her. ◇ In returning and rest you shall be saved; in quietness and confidence shall be your strength. ◇ Meditate within your heart on your bed, and be still.

Rest in the Lord, and wait patiently for Him; do not fret because of him who prospers in his way, because of the man who brings wicked schemes to pass.

He will not be afraid of evil tidings; his heart is steadfast, trusting in the Lord. His heart is established.

Whoever believes will not act hastily.

RUTH 3:18.IS 7:4.PS 46:10.JOHN 11:40.IS 2:17.LUKE 10:39.LUKE 10:42.IS 30:15.PS 4:4.PS 37:7.PS 112:7-8.IS 28:16

He is the head of the body, the church. ◊ He . . . gave Him to be head over all things to the church, which is His body, the fullness of Him who fills all in all. ◊ We are members of His body, of His flesh and of His bones.

A body You have prepared for Me. ◊ Your eyes saw my substance, being yet unformed. And in Your book they all were written, the days fashioned for me, when as yet there were none of them.

They were Yours, You gave them to Me. ◊ He chose us in Him before the foundation of the world. ◊ Whom He foreknew, He also predestined to be conformed to the image of His Son.

Grow up in all things into Him who is the head—Christ—from whom the whole body, joined and knit together by what every joint supplies, . . . causes growth of the body for the edifying of itself in love.

1 COR 12:12.COL 1:18.EPH 1:22-23.EPH 5:30.HEB 10:5.PS 139:16.JOHN 17:6.EPH 1:4.ROM 8:29.EPH 4:15-16

## September 5

As the body is one and has many members, . . . so also is Christ.

## September 6

**Let us lift our hearts and hands to God in heaven.**

Who is like the Lord our God, who dwells on high, who humbles Himself to behold the things that are in the heavens and in the earth? ◊ To You, O Lord, I lift up my soul. ◊ I spread out my hands to You; my soul longs for You like a thirsty land. Do not hide Your face from me, lest I be like those who go down into the pit. Cause me to hear Your lovingkindness in the morning, for in You do I trust; cause me to know the way in which I should walk, for I lift up my soul to You.

Because Your lovingkindness is better than life, my lips shall praise You. Thus I will bless You while I live; I will lift up my hands in Your name. ◊ Rejoice the soul of Your servant, for to You, O Lord, I lift up my soul. For You, Lord, are good, and ready to forgive, and abundant in mercy to all those who call upon You.

Whatever you ask in My name, that I will do.

LAM 3:41.PS 113:5-6.PS 25:1.PS 143:6-8.PS 86:4-5.JOHN 14:13

Hope . . . is laid up for you in heaven. ◇ If in this life only we have hope in Christ, we are of all men the most pitiable. ◇ We must through many tribulations enter the kingdom of God. ◇ Whoever does not bear his cross and come after Me cannot be My disciple. ◇ No one should be shaken by these afflictions; for you yourselves know that we are appointed to this.

Rejoice in the Lord always. Again I will say, rejoice! ◇ The God of hope fill you with all joy and peace in believing, that you may abound in hope by the power of the Holy Spirit. ◇ Blessed be the God and Father of our Lord Jesus Christ, who according to His abundant mercy has begotten us again to a living hope through the resurrection of Jesus Christ from the dead. ◇ Whom having not seen you love. Though now you do not see Him, yet believing, you rejoice with joy inexpressible and full of glory. ◇ Through [Him] also we have access by faith into this grace in which we stand, and rejoice in hope of the glory of God.

ROM 12:12.COL 1:5.1 COR 15:19.ACTS 14:22.LUKE 14:27.1 THESS 3:3.PHIL 4:4.ROM 15:13.1 PET 1:3.1 PET 1:8.ROM 5:2

## September 7

Rejoicing in hope.

## September 8

You have been weighed in the balances, and found wanting.

The Lord is the God of knowledge; and by Him actions are weighed. ◊ What is highly esteemed among men is an abomination in the sight of God. ◊ The Lord does not see as man sees; for man looks at the outward appearance, but the Lord looks at the heart. ◊ Do not be deceived, God is not mocked; for whatever a man sows, that he will also reap. For he who sows to his flesh will of the flesh reap corruption, but he who sows to the Spirit will of the Spirit reap everlasting life.

What is a man profited if he gains the whole world, and loses his own soul? Or what will a man give in exchange for his soul? ◊ What things were gain to me, these I have counted loss for Christ.

Behold, You desire truth in the inward parts. ◊ You have tested my heart; You have visited me in the night; You have tried me and have found nothing.

DAN 5:27.1 SAM 2:3.LUKE 16:15.1 SAM 16:7.GAL 6:7-8.MATT 16:26.PHIL 3:7.PS 51:6.PS 17:3

You say, "I am rich, have become wealthy, and have need of nothing"—and do not know that you are wretched, miserable, poor, blind, and naked—I counsel you to buy from Me gold refined in the fire, that you may be rich. . . . As many as I love, I rebuke and chasten. Therefore be zealous and repent.

Blessed are those who hunger and thirst for righteousness, for they shall be filled. ◊ When the poor and needy seek water, and there is none, and their tongues fail for thirst, I, the Lord, will hear them; I, the God of Israel, will not forsake them. ◊ I am the Lord your God, . . . open your mouth wide, and I will fill it.

Why do you spend money for what is not bread, and your wages for what does not satisfy? Listen diligently to Me, and eat what is good, and let your soul delight itself in abundance. ◊ I am the bread of life. He who comes to Me shall never hunger, and he who believes in Me shall never thirst.

LUKE 1:53.REV 3:17-19.MATT 5:6.IS 41:17.PS 81:10.IS 55:2.JOHN 6:35

## September 9

He has filled the hungry with good things, and the rich He has sent away empty.

## September 10

I will give them one heart and one way, that they may fear Me forever, for the good of them and their children after them.

I will give you a new heart and put a new spirit within you. ◊ Good and upright is the Lord; therefore He teaches sinners in the way. The humble He guides in justice, and the humble He teaches His way. All the paths of the Lord are mercy and truth, to such as keep His covenant and His testimonies.

That they all may be one, as You, Father, are in Me, and I in You; that they also may be one in Us, that the world may believe that You sent Me.

I . . . beseech you to have a walk worthy of the calling with which you were called, with all lowliness and gentleness, . . . endeavoring to keep the unity of the Spirit in the bond of peace. There is one body and one Spirit, just as you were called in one hope of your calling; one Lord, one faith, one baptism; one God and Father of all, who is above all, and through all, and in you all.

JER 32:39.EZEK 36:26.PS 25:8-10.JOHN 17:21.EPH 4:1-6

You shall not follow a crowd to do evil.

Do you not know that friendship with the world is enmity with God? Whoever therefore wants to be a friend of the world makes himself an enemy of God.

What fellowship has righteousness with lawlessness? And what communion has light with darkness? And what accord has Christ with Belial? Or what part has a believer with an unbeliever? And what agreement has the temple of God with idols? ◊ Do not love the world or the things in the world. If anyone loves the world, the love of the Father is not in him. . . . The world is passing away, and the lust of it; but he who does the will of God abides forever.

You once walked according to the course of this world, according to the prince of the power of the air, the spirit who now works in the sons of disobedience. ◊ You have not so learned Christ, if indeed you have heard Him, . . . as the truth is in Jesus.

ROM 12:2.EX 23:2.JAMES 4:4.2 COR 6:14-16.1 JOHN 2:15,17.EPH 2:2.EPH 4:20-21

## September 11

Do not be conformed to this world, but be transformed by the renewing of your mind.

## September 12

**I have seen his ways, and will heal him.**

I am the Lord who heals you.

O Lord, You have searched me and known me. You know my sitting down and my rising up; You understand my thought afar off. You comprehend my path and my lying down, and are acquainted with all my ways. ◊ You have set our iniquities before You, our secret sins in the light of Your countenance. ◊ All things are naked and open to the eyes of Him to whom we must give account.

"Come now, and let us reason together," says the Lord, "though your sins are like scarlet, they shall be as white as snow; though they are red like crimson, they shall be as wool." ◊ He is gracious to him, and says, "Deliver him from going down to the Pit; I have found a ransom." ◊ He was wounded for our transgressions, He was bruised for our iniquities; the chastisement for our peace was upon Him, and by His stripes we are healed. ◊ He has sent Me to heal the brokenhearted. ◊ Your faith has made you well. Go in peace, and be healed of your affliction.

IS 57:18.EX 15:26.PS 139:1-3.PS 90:8.HEB 4:13.IS 1:18.JOB 33:24.IS 53:5.IS 61:1.MARK 5:34

My soul longs, yes, even faints for the courts of the Lord; my heart and my flesh cry out for the living God. ◊ O God, You are my God; early will I seek You; my soul thirsts for You; my flesh longs for You in a dry and thirsty land where there is no water. So I have looked for You in the sanctuary, to see Your power and Your glory.

Ho! Everyone who thirsts, come to the waters; and you who have no money, come, buy and eat. Yes, come, buy wine and milk without money and without price. ◊ The Spirit and the bride say, "Come!" And let him who hears say, "Come!" And let him who thirsts come. And whoever desires, let him take the water of life freely. ◊ Whoever drinks of the water that I shall give him will never thirst. But the water that I shall give him will become in him a fountain of water springing up into everlasting life. ◊ My blood is drink indeed.

Eat, O friends! Drink, yes, drink deeply, O beloved ones!

JOHN 7:37.PS 84:2.PS 63:1-2.IS 55:1.REV 22:17.JOHN 4:14.JOHN 6:55.SONG 5:1

## September 13

If anyone thirsts, let him come to Me and drink.

## September 14

I, even I, am He who comforts you.

Blessed be the God and Father of our Lord Jesus Christ, the Father of mercies and God of all comfort, who comforts us in all our tribulation, that we may be able to comfort those who are in any trouble, with the comfort with which we ourselves are comforted by God. ◊ As a father pities his children, so the Lord pities those who fear Him. For He knows our frame; He remembers that we are dust. ◊ As one whom his mother comforts, so I will comfort you. ◊ [Cast] all your care upon Him, for He cares for you.

You, O Lord, are a God full of compassion, and gracious, longsuffering and abundant in mercy and truth.

He will give you another Helper, . . . even the Spirit of truth. ◊ The Spirit . . . helps in our weaknesses.

God will wipe away every tear from their eyes; there shall be no more death, nor sorrow, nor crying; and there shall be no more pain, for the former things have passed away.

IS 51:12.2 COR 1:3-4.PS 103:13-14.IS 66:13.1 PET 5:7.PS 86:15.JOHN 14:16-17.ROM 8:26.REV 21:4

What then? Shall we sin because we are not under law but under grace? Certainly not! ◊ My brethren, you . . . have become dead to the law through the body of Christ, that you may be married to another, even to Him who was raised from the dead, that we should bear fruit to God. ◊ Being without law toward God, but under law toward Christ. ◊ The sting of death is sin, and the strength of sin is the law. But thanks be to God, who gives us the victory through our Lord Jesus Christ.

The law of the Spirit of life in Christ Jesus has made me free from the law of sin and death. ◊ Whoever commits sin is a slave of sin. ◊ If the Son makes you free, you shall be free indeed.

Stand fast therefore in the liberty by which Christ has made us free, and do not be entangled again with a yoke of bondage.

ROM 6:14.ROM 6:15.ROM 7:4.1 COR 9:21.1 COR 15:56-57.ROM 8:2.JOHN 8:34.JOHN 8:36.GAL 5:1

## September 15

Sin shall not have dominion over you, for you are not under law but under grace.

## September 16

**The LORD weighs the hearts.**

The Lord knows the way of the righteous, but the way of the ungodly shall perish. ◊ The Lord will show who is His and who is holy. ◊ Your Father who sees in secret will Himself reward you openly.

Search me, O God, and know my heart; try me, and know my anxieties; and see if there is any wicked way in me, and lead me in the way everlasting. ◊ There is no fear in love; but perfect love casts out fear.

Lord, all my desire is before You; and my sighing is not hidden from You. ◊ When my spirit was overwhelmed within me, then You knew my path. ◊ He who searches the hearts knows what the mind of the Spirit is, because He makes intercession for the saints according to the will of God.

The solid foundation of God stands, having this seal: "The Lord knows those who are His," and, "Let everyone who names the name of Christ depart from iniquity."

PROV 21:2.PS 1:6.NUM 16:5.MATT 6:4.PS 139:23-24.
1 JOHN 4:18.PS 38:9.PS 142:3.ROM 8:27.2 TIM 2:19

The sacrifices of God are a broken spirit, a broken and a contrite heart—these, O God, You will not despise. ◊ He heals the broken-hearted and binds up their wounds. ◊ Thus says the High and Lofty One who inhabits eternity, whose name is Holy: "I dwell in the high and holy place, with him who has a contrite and humble spirit, to revive the spirit of the humble, and to revive the heart of the contrite ones. For I will not contend forever, nor will I always be angry; for the spirit would fail before Me, and the souls which I have made."

I will seek what was lost and bring back what was driven away, bind up the broken and strengthen what was sick. ◊ Therefore strengthen the hands which hang down, and the feeble knees, and make straight paths for your feet, so that what is lame may not be dislocated, but rather be healed. ◊ Behold, your God . . . will come and save you.

MATT 12:20.PS 51:17.PS 147:3.IS 57:15-16.EZEK 34:16.HEB 12:12-13.IS 35:4

## September 17

A bruised reed He will not break.

## September 18

Open my eyes, that I may see wondrous things from Your law.

He opened their understanding, that they might comprehend the Scriptures. ◊ It has been given to you to know the mysteries of the kingdom of heaven, but to them it has not been given. ◊ I thank You, Father, Lord of heaven and earth, because You have hidden these things from the wise and prudent and have revealed them to babes. Even so, Father, for so it seemed good in Your sight. ◊ We have received, not the spirit of the world, but the Spirit who is from God, that we might know the things that have been freely given to us by God. ◊ How precious also are Your thoughts to me, O God! How great is the sum of them! If I should count them, they would be more in number than the sand. ◊ Oh, the depth of the riches both of the wisdom and knowledge of God! How unsearchable are His judgments and His ways past finding out! For who has known the mind of the Lord? Or who has become His counselor? . . . For of Him and through Him and to Him are all things, to whom be glory forever. Amen.

PS 119:18.LUKE 24:45.MATT 13:11.MATT 11:25-26. 1 COR 2:12.PS 139:17-18.ROM 11:33-34,36

I will proclaim the name of the Lord before you. I will be gracious to whom I will be gracious. ◊ He is gracious to him, and says, "Deliver him from going down to the Pit; I have found a ransom." ◊ Being justified freely by His grace through the redemption that is in Christ Jesus, whom God set forth to be a propitiation by His blood, through faith, to demonstrate His righteousness, because in His forbearance God had passed over the sins that were previously committed. ◊ Grace and truth came through Jesus Christ.

By grace you have been saved through faith, and that not of yourselves; it is the gift of God. ◊ Grace, mercy, and peace from God our Father and Jesus Christ our Lord. ◊ To each one of us grace was given according to the measure of Christ's gift. ◊ As each one has received a gift, minister it to one another, as good stewards of the manifold grace of God. ◊ He gives more grace.

Grow in the grace and knowledge of our Lord and Savior Jesus Christ. To Him be the glory both now and forever.

The God of all grace.

1 PET 5:10.EX 33:19.JOB 33:24.ROM 3:24-25.JOHN 1:17.EPH 2:8.1 TIM 1:2.EPH 4:7.1 PET 4:10.JAMES 4:6. 2 PET 3:18

## September 20

Happy is the man who finds wisdom, and the man who gains understanding.

Whoever finds me finds life, and obtains favor from the Lord.

Thus says the Lord: "Let not the wise man glory in his wisdom, let not the mighty man glory in his might, . . . but let him who glories glory in this, that he understands and knows Me, that I am the Lord." ◇ The fear of the Lord is the beginning of wisdom.

What things were gain to me, these I have counted loss for Christ. But indeed I also count all things loss for the excellence of the knowledge of Christ Jesus my Lord, for whom I have suffered the loss of all things, and count them as rubbish, that I may gain Christ. ◇ In [Him] are hidden all the treasures of wisdom and knowledge. ◇ Counsel is mine, and sound wisdom; I am understanding, I have strength.

Christ Jesus . . . became for us wisdom . . . and righteousness and sanctification and redemption.

He who wins souls is wise.

PROV 3:13.PROV 8:35.JER 9:23-24.PROV 9:10.PHIL 3:7-8.COL 2:3.PROV 8:14.1 COR 1:30.PROV 11:30

Surely the wrath of man shall praise You; with the remainder of wrath You shall gird Yourself. ◊ You meant evil against me; but God meant it for good.

All things are yours: whether . . . the world or life or death, or things present or things to come all are yours. And you are Christ's, and Christ is God's. ◊ All things are for your sakes, that grace, having spread through the many, may cause thanksgiving to abound to the glory of God. Therefore we do not lose heart. Even though our outward man is perishing, yet the inward man is being renewed day by day. For our light affliction, which is but for a moment, is working for us a far more exceeding and eternal weight of glory.

My brethren, count it all joy when you fall into various trials, knowing that the testing of your faith produces patience. But let patience have its perfect work, that you may be perfect and complete, lacking nothing.

ROM 8:28.PS 76:10.GEN 50:20.1 COR 3:21-23.2 COR 4:15-17.JAMES 1:2-4

We know that all things work together for good to those who love God.

## September 22

Like an apple tree among the trees of the woods, so is my beloved among the sons. I sat down in his shade with great delight, and his fruit was sweet to my taste. ◊ For who in the heavens can be compared to the Lord? Who among the sons of the mighty can be likened to the Lord?

My beloved is white and ruddy, chief among ten thousand. ◊ One pearl of great price. ◊ The ruler over the kings of the earth.

His head is like the finest gold; his locks are wavy, and black as a raven. ◊ Head over all things. ◊ He is the head of the body, the church.

His cheeks are like a bed of spices, like banks of scented herbs. ◊ He could not be hidden.

His lips are lilies, dripping liquid myrrh. ◊ No man ever spoke like this Man!

His countenance is like Lebanon, excellent as the cedars. ◊ Make Your face shine upon Your servant. ◊ Lord, lift up the light of Your countenance upon us.

PS 104:34.SONG 2:3.PS 89:6.SONG 5:10.MATT 13:46.REV 1:5.SONG 5:11.EPH 1:22.COL 1:18.SONG 5:13.MARK 7:24.SONG 5:13.JOHN 7:46.SONG 5:15.PS 31:16.PS 4:6

Beloved, do not think it strange concerning the fiery trial which is to try you, as though some strange thing happened to you. ◊ If you endure chastening, God deals with you as with sons; for what son is there whom a father does not chasten? But if you are without chastening, of which all have become partakers, then you are illegitimate and not sons.

The Lord your God is testing you to know whether you love the Lord your God with all your heart and with all your soul.

The Lord will not forsake His people, for His great name's sake, because it has pleased the Lord to make you His people. ◊ Can a woman forget her nursing child, and not have compassion on the son of her womb? Surely they may forget, yet I will not forget you. ◊ Happy is he who has the God of Jacob for his help, whose hope is in the Lord his God.

Shall God not avenge His own elect who cry out day and night to Him, though He bears long with them? I tell you that He will avenge them speedily.

Our God did not forsake us.

EZRA 9:9.1 PET 4:12.HEB 12:7-8.DEUT 13:3.1 SAM 12:22.IS 49:15.PS 146:5.LUKE 18:7-8

## September 24

It is good for me to draw near to God.

Lord, I have loved the habitation of Your house, and the place where Your glory dwells. ◊ A day in Your courts is better than a thousand. I would rather be a doorkeeper in the house of my God than dwell in the tents of wickedness. ◊ Blessed is the man whom You choose, and cause to approach You, that he may dwell in Your courts. We shall be satisfied with the goodness of Your house, of Your holy temple.

The Lord is good to those who wait for Him, to the soul who seeks Him. ◊ Therefore the Lord will wait, that He may be gracious to you; and therefore He will be exalted, that He may have mercy on you. For the Lord is a God of justice; blessed are all those who wait for Him.

Therefore, brethren, having boldness to enter the Holiest by the blood of Jesus, by a new and living way which He consecrated for us, . . . let us draw near with a true heart in full assurance of faith, having our hearts sprinkled from an evil conscience.

PS 73:28.PS 26:8.PS 84:10.PS 65:4.LAM 3:25.IS 30:18.HEB 10:19-20,22

Now for a little while, if need be, you have been grieved by various trials, that the genuineness of your faith, being much more precious than gold that perishes, though it is tested by fire, may be found to praise, honor, and glory at the revelation of Jesus Christ. ◊ We also glory in tribulations, knowing that tribulation produces perseverance; and perseverance, character; and character, hope.

It is good that one should hope and wait quietly for the salvation of the Lord. ◊ You have a better and an enduring possession for yourselves in heaven. Do not cast away your confidence, which has great reward. For you have need of endurance, so that after you have done the will of God, you may receive the promise. ◊ Our Lord Jesus Christ Himself, and our God and Father, who has loved us and given us everlasting consolation and good hope by grace, comfort your hearts.

JAMES 1:4.1 PET 1:6-7.ROM 5:3-4.LAM 3:26.HEB 10:34-36.2 THESS 2:16-17

## September 25

Let patience have its perfect work, that you may be perfect and complete, lacking nothing.

## September 26

A God of truth
and without
injustice;
righteous and
upright is He.

Him who judges righteously. ◊ We must all appear before the judgment seat of Christ, that each one may receive the things done in the body, according to what he has done, whether good or bad. ◊ Each of us shall give account of himself to God. ◊ The soul who sins shall die.

"Awake, O sword, against My Shepherd, against the Man who is My Companion," says the Lord of hosts. "Strike the Shepherd." ◊ The Lord has laid on Him the iniquity of us all. ◊ Mercy and truth have met together; righteousness and peace have kissed each other. ◊ Mercy triumphs over judgment.

The wages of sin is death, but the gift of God is eternal life in Christ Jesus our Lord.

A just God and a Savior; there is none besides Me. ◊ Just and the justifier of the one who has faith in Jesus. ◊ Justified freely by His grace through the redemption that is in Christ Jesus.

DEUT 32:4.1 PET 2:23.2 COR 5:10.ROM 14:12.EZEK 18:4.ZECH 13:7.IS 53:6.PS 85:10.JAMES 2:13.ROM 6:23.IS 45:21.ROM 3:26.ROM 3:24

Everyone who is proud in heart is an abomination to the Lord; though they join forces, none will go unpunished.

O Lord, You are our Father; we are the clay, and You our potter; and all we are the work of Your hand. Do not be furious, O Lord, nor remember iniquity forever; indeed, please look—we all are Your people! ◊ You have chastised me, and I was chastised, like an untrained bull; restore me, and I will return, for You are the Lord my God. Surely, after my turning, I repented; and after I was instructed, I struck myself on the thigh; I was ashamed, yes, even humiliated, because I bore the reproach of my youth. ◊ It is good for a man to bear the yoke in his youth.

Affliction does not come from the dust, nor does trouble spring from the ground; yet man is born to trouble, as the sparks fly upward.

1 PET 5:6.PROV 16:5.IS 64:8-9.JER 31:18-19.LAM 3:27.JOB 5:6-7

Humble yourselves under the mighty hand of God, that He may exalt you in due time.

## September 28

O Lord our God, other masters besides You have had dominion over us; but by You only we make mention of Your name. ◇ We have become like those of old, over whom You never ruled, those who were never called by Your name.

All peoples of the earth shall see that you are called by the name of the Lord, and they shall be afraid of you. ◇ The Lord will not forsake His people, for His great name's sake, because it has pleased the Lord to make you His people.

O Lord, hear! O Lord, forgive! O Lord, listen and act! Do not delay for Your own sake, my God, for Your city and Your people are called by Your name. ◇ Help us, O God of our salvation, for the glory of Your name; and deliver us, and provide atonement for our sins, for Your name's sake! Why should the nations say, "Where is their God?" ◇ The name of the Lord is a strong tower; the righteous run to it and are safe.

NUM 6:27.IS 26:13.IS 63:19.DEUT 28:10.1 SAM 12:22.DAN 9:19.PS 79:9-10.PROV 18:10

The love of Christ . . . passes knowledge. ◊ Greater love has no one than this, than to lay down one's life for his friends. ◊ You know the grace of our Lord Jesus Christ, that though He was rich, yet for your sakes He became poor, that you through His poverty might become rich. ◊ Beloved, if God so loved us, we also ought to love one another. ◊ Be kind to one another, tenderhearted, forgiving one another, just as God in Christ also forgave you. ◊ [Bear] with one another, and [forgive] one another, if anyone has a complaint against another; even as Christ forgave you. ◊ For even the Son of Man did not come to be served, but to serve, and to give His life a ransom for many. ◊ Christ . . . suffered for us, leaving us an example, that you should follow His steps.

You also ought to wash one another's feet. For I have given you an example, that you should do as I have done to you. ◊ We also ought to lay down our lives for the brethren.

1 JOHN 3:16.EPH 3:19.JOHN 15:13.2 COR 8:9.1 JOHN 4:11.EPH 4:32.COL 3:13.MARK 10:45.1 PET 2:21.JOHN 13:14-15.1 JOHN 3:16

By this we know love, because He laid down His life for us.

## September 30

He knows the way that I take; when He has tested me, I shall come forth as gold.

He knows our frame. ◊ He does not afflict willingly, nor grieve the children of men.

The solid foundation of God stands, having this seal: "The Lord knows those who are His," and, "Let everyone who names the name of Christ depart from iniquity." But in a great house there are not only vessels of gold and silver, but also of wood and clay, some for honor and some for dishonor. Therefore if anyone cleanses himself from the latter, he will be a vessel for honor, sanctified and useful for the Master, prepared for every good work.

He will sit as a refiner and a purifier of silver; He will purify the sons of Levi, and purge them as gold and silver, that they may offer to the Lord an offering in righteousness. ◊ I . . . will refine them as silver is refined. . . . They will call on My name, and I will answer them. I will say, "This is My people"; and each one will say, "The Lord is my God."

JOB 23:10.PS 103:14.LAM 3:33.2 TIM 2:19-21.MAL 3:3.ZECH 13:9

Everyone who competes for the prize is temperate in all things. Now they do it to obtain a perishable crown, but we for an imperishable crown. Therefore I run thus: not with uncertainty. Thus I fight: not as one who beats the air. But I discipline my body and bring it into subjection, lest, when I have preached to others, I myself should become disqualified.

Do not be drunk with wine, in which is dissipation; but be filled with the Spirit.

If anyone desires to come after Me, let him deny himself, and take up his cross, and follow Me.

Let us not sleep, as others do, but let us watch and be sober. For those who sleep, sleep at night, and those who get drunk are drunk at night. But let us who are of the day be sober. ◊ Denying ungodliness and worldly lusts, we should live soberly, righteously, and godly in the present age, looking for the blessed hope and glorious appearing of our great God and Savior Jesus Christ.

GAL 5:22-23.1 COR 9:25-27.EPH 5:18.MATT 16:24.1 THESS 5:6-8.TITUS 2:12-13

## October 1

The fruit of the Spirit is . . . self-control.

## October 2

The goat shall bear on itself all their iniquities to an uninhabited land; and he shall release the goat in the wilderness.

As far as the east is from the west, so far has He removed our transgressions from us. ◊ "In those days and in that time," says the Lord, "the iniquity of Israel shall be sought, but there shall be none; and the sins of Judah, but they shall not be found; for I will pardon those whom I preserve." ◊ You will cast all our sins into the depths of the sea. ◊ Who is a God like You, pardoning iniquity?

All we like sheep have gone astray; we have turned, every one, to his own way; and the Lord has laid on Him the iniquity of us all. ◊ He shall bear their iniquities. Therefore I will divide Him a portion with the great, and He shall divide the spoil with the strong, because He poured out His soul unto death, and He was numbered with the transgressors, and He bore the sin of many, and made intercession for the transgressors. ◊ The Lamb of God who takes away the sin of the world!

LEV 16:22.PS 103:12.JER 50:20.MIC 7:19.MIC 7:18.IS 53:6.IS 53:11-12.JOHN 1:29

Many waters cannot quench love, nor can the floods drown it. . . . Love is as strong as death. ◊ Greater love has no one than this, than to lay down one's life for his friends.

[He] Himself bore our sins in His own body on the tree, that we, having died to sins, might live for righteousness by whose stripes you were healed. ◊ In Him we have redemption through His blood, the forgiveness of sins, according to the riches of His grace. ◊ You were washed, . . . you were sanctified, . . . you were justified in the name of the Lord Jesus and by the Spirit of our God. ◊ You are a chosen generation, a royal priesthood, a holy nation, His own special people, that you may proclaim the praises of Him who called you out of darkness into His marvelous light. ◊ I beseech you . . . brethren, by the mercies of God, that you present your bodies a living sacrifice, holy, acceptable to God, which is your reasonable service.

REV 1:5.SONG 8:7,6.JOHN 15:13.1 PET 2:24.EPH 1:7.
1 COR 6:11.1 PET 2:9.ROM 12:1

## October 3

To Him who loved us and washed us from our sins in His own blood.

## October 4

Moses did not know that the skin of his face shone while he talked with Him.

Not unto us, O Lord, not unto us, but to Your name give glory. ◊ Lord, when did we see You hungry and feed You, or thirsty and give You drink? ◊ In lowliness of mind let each esteem others better than himself. . . . Be clothed with humility.

[Jesus] was transfigured before them. His face shone like the sun, and His clothes became as white as the light. ◊ All who sat in the council, looking steadfastly at [Stephen], saw his . . . face as the face of an angel. ◊ The glory which You gave Me I have given them. ◊ We all, with unveiled face, beholding as in a mirror the glory of the Lord, are being transformed into the same image from glory to glory, just as by the Spirit of the Lord.

You are the light of the world. A city that is set on a hill cannot be hidden. Nor do they light a lamp and put it under a basket, but on a lampstand, and it gives light to all who are in the house.

EX 34:29.PS 115:1.MATT 25:37.PHIL 2:3.1 PET 5:5.MATT 17:2.ACTS 6:15.JOHN 17:22.2 COR 3:18.MATT 5:14-15

Why are you cast down, O my soul? And why are you disquieted within me? Hope in God; for I shall yet praise Him, the help of my countenance and my God. ◊ Lord, You have heard the desire of the humble; You will prepare their heart; You will cause Your ear to hear. ◊ For You, Lord, are good, and ready to forgive, and abundant in mercy to all those who call upon You.

Jacob said to his household, . . . "Let us arise and go up to Bethel; and I will make an altar there to God, who answered me in the day of my distress and has been with me in the way which I have gone. ◊ Bless the Lord, O my soul, and forget not all His benefits.

I love the Lord, because He has heard My voice and my supplications. Because He has inclined His ear to me, therefore I will call upon Him as long as I live. The pains of death encompassed me, and the pangs of Sheol laid hold of me; I found trouble and sorrow. Then I called upon the name of the Lord.

PS 50:15.PS 42:11.PS 10:17.PS 86:5.GEN 35:2-3.PS 103:2.PS 116:1-4

## October 5

Call upon Me in the day of trouble; I will deliver you, and you shall glorify Me.

## October 6

**The Lord God Omnipotent reigns!**

I know that You can do everything. ◇ The things which are impossible with men are possible with God. ◇ He does according to His will in the army of heaven and among the inhabitants of the earth. No one can restrain His hand or say to Him, "What have You done?" ◇ There is no one who can deliver out of My hand; I work, and who will reverse it? ◇ Abba, Father, all things are possible for You.

"Do you believe that I am able to do this?" They said to Him, "Yes, Lord." Then He touched their eyes, saying, "According to your faith let it be to you." ◇ "Lord, if You are willing, You can make me clean." Then Jesus put out His hand and touched him, saying, "I am willing; be cleansed." ◇ Mighty God. ◇ All authority has been given to Me in heaven and on earth.

Some trust in chariots, and some in horses; but we will remember the name of the Lord our God. ◇ Be strong and courageous; do not be afraid nor dismayed, . . . for there are more with us than with him.

REV 19:6.JOB 42:2.LUKE 18:27.DAN 4:35.IS 43:13.MARK 14:36.MATT 9:28-29.MATT 8:2-3.IS 9:6.MATT 28:18.PS 20:7.2 CHR 32:7

Blessed are the meek.

I returned and saw under the sun that the race is not to the swift, nor the battle to the strong, nor bread to the wise, nor riches to men of understanding, nor favor to men of skill. ◊ A man's heart plans his way, but the Lord directs his steps.

Unto You I lift up my eyes, O You who dwell in the heavens. Behold, as the eyes of servants look to the hand of their masters, as the eyes of a maid to the hand of her mistress, so our eyes look to the Lord our God. ◊ Cause me to know the way in which I should walk, for I lift up my soul to You.

O our God, will You not judge them? For we have no power against this great multitude that is coming against us; nor do we know what to do, but our eyes are upon You.

If any of you lacks wisdom, let him ask of God, who gives to all liberally and without reproach, and it will be given to him.

When He, the Spirit of truth, has come, He will guide you into all truth.

PS 25:9.MATT 5:5.ECCL 9:11.PROV 16:9.PS 123:1-2.PS 143:8.2 CHR 20:12.JAMES 1:5.JOHN 16:13

## October 8

I will not fear.
What can man do
to me?

Who shall separate us from the love of Christ? Shall tribulation, or distress, or persecution, or famine, or nakedness, or peril, or sword? . . . Yet in all these things we are more than conquerors through Him who loved us.

My friends, do not be afraid of those who kill the body, and after that have no more that they can do. But I will show you whom you should fear: Fear Him who, after He has killed, has power to cast into hell; yes, I say to you, fear Him!

Blessed are those who are persecuted for righteousness' sake, for theirs is the kingdom of heaven. Blessed are you when they revile and persecute you, and say all kinds of evil against you falsely for My sake. Rejoice and be exceedingly glad, for great is your reward in heaven. ◊ None of these things move me; nor do I count my life dear to myself, so that I may finish my race with joy. ◊ I will speak of Your testimonies . . . before kings, and will not be ashamed.

HEB 13:6.ROM 8:35,37.LUKE 12:4-5.MATT
5:10-12.ACTS 20:24.PS 119:46

The Lord is not slack concerning His promise, as some count slackness, but is longsuffering toward us, not willing that any should perish but that all should come to repentance. ◊ The longsuffering of our Lord is salvation.

For this reason I obtained mercy, that in me first Jesus Christ might show all longsuffering, as a pattern to those who are going to believe on Him for everlasting life. ◊ Whatever things were written before were written for our learning, that we through the patience and comfort of the Scriptures might have hope.

Do you despise the riches of His goodness, forbearance, and longsuffering, not knowing that the goodness of God leads you to repentance? ◊ Rend your heart, and not your garments; return to the Lord your God, for He is gracious and merciful, slow to anger, and of great kindness; and He relents from doing harm.

NEH 9:17.2 PET 3:9.2 PET 3:15.1 TIM 1:16.ROM 15:4.ROM 2:4.JOEL 2:13

## October 9

You are God, ready to pardon, gracious and merciful.

## October 10

**The whole family in heaven and earth.**

One God and Father of all, who is above all, and through all, and in you all. ◊ You are all sons of God through faith in Christ Jesus. ◊ That in the dispensation of the fullness of the times He might gather together in one all things in Christ, both which are in heaven and which are on earth in Him.

He is not ashamed to call them brethren. ◊ Here are My mother and My brothers! For whoever does the will of My Father in heaven is My brother and sister and mother. ◊ Go to My brethren and say to them, "I am ascending to My Father and your Father."

I saw under the altar the souls of those who had been slain for the word of God and for the testimony which they held. . . . And a white robe was given to each of them; and it was said to them that they should rest a little while longer, until both the number of their fellow servants and their brethren, who would be killed as they were, was completed. ◊ That they should not be made perfect apart from us.

EPH 3:15.EPH 4:6.GAL 3:26.EPH 1:10.HEB 2:11.MATT 12:49-50.JOHN 20:17.REV 6:9,11.HEB 11:40

How long, O Lord? Will You forget me forever? How long will You hide Your face from me? How long shall I take counsel in my soul, having sorrow in my heart daily? ◊ Do not hide Your face from me; do not turn Your servant away in anger; You have been my help; do not leave me nor forsake me, O God of my salvation.

He shall call upon Me, and I will answer him; I will be with him in trouble; I will deliver him and honor him. ◊ The Lord is near to all who call upon Him, to all who call upon Him in truth. He will fulfill the desire of those who fear Him; He also will hear their cry and save them.

I will not leave you orphans; I will come to you. ◊ Lo, I am with you always, even to the end of the age.

God is our refuge and strength, a very present help in trouble. ◊ Truly my soul silently waits for God; from Him comes my salvation. . . . My soul, wait silently for God alone, for my expectation is from Him.

PS 22:11.PS 13:1-2.PS 27:9.PS 91:15.PS 145:18-19.JOHN 14:18.MATT 28:20.PS 46:1.PS 62:1,5

## October 11

Be not far from Me, for trouble is near.

## October 12

It pleased the Father that in Him all the fullness should dwell, and by Him to reconcile all things to Himself, . . . having made peace through the blood of His cross. ◊ Mercy and truth have met together; righteousness and peace have kissed each other.

I know the thoughts that I think toward you, says the Lord, thoughts of peace and not of evil. ◊ "Come now, and let us reason together," says the Lord, "though your sins are like scarlet, they shall be as white as snow; though they are red like crimson, they shall be as wool."

Who is a God like You, pardoning iniquity?

Now acquaint yourself with Him, and be at peace. ◊ Work out your own salvation with fear and trembling; for it is God who works in you both to will and to do for His good pleasure. ◊ Lord, You will establish peace for us, for You have also done all our works in us.

2 COR 5:19.COL 1:19-20.PS 85:10.JER 29:11.IS 1:18.MIC 7:18.JOB 22:21.PHIL 2:12-13.IS 26:12

Thus says the High and Lofty One who inhabits eternity, whose name is Holy: "I dwell in the high and holy place, with him who has a contrite and humble spirit, to revive the spirit of the humble, and to revive the heart of the contrite ones." ◊ The sacrifices of God are a broken spirit, a broken and a contrite heart—these, O God, You will not despise. ◊ Though the Lord is on high, yet He regards the lowly; but the proud He knows from afar. ◊ Humble yourselves under the mighty hand of God, that He may exalt you in due time. ◊ God resists the proud, but gives grace to the humble. Therefore submit to God.

You, Lord, are good, and ready to forgive, and abundant in mercy to all those who call upon You. Give ear, O Lord, to my prayer; and attend to the voice of my supplications. In the day of my trouble I will call upon You, for You will answer me.

DAN 10:12.IS 57:15.PS 51:17.PS 138:6.1 PET 5:6.JAMES 4:6-7.PS 86:5-7

From the first day that you set your heart to understand, and to humble yourself before your God, your words were heard.

## October 14

Christ died and rose and lived again, that He might be Lord of both the dead and the living.

It pleased the Lord to bruise Him; He has put Him to grief. When You make His soul an offering for sin, He shall see His seed, He shall prolong His days, and the pleasure of the Lord shall prosper in His hand. He shall see the travail of His soul, and be satisfied. By His knowledge My righteous Servant shall justify many, for He shall bear their iniquities. ◊ Ought not the Christ to have suffered these things and to enter into His glory? ◊ We judge thus: that if One died for all, then all died; and He died for all, that those who live should live no longer for themselves, but for Him who died for them and rose again.

Let all the house of Israel know assuredly that God has made this Jesus, whom you crucified, both Lord and Christ. ◊ He indeed was foreordained before the foundation of the world, but was manifest in these last times for you who through Him believe in God.

ROM 14:9.IS 53:10-11.LUKE 24:26.2 COR 5:14-15.ACTS 2:36.1 PET 1:20-21

The Lord is my rock, my fortress and my deliverer; the God of my strength, in Him I will trust, my shield and the horn of my salvation, my stronghold and my refuge; my Savior. ◊ The Lord is my strength and my shield; my heart trusted in Him, and I am helped; therefore my heart greatly rejoices, and with my song I will praise Him.

When the enemy comes in like a flood, the Spirit of the Lord will lift up a standard against him. ◊ We may boldly say: "The Lord is my helper; I will not fear. What can man do to me?"

The Lord is my light and my salvation; whom shall I fear? The Lord is the strength of my life; of whom shall I be afraid?

As the mountains surround Jerusalem, so the Lord surrounds His people from this time forth and forever. ◊ Because You have been my help, therefore in the shadow of Your wings I will rejoice.

For Your name's sake, lead me and guide me.

PS 59:9.2 SAM 22:2-3.PS 28:7.IS 59:19.HEB 13:6.PS 27:1.PS 125:2.PS 63:7.PS 31:3

## October 16

Whatever your hand finds to do, do it with your might; for there is no work or device or knowledge or wisdom in the grave where you are going. ◊ Whatever you do, do it heartily, as to the Lord and not to men, knowing that from the Lord you will receive the reward of the inheritance; for you serve the Lord Christ. ◊ Whatever good anyone does, he will receive the same from the Lord.

I must work the works of Him who sent Me while it is day; the night is coming when no one can work. ◊ Did you not know that I must be about My Father's business? ◊ Zeal for Your house has eaten Me up.

Brethren, be even more diligent to make your calling and election sure, for if you do these things you will never stumble. ◊ We desire that each one of you show the same diligence to the full assurance of hope until the end, that you do not become sluggish, but imitate those who through faith and patience inherit the promises. ◊ Run in such a way that you may obtain it.

ROM 12:11.ECCL 9:10.COL 3:23-24.EPH 6:8.JOHN 9:4.LUKE 2:49.JOHN 2:17.2 PET 1:10.HEB 6:11-12. 1 COR 9:24

In the Lord I have righteousness and strength. To Him men shall come, and all shall be ashamed who are incensed against Him. In the Lord all the descendants of Israel shall be justified, and shall glory. ◊ Be glad in the Lord and rejoice, you righteous; and shout for joy, all you upright in heart!

The righteousness of God apart from the law is revealed, being witnessed by the Law and the Prophets, even the righteousness of God which is through faith in Jesus Christ to all and on all who believe. . . . to demonstrate at the present time His righteousness, that He might be just and the justifier of the one who has faith in Jesus.

Rejoice in the Lord always. Again I will say, rejoice! ◊ Jesus Christ, whom having not seen you love. Though now you do not see Him, yet believing, you rejoice with joy inexpressible and full of glory.

PS 89:16.IS 45:24-25.PS 32:11.ROM 3:21-22,26.PHIL 4:4.
1 PET 1:7-8

## October 17

In Your name they rejoice all day long, and in Your righteousness they are exalted.

## October 18

One of the soldiers pierced His side with a spear, and immediately blood and water came out.

Behold, the blood of the covenant which the Lord has made with you. ◊ The life of the flesh is in the blood, and I have given it to you upon the altar to make atonement for your souls. ◊ It is not possible that the blood of bulls and goats could take away sins.

"This is My blood of the new covenant, which is shed for many." ◊ With His own blood He entered the Most Holy Place . . . having obtained eternal redemption. ◊ Peace through the blood of His cross.

You were not redeemed with corruptible things, like silver or gold, . . . but with the precious blood of Christ, as of a lamb without blemish and without spot. He indeed was foreordained . . . , but was manifest in these last times for you.

Then I will sprinkle clean water on you, and you shall be clean; I will cleanse you . . . from all your idols. ◊ Let us draw near with a true heart in full assurance of faith, having our hearts sprinkled from an evil conscience.

JOHN 19:34.EX 24:8.LEV 17:11.HEB 10:4.MARK 14:24.HEB 9:12.COL 1:20.1 PET 1:18-20.EZEK 36:25.HEB 10:22

Surely the wrath of man shall praise You; with the remainder of wrath You shall gird Yourself. ◇ The king's heart is in the hand of the Lord, like the rivers of water; He turns it wherever He wishes. ◇ When a man's ways please the Lord, he makes even his enemies to be at peace with him.

I wait for the Lord, my soul waits, and in His word I do hope. My soul waits for the Lord more than those who watch for the morning I say, more than those who watch for the morning. ◇ I sought the Lord, and He heard me, and delivered me from all my fears.

The eternal God is your refuge, and underneath are the everlasting arms; He will thrust out the enemy from before you, and will say, "Destroy!" ◇ Blessed is the man who trusts in the Lord, and whose hope is the Lord.

What then shall we say to these things? If God is for us, who can be against us?

PROV 3:26.PS 76:10.PROV 21:1.PROV 16:7.PS 130:5-6.PS 34:4.DEUT 33:27.JER 17:7.ROM 8:31

# October 19

The LORD will be your confidence, and will keep your foot from being caught.

## October 20

I delight in the law of God according to the inward man.

Oh, how I love Your law! It is my meditation all the day. ◊ Your words were found, and I ate them, and Your word was to me the joy and rejoicing of my heart. ◊ I sat down in his shade with great delight, and his fruit was sweet to my taste. ◊ I have treasured the words of His mouth more than my necessary food.

I delight to do Your will, O my God, and Your law is within my heart. ◊ My food is to do the will of Him who sent Me, and to finish His work.

The statutes of the Lord are right, rejoicing the heart; the commandment of the Lord is pure, enlightening the eyes. . . . More to be desired are they than gold, yea, than much fine gold; sweeter also than honey and the honeycomb. ◊ Be doers of the word, and not hearers only, deceiving yourselves. For if anyone is a hearer of the word and not a doer, he is like a man observing his natural face in a mirror.

ROM 7:22.PS 119:97.JER 15:16.SONG 2:3.JOB 23:12.PS 40:8.JOHN 4:34.PS 19:8,10.JAMES 1:22-23

This is My beloved Son, in whom I am well pleased. ◊ Behold what manner of love the Father has bestowed on us, that we should be called children of God!

His Son, whom He has appointed heir of all things. ◊ If children, then heirs — heirs of God and joint heirs with Christ, if indeed we suffer with Him, that we may also be glorified together.

I and My Father are one. ◊ The Father is in Me, and I in Him. ◊ My Father and your Father, and . . . My God and your God. ◊ I in them, and You in Me; that they may be made perfect in one.

The church, which is His body, the fullness of Him who fills all in all.

Having these promises, beloved, let us cleanse ourselves from all filthiness of the flesh and spirit, perfecting holiness in the fear of God.

JOHN 1:16.MATT 17:5.1 JOHN 3:1.HEB 1:2.ROM 8:17.JOHN 10:30.JOHN 10:38.JOHN 20:17.JOHN 17:23.EPH 1:22-23.2 COR 7:1

## October 22

O God, my heart is steadfast.

The Lord is my light and my salvation; whom shall I fear? The Lord is the strength of my life; of whom shall I be afraid?

You will keep him in perfect peace, whose mind is stayed on You, because he trusts in You. ◊ He will not be afraid of evil tidings; his heart is steadfast, trusting in the Lord. His heart is established; he will not be afraid, until he sees his desire upon his enemies.

Whenever I am afraid, I will trust in You. ◊ In the time of trouble He shall hide me in His pavilion; in the secret place of His tabernacle He shall hide me; He shall set me high upon a rock. And now my head shall be lifted up above my enemies all around me; therefore I will offer sacrifices of joy in His tabernacle; I will sing, yes, I will sing praises to the Lord.

May the God of all grace, who called us to His eternal glory by Christ Jesus, after you have suffered a while, perfect, establish, strengthen, and settle you. To Him be the glory and the dominion forever and ever.

PS 108:1.PS 27:1.IS 26:3.PS 112:7-8.PS 56:3.PS 27:5-6.
1 PET 5:10-11

A little that a righteous man has is better than the riches of many wicked. ◊ Better is a little with the fear of the Lord, than great treasure with trouble. ◊ Godliness with contentment is great gain. . . . Having food and clothing, with these we shall be content.

Give me neither poverty nor riches—feed me with the food You prescribe for me; lest I be full and deny You, and say, "Who is the Lord?" Or lest I be poor and steal, and profane the name of my God. ◊ Give us this day our daily bread.

Do not worry about your life, what you will eat or what you will drink; nor about your body, what you will put on. Is not life more than food and the body more than clothing? ◊ "When I sent you without money bag, sack, and sandals, did you lack anything?" So they said, "Nothing." ◊ Let your conduct be without covetousness, and be content with such things as you have. For He Himself has said, "I will never leave you nor forsake you."

LUKE 12:15.PS 37:16.PROV 15:16.1 TIM 6:6,8.PROV 30:8-9.MATT 6:11.MATT 6:25.LUKE 22:35.HEB 13:5

One's life does not consist in the abundance of the things he possesses.

## October 24

*I have been cast out of Your sight; yet I will look again toward Your holy temple.*

Zion said, "The Lord has forsaken me, and my Lord has forgotten me." Can a woman forget her nursing child, and not have compassion on the son of her womb? Surely they may forget, yet I will not forget you.

I have forgotten prosperity. And I said, "My strength and my hope have perished from the Lord." ◊ Awake! Why do You sleep, O Lord? Arise! Do not cast us off forever. ◊ Why do you say, O Jacob, and speak, O Israel: "My way is hidden from the Lord, and my just claim is passed over by my God?" ◊ "With a little wrath I hid My face from you for a moment; but with everlasting kindness I will have mercy on you," says the Lord, your Redeemer.

Why are you cast down, O my soul? And why are you disquieted within me? Hope in God; for I shall yet praise Him, the help of my countenance. ◊ We are hard pressed on every side, yet not crushed; we are perplexed, but not in despair; persecuted, but not forsaken; struck down, but not destroyed.

JON 2:4.IS 49:14-15.LAM 3:17-18.PS 44:23.IS 40:27.IS 54:8.PS 43:5.2 COR 4:8-9

I say to you that if two of you agree on earth concerning anything that they ask, it will be done for them by My Father in heaven. "For where two or three are gathered together in My name, I am there in the midst of them." ◊ He who has My commandments and keeps them, it is he who loves Me. And he who loves Me will be loved by My Father, and I will love him and manifest Myself to him.

"Lord, how is it that You will manifest Yourself to us, and not to the world?" . . . "If anyone loves Me, he will keep My word; and My Father will love him, and We will come to him and make Our home with him."

Now to Him who is able to keep you from stumbling, and to present you faultless before the presence of His glory with exceeding joy, to God our Savior, who alone is wise, be glory and majesty, dominion and power, both now and forever. Amen.

MATT 28:20.MATT 18:19-20.JOHN 14:21.JOHN 14:22-23.JUDE 1:24-25

Lo, I am with you always, even to the end of the age.

## October 26

**The LORD reigns.**

"Do you not fear Me?" says the Lord. "Will you not tremble at My presence, who have placed the sand as the bound of the sea, by a perpetual decree, that it cannot pass beyond it? And though its waves toss to and fro, yet they cannot prevail; though they roar, yet they cannot pass over it." ◊ Exaltation comes neither from the east nor from the west nor from the south. But God is the Judge: He puts down one, and exalts another.

He changes the times and the seasons; He removes kings and raises up kings; He gives wisdom to the wise and knowledge to those who have understanding. ◊ You will hear of wars and rumors of wars. See that you are not troubled.

If God is for us, who can be against us? ◊ Are not two sparrows sold for a copper coin? And not one of them falls to the ground apart from your Father's will. The very hairs of your head are all numbered. Do not fear therefore; you are of more value than many sparrows.

PS 99:1.JER 5:22.PS 75:6-7.DAN 2:21.MATT 24:6.ROM 8:31.MATT 10:29-31

Then the priest shall command to take for him who is to be cleansed two living and clean birds, cedar wood, scarlet, and hyssop. And the priest shall command that one of the birds be killed in an earthen vessel over running water. As for the living bird, he shall take it, the cedar wood and the scarlet and the hyssop, and dip them and the living bird in the blood of the bird that was killed over the running water. And he shall sprinkle it seven times on him who is to be cleansed from the leprosy, and shall pronounce him clean, and shall let the living bird loose in the open field.

Behold, a man who was full of leprosy saw Jesus; and he fell on his face and implored Him, saying, "Lord, if You are willing, You can make me clean." ◊ And Jesus, moved with compassion, put out His hand and touched him, and said to him, "I am willing; be cleansed." As soon as He had spoken, immediately the leprosy left him, and he was cleansed.

MATT 8:17.LEV 14:4-7.LUKE 5:12.MARK 1:41-42

He Himself took our infirmities and bore our sicknesses.

## October 28

He saw that there was no man, and wondered that there was no intercessor; therefore His own arm brought salvation for Him.

Sacrifice and offering You did not desire; my ears You have opened; burnt offering and sin offering You did not require. Then I said, "Behold, I come; in the scroll of the Book it is written of me. I delight to do Your will, O my God, and Your law is within my heart." ◊ I lay down My life that I may take it again. No one takes it from Me, but I lay it down of Myself. I have power to lay it down, and I have power to take it again.

There is no other God besides Me, a just God and a Savior; there is none besides Me. Look to Me, and be saved, all you ends of the earth! For I am God, and there is no other. ◊ There is no other name under heaven given among men by which we must be saved.

You know the grace of our Lord Jesus Christ, that though He was rich, yet for your sakes He became poor, that you through His poverty might become rich.

IS 59:16.PS 40:6-8.JOHN 10:17-18.IS 45:21-22.ACTS 4:12.2 COR 8:9

May my meditation be sweet to Him. ◊ My beloved is . . . chief among ten thousand. ◊ A chief cornerstone, elect, precious, and he who believes on Him will by no means be put to shame. ◊ You are fairer than the sons of men; grace is poured upon Your lips. ◊ God . . . has highly exalted Him and given Him the name which is above every name. ◊ It pleased the Father that in Him all the fullness should dwell.

Whom having not seen you love. Though now you do not see Him, yet believing, you rejoice with joy inexpressible and full of glory.

I also count all things loss for the excellence of the knowledge of Christ Jesus my Lord, for whom I have suffered the loss of all things, and count them as rubbish, that I may gain Christ and be found in Him, not having my own righteousness, which is from the law, but that which is through faith in Christ, the righteousness which is from God by faith.

SONG 5:16.PS 104:34.SONG 5:10.1 PET 2:6.PS 45:2.PHIL 2:9.COL 1:19.1 PET 1:8.PHIL 3:8-9

## October 29

He is altogether lovely.

## October 30

It is good that one should hope and wait quietly for the salvation of the LORD.

Has God forgotten to be gracious? Has He in anger shut up His tender mercies? ◊ I said in my haste, "I am cut off from before Your eyes"; nevertheless You heard the voice of my supplications when I cried out to You.

Shall God not avenge His own elect who cry out day and night to Him, though He bears long with them? I tell you that He will avenge them speedily. ◊ Wait for the Lord, and He will save you. ◊ Rest in the Lord, and wait patiently for Him; do not fret because of him who prospers in his way, because of the man who brings wicked schemes to pass.

You will not need to fight in this battle. Position yourselves, stand still and see the salvation of the Lord.

Let us not grow weary while doing good, for in due season we shall reap if we do not lose heart. ◊ See how the farmer waits for the precious fruit of the earth, waiting patiently for it until it receives the early and latter rain.

LAM 3:26.PS 77:9.PS 31:22.LUKE 18:7-8.PROV 20:22.PS 37:7.2 CHR 20:17.GAL 6:9.JAMES 5:7

Who has directed the Spirit of the Lord, or as His counselor has taught Him?

God has chosen the foolish things of the world to put to shame the wise, and God has chosen the weak things of the world to put to shame the things which are mighty; and the base things of the world and the things which are despised God has chosen, and the things which are not, to bring to nothing the things that are, that no flesh should glory in His presence.

The wind blows where it wishes, and you hear the sound of it, but cannot tell where it comes from and where it goes. So is everyone who is born of the Spirit. ◊ Born, not of blood, nor of the will of the flesh, nor of the will of man, but of God.

My Spirit remains among you; do not fear! ◊ The battle is not yours, but God's. ◊ The Lord does not save with sword and spear; for the battle is the Lord's.

ZECH 4:6.IS 40:13.1 COR 1:27-29.JOHN 3:8.JOHN 1:13.HAG 2:5.2 CHR 20:15.1 SAM 17:47

## October 31

"Not by might nor by power, but by My Spirit," says the LORD of hosts.

## November 1

Blessed is the man who listens to me, watching daily at my gates, waiting at the posts of my doors.

Behold, as the eyes of servants look to the hand of their masters, as the eyes of a maid to the hand of her mistress, so our eyes look to the Lord our God, until He has mercy on us.

This shall be a continual burnt offering throughout your generations at the door of the tabernacle of meeting before the Lord, where I will meet you to speak with you. ◊ In every place where I record My name I will come to you, and I will bless you.

Where two or three are gathered together in My name, I am there in the midst of them.

The hour is coming, and now is, when the true worshipers will worship the Father in spirit and truth; for the Father is seeking such to worship Him. God is Spirit, and those who worship Him must worship in spirit and truth.

Praying always with all prayer and supplication in the Spirit. ◊ Pray without ceasing.

PROV 8:34.PS 123:2.EX 29:42.EX 20:24.MATT 18:20.JOHN 4:23-24.EPH 6:18.1 THESS 5:17

For to this you were called, because
Christ also suffered for us, leaving us an
example, that you should follow His
steps: who committed no sin, nor was
guile found in His mouth; who, when
He was reviled, did not revile in return;
. . . but committed Himself to Him who
judges righteously. ◊ Consider Him
who endured such hostility from sinners
against Himself, lest you become weary
and discouraged in your souls.

Let us lay aside every weight, and the
sin which so easily ensnares us, and let
us run with endurance the race that is
set before us, looking unto Jesus, the
author and finisher of our faith, who for
the joy that was set before Him endured
the cross, despising the shame, and has
sat down at the right hand of the throne
of God.

Finally, brethren, whatever things are
true, whatever things are noble,
whatever things are just, whatever
things are pure, whatever things are
lovely, whatever things are of good
report, if there is any virtue and if there
is anything praiseworthy meditate on
these things.

1 THESS 5:15.1 PET 2:21-23.HEB 12:3.HEB 12:1-2.
PHIL 4:8

## November 2

**Always pursue
what is good.**

## November 3

To you who believe, He is precious; but to those who are disobedient, . . . a stone of stumbling and a rock of offense. ◊ The way of the Lord is strength for the upright, but destruction will come to the workers of iniquity.

He who has ears to hear, let him hear! ◊ Whoever is wise will observe these things, and they will understand the lovingkindness of the Lord. ◊ The lamp of the body is the eye. If therefore your eye is good, your whole body will be full of light. ◊ If anyone wants to do His will, he shall know concerning the doctrine, whether it is from God.

Whoever has, to him more will be given, and he will have abundance.

He who is of God hears God's words; therefore you do not hear, because you are not of God. ◊ You are not willing to come to Me that you may have life. ◊ My sheep hear My voice, and I know them, and they follow Me.

HOS 14:9.1 PET 2:7-8.PROV 10:29.MATT 11:15.PS 107:43.MATT 6:22.JOHN 7:17.MATT 13:12.JOHN 8:47.JOHN 5:40.JOHN 10:27

Beloved, do not think it strange concerning the fiery trial which is to try you, as though some strange thing happened to you; but rejoice to the extent that you partake of Christ's sufferings, that when His glory is revealed, you may also be glad with exceeding joy. ◊ The exhortation . . . speaks to you as to sons: "My son, do not despise the chastening of the Lord, nor be discouraged when you are rebuked by Him." ◊ Now no chastening seems to be joyful for the present, but grievous; nevertheless, afterward it yields the peaceable fruit of righteousness to those who have been trained by it.

We do not have a High Priest who cannot sympathize with our weaknesses, but was in all points tempted as we are, yet without sin. ◊ For in that He Himself has suffered, being tempted, He is able to aid those who are tempted. ◊ God is faithful, who will not allow you to be tempted beyond what you are able.

1 PET 1:6.1 PET 4:12-13.HEB 12:5.HEB 12:11.HEB 4:15.HEB 2:18.1 COR 10:13

Now for a little while, if need be, you have been grieved by various trials.

## November 5

Take for yourself quality spices . . . And you shall make from these a holy anointing oil.

It shall not be poured on man's flesh; nor shall you make any other like it, according to its composition. It is holy, and it shall be holy to you. ◊ One Spirit. ◊ Diversities of gifts, but the same Spirit.

Your God, has anointed You with the oil of gladness more than Your companions. ◊ God anointed Jesus of Nazareth with the Holy Spirit and with power. ◊ God does not give the Spirit by measure.

Of His fullness we have all received. ◊ As the same anointing teaches you concerning all things, and is true, and is not a lie, and just as it has taught you, you will abide in Him. ◊ He who . . . has anointed us is God, who also has sealed us and given us the Spirit in our hearts as a deposit.

The fruit of the Spirit is love, joy, peace, longsuffering, kindness, goodness, faithfulness, gentleness, self-control. Against such there is no law.

EX 30:23-25.EX 30:32.EPH 4:4.1 COR 12:4.PS 45:7.ACTS 10:38.JOHN 3:34.JOHN 1:16.1 JOHN 2:27.2 COR 1:21-22.GAL 5:22-23

I am the resurrection and the life. He who believes in Me, though he may die, he shall live. ◊ God has given us eternal life, and this life is in His Son. He who has the Son has life; he who does not have the Son of God does not have life.

For the Lord Himself will descend from heaven with a shout, with the voice of an archangel, and with the trumpet of God. And the dead in Christ will rise first. Then we who are alive and remain shall be caught up together with them in the clouds to meet the Lord in the air. And thus we shall always be with the Lord. Therefore comfort one another with these words. ◊ When He is revealed, we shall be like Him, for we shall see Him as He is. ◊ It is sown in dishonor, it is raised in glory. It is sown in weakness, it is raised in power.

If I go and prepare a place for you, I will come again and receive you to Myself; that where I am, there you may be also.

COL 3:4.JOHN 11:25.1 JOHN 5:11-12.1 THESS 4:16-18. 1 JOHN 3:2.1 COR 15:43.JOHN 14:3

## November 6

When Christ who is our life appears, then you also will appear with Him in glory.

# November 7

Oh, taste and see that the Lord is good; blessed is the man who trusts in Him! ◊ How great is Your goodness, which You have laid up for those who fear You.

This people I have formed for Myself; they shall declare My praise. ◊ Having predestined us to adoption as sons by Jesus Christ to Himself, according to the good pleasure of His will, to the praise of the glory of His grace, by which He has made us accepted in the Beloved. . . . that we who first trusted in Christ should be to the praise of His glory.

How great is their goodness and how great their beauty! ◊ The Lord is good to all, and His tender mercies are over all His works. All Your works shall praise You, O Lord, and Your saints shall bless You. They shall speak of the glory of Your kingdom, and talk of Your power, to make known to the sons of men His mighty acts, and the glorious majesty of His kingdom.

PS 107:8.PS 34:8.PS 31:19.IS 43:21.EPH 1:5-6,12.ZECH 9:17.PS 145:9-12

Gird up the loins of your mind, be sober, and rest your hope fully upon the grace that is to be brought to you at the revelation of Jesus Christ. ◊ Stand therefore, having girded your waist with truth, having put on the breastplate of righteousness, . . . above all, taking the shield of faith with which you will be able to quench all the fiery darts of the wicked one. And take the helmet of salvation, and the sword of the Spirit, which is the word of God.

He will swallow up death forever, and the Lord God will wipe away tears from all faces; the rebuke of His people He will take away from all the earth; for the Lord has spoken. And it will be said in that day: "Behold, this is our God; we have waited for Him, and He will save us. This is the Lord; . . . we will be glad and rejoice in His salvation."

Faith is the substance of things hoped for, the evidence of things not seen.

1 THESS 5:8.1 PET 1:13.EPH 6:14.EPH 6:16-17.IS 25:8-9.HEB 11:1

## November 8

Let us who are of the day be sober, putting on the breastplate of faith and love, and as a helmet the hope of salvation.

# November 9

I have given help to one who is mighty; I have exalted one chosen from the people.

I, even I, am the Lord, and besides Me there is no savior. ◊ There is one God and one Mediator between God and men, the Man Christ Jesus. ◊ There is no other name under heaven given among men by which we must be saved.

The . . . Mighty God. ◊ Made Himself of no reputation, taking the form of a servant, and coming in the likeness of men. And being found in appearance as a man, He humbled Himself and became obedient to the point of death, even the death of the cross. Therefore God also has highly exalted Him and given Him the name which is above every name. ◊ We see Jesus, who was made a little lower than the angels, for the suffering of death crowned with glory and honor, that He, by the grace of God, might taste death for everyone. ◊ Inasmuch . . . as the children have partaken of flesh and blood, He Himself likewise shared in the same.

PS 89:19.IS 43:11.1 TIM 2:5.ACTS 4:12.IS 9:6.PHIL 2:7-9.HEB 2:9.HEB 2:14

I beseech you . . . brethren, by the mercies of God, that you present your bodies a living sacrifice, holy, acceptable to God, which is your reasonable service. And do not be conformed to this world, but be transformed by the renewing of your mind, that you may prove what is that good and acceptable and perfect will of God. ◊ Just as you presented your members as slaves of uncleanness, and of lawlessness leading to more lawlessness, so now present your members as slaves of righteousness for holiness. ◊ In Christ Jesus neither circumcision nor uncircumcision avails anything, but a new creation. And as many as walk according to this rule, peace and mercy be upon them.

By this My Father is glorified, that you bear much fruit; so you will be My disciples. ◊ I chose you and appointed you that you should go and bear fruit, and that your fruit should remain, that whatever you ask the Father in My name He may give you.

COL 1:10.ROM 12:1-2.ROM 6:19.GAL 6:15-16.JOHN 15:8.JOHN 15:16

## November 10

Fruitful in every good work and increasing in the knowledge of God.

## November 11

**He led them on safely.**

I traverse the way of righteousness, in the midst of the paths of justice.

Behold, I send an Angel before you to keep you in the way and to bring you into the place which I have prepared. ◊ In all their affliction He was afflicted, and the Angel of His Presence saved them; in His love and in His pity He redeemed them; and He bore them and carried them all the days of old.

They did not gain possession of the land by their own sword, nor did their own arm save them; but it was Your right hand, Your arm, and the light of Your countenance, because You favored them. ◊ So You lead Your people, to make Yourself a glorious name.

Lead me, O Lord, in Your righteousness because of my enemies; make Your way straight before my face. ◊ Oh, send out Your light and Your truth! Let them lead me; let them bring me to Your holy hill and to Your tabernacle. Then I will go to the altar of God, to God my exceeding joy; and on the harp I will praise You, O God, my God.

PS 78:53.PROV 8:20.EX 23:20.IS 63:9.PS 44:3.IS 63:14.PS 5:8.PS 43:3-4

Peter remembered the word of Jesus who had said to him, "Before the rooster crows, you will deny Me three times." Then he went out and wept bitterly. ◊ If we confess our sins, He is faithful and just to forgive us our sins and to cleanse us from all unrighteousness. ◊ The blood of Jesus Christ His Son cleanses us from all sin.

My iniquities have overtaken me, so that I am not able to look up; they are more than the hairs of my head; therefore my heart fails me. Be pleased, O Lord, to deliver me; O Lord, make haste to help me!

So you, by the help of your God, return; observe mercy and justice, and wait on your God continually.

The sacrifices of God are a broken spirit, a broken and a contrite heart—these, O God, You will not despise. ◊ He heals the broken-hearted and binds up their wounds. ◊ He has shown you, O man, what is good; and what does the Lord require of you but to do justly, to love mercy, and to walk humbly with your God?

**2 COR 7:10.MATT 26:75.1 JOHN 1:9.1 JOHN 1:7.PS 40:12-13.HOS 12:6.PS 51:17.PS 147:3.MIC 6:8**

Godly sorrow produces repentance to salvation, not to be regretted.

## November 13

Christ . . . loved the church and gave Himself for it, . . . that He might sanctify and cleanse it with the washing of water by the word.

Walk in love, as Christ also has loved us and given Himself for us, an offering and a sacrifice to God for a sweet-smelling aroma. ◊ Love one another fervently with a pure heart, having been born again, not of corruptible seed but incorruptible, through the word of God which lives and abides forever.

Sanctify them by Your truth. Your word is truth. ◊ Unless one is born of water and the Spirit, he cannot enter the kingdom of God. ◊ Not by works of righteousness which we have done, but according to His mercy He saved us, through the washing of regeneration and renewing of the Holy Spirit. ◊ Your word has given me life.

The law of the Lord is perfect, converting the soul; the testimony of the Lord is sure, making wise the simple; the statutes of the Lord are right, rejoicing the heart; the commandment of the Lord is pure, enlightening the eyes.

EPH 5:25-26.EPH 5:2.1 PET 1:22-23.JOHN 17:17.JOHN 3:5.TITUS 3:5.PS 119:50.PS 19:7-8

The steps of a good man are ordered by the Lord, and He delights in his way. Though he fall, he shall not be utterly cast down; for the Lord upholds him with His hand. ◊ In the fear of the Lord there is strong confidence, and His children will have a place of refuge. ◊ Who are you that you should be afraid of a man who will die, and of the son of a man who will be made like grass? And you forget the Lord your Maker.

I am with you to deliver you. ◊ Be strong and of good courage, do not fear nor be afraid of them; for the Lord your God, He is the One who goes with you. He will not leave you nor forsake you.

I will sing of Your power; yes, I will sing aloud of Your mercy in the morning; for You have been my defense and refuge in the day of my trouble. ◊ You are my hiding place; You shall preserve me from trouble; You shall surround me with songs of deliverance.

PS 40:17.PS 37:23-24.PROV 14:26.IS 51:12-13.JER 1:8.DEUT 31:6.PS 59:16.PS 32:7

You are my help and my deliverer; do not delay, O my God.

## November 15

**God is faithful, by whom you were called into the fellowship of His Son, Jesus Christ our Lord.**

Let us hold fast the confession of our hope without wavering, for He who promised is faithful. ◊ God has said: "I will dwell in them and walk among them. I will be their God, and they shall be My people." ◊ Truly our fellowship is with the Father and with His Son Jesus Christ. ◊ Rejoice to the extent that you partake of Christ's sufferings, that when His glory is revealed, you may also be glad with exceeding joy.

That you, being rooted and grounded in love, may be able to comprehend with all the saints what is the width and length and depth and height—to know the love of Christ which passes knowledge; that you may be filled with all the fullness of God.

Whoever confesses that Jesus is the Son of God, God abides in him, and he in God. ◊ He who keeps His commandments abides in Him, and He in him.

1 COR 1:9.HEB 10:23.2 COR 6:16.1 JOHN 1:3.1 PET 4:13.EPH 3:17-19.1 JOHN 4:15.1 JOHN 3:24

You are already clean because of the word which I have spoken to you. ◊ Let the word of Christ dwell in you richly in all wisdom.

How can a young man cleanse his way? By taking heed according to Your word. With my whole heart I have sought You; oh, let me not wander from Your commandments!

When wisdom enters your heart, and knowledge is pleasant to your soul, discretion will preserve you; understanding will keep you.

My foot has held fast to His steps; I have kept His way and not turned aside. I have not departed from the commandment of His lips; I have treasured the words of His mouth more than my necessary food. ◊ I have more understanding than all my teachers, for Your testimonies are my meditation. ◊ If you abide in My word, you are My disciples indeed. And you shall know the truth, and the truth shall make you free.

JOHN 17:17.JOHN 15:3.COL 3:16.PS 119:9-10.PROV 2:10-11.JOB 23:11-12.PS 119:99.JOHN 8:31-32

## November 16

Sanctify them by Your truth. Your word is truth.

## November 17

**Your thoughts are very deep.**

We . . . do not cease to pray for you, and to ask that you may be filled with the knowledge of His will in all wisdom and spiritual understanding. ◊ That you, being rooted and grounded in love, may be able to comprehend with all the saints what is the width and length and depth and height—to know the love of Christ which passes knowledge; that you may be filled with all the fullness of God.

Oh, the depth of the riches both of the wisdom and knowledge of God! How unsearchable are His judgments and His ways past finding out! ◊ "My thoughts are not your thoughts, nor are your ways My ways," says the Lord. "For as the heavens are higher than the earth, so are My ways higher than your ways, and My thoughts than your thoughts." ◊ Many, O Lord my God, are Your wonderful works which You have done; and Your thoughts which are toward us cannot be recounted to You in order; if I would declare and speak of them, they are more than can be numbered.

PS 92:5.COL 1:9.EPH 3:17-19.ROM 11:33.IS 55:8-9.PS 40:5

Let us fall into the hand of the Lord, for His mercies are great. ◊ "I am with you," says the Lord, "to save you; . . . I will correct you in justice, and will not let you go altogether unpunished." ◊ He will not always strive with us, nor will He keep His anger forever. He has not dealt with us according to our sins, nor punished us according to our iniquities. . . . For He knows our frame; He remembers that we are dust. ◊ I will spare them as a man spares his own son who serves him.

God is faithful, who will not allow you to be tempted beyond what you are able, but with the temptation will also make the way of escape, that you may be able to bear it. ◊ Satan has asked for you, that he may sift you as wheat. But I have prayed for you, that your faith should not fail.

You have been a strength to the poor, a strength to the needy in his distress, a refuge from the storm, a shade from the heat; for the blast of the terrible ones is as a storm against the wall.

IS 27:8.2 SAM 24:14.JER 30:11.PS 103:9-10,14.MAL 3:17.1 COR 10:13.LUKE 22:31-32.IS 25:4

## November 18

He removes it by His rough wind in the day of the east wind.

## November 19

**By their fruits you will know them.**

Little children, let no one deceive you. He who practices righteousness is righteous, just as He is righteous. ◊ Does a spring send forth fresh water and bitter from the same opening? Can a fig tree, my brethren, bear olives, or a grapevine bear figs? Thus no spring can yield both salt water and fresh. Who is wise and understanding among you? Let him show by good conduct that his works are done in the meekness of wisdom. ◊ Having your conduct honorable among the Gentiles, that when they speak against you as evildoers, they may, by your good works which they observe, glorify God in the day of visitation.

Either make the tree good and its fruit good, or else make the tree bad and its fruit bad; for a tree is known by its fruit. ◊ A good man out of the good treasure of his heart brings forth good things, and an evil man out of the evil treasure brings forth evil things.

What more could have been done to My vineyard that I have not done in it?

MATT 7:20.1 JOHN 3:7.JAMES 3:11-13.1 PET 2:12.MATT 12:33.MATT 12:35.IS 5:4

When you pass through the waters, I will be with you; and through the rivers, they shall not overflow you. When you walk through the fire, you shall not be burned, nor shall the flame scorch you. For I am the Lord your God, the Holy One of Israel, your Savior. ◊ I will bring the blind by a way they did not know; I will lead them in paths they have not known. I will make darkness light before them, and crooked places straight. These things I will do for them, and not forsake them.

Yea, though I walk through the valley of the shadow of death, I will fear no evil; for You are with me; Your rod and Your staff, they comfort me. ◊ Whenever I am afraid, I will trust in You. In God (I will praise His word), in God I have put my trust; I will not fear. What can flesh do to me? ◊ The Lord is my light and my salvation; whom shall I fear? The Lord is the strength of my life; of whom shall I be afraid?

MIC 7:8.IS 43:2-3.IS 42:16.PS 23:4.PS 56:3-4.PS 27:1

When I sit in darkness, the Lord will be a light to me.

## November 21

**The one who comes to Me I will by no means cast out.**

It will be that when he cries to Me, I will hear, for I am gracious. ◊ I will not cast them away, nor shall I abhor them, to utterly destroy them and break My covenant with them; for I am the Lord their God. ◊ I will remember My covenant with you in the days of your youth, and I will establish an everlasting covenant with you.

"Come now, and let us reason together," says the Lord, "though your sins are like scarlet, they shall be as white as snow; though they are red like crimson, they shall be as wool." ◊ Let the wicked forsake his way, and the unrighteous man his thoughts; let him return to the Lord, and He will have mercy on him; and to our God, for He will abundantly pardon. ◊ "Lord, remember me when You come into Your kingdom." And Jesus said to him, "Assuredly, I say to you, today you will be with Me in Paradise."

A bruised reed He will not break, and smoking flax He will not quench.

JOHN 6:37.EX 22:27.LEV 26:44.EZEK 16:60.IS 1:18.IS 55:7.LUKE 23:42-43.IS 42:3

God is Spirit, and those who worship Him must worship in spirit and truth. ◊ We . . . have access by one Spirit to the Father.

O My Father, if it is possible, let this cup pass from Me; nevertheless, not as I will, but as You will.

The Spirit . . . helps in our weaknesses. For we do not know what we should pray for as we ought, but the Spirit Himself makes intercession for us with groanings which cannot be uttered. Now He who searches the hearts knows what the mind of the Spirit is, because He makes intercession for the saints according to the will of God. ◊ This is the confidence that we have in Him, that if we ask anything according to His will, He hears us. ◊ When He, the Spirit of truth, has come, He will guide you into all truth.

Praying always with all prayer and supplication in the Spirit, being watchful to this end with all perseverance and supplication.

JUDE 1:20.JOHN 4:24.EPH 2:18.MATT 26:39.ROM 8:26-27.1 JOHN 5:14.JOHN 16:13.EPH 6:18

Praying in the Holy Spirit.

## November 23

Whoever listens to me will dwell safely, and will be secure, without fear of evil.

Lord, You have been our dwelling place in all generations. ◊ He who dwells in the secret place of the Most High shall abide under the shadow of the Almighty. . . . His truth shall be your shield and buckler.

Your life is hidden with Christ in God. ◊ He who touches you touches the apple of His eye. ◊ Stand still, and see the salvation of the Lord. . . . The Lord will fight for you, and you shall hold your peace. ◊ God is our refuge and strength, a very present help in trouble. Therefore we will not fear.

Jesus spoke to them, saying, "Be of good cheer! It is I; do not be afraid." ◊ "Why are you troubled? And why do doubts arise in your hearts? Behold My hands and My feet, that it is I Myself. Handle Me and see, for a spirit does not have flesh and bones as you see I have." ◊ I know whom I have believed and am persuaded that He is able to keep what I have committed to Him until that Day.

PROV 1:33.PS 90:1.PS 91:1,4.COL 3:3.ZECH 2:8.EX 14:13-14.PS 46:1-2.MATT 14:27.LUKE 24:38-39.2 TIM 1:12

Both He who sanctifies and those who are being sanctified are all of one, for which reason He is not ashamed to call them brethren, saying, "I will declare your name to My brethren; in the midst of the congregation I will sing praise to You." ◊ In Christ Jesus neither circumcision nor uncircumcision avails anything, but faith working through love. ◊ You are My friends if you do whatever I command you. ◊ Blessed are those who hear the word of God and keep it!

Not everyone who says to Me, "Lord, Lord," shall enter the kingdom of heaven, but he who does the will of My Father in heaven. ◊ My food is to do the will of Him who sent Me.

If we say that we have fellowship with Him, and walk in darkness, we lie and do not practice the truth. ◊ Whoever keeps His word, truly the love of God is perfected in him. By this we know that we are in Him.

LUKE 8:21.HEB 2:11-12.GAL 5:6.JOHN 15:14.LUKE 11:28.MATT 7:21.JOHN 4:34.1 JOHN 1:6.1 JOHN 2:5

## November 24

My mother and My brothers are these who hear the word of God and do it.

## November 25

Having been set free from sin, you became slaves of righteousness.

You cannot serve God and mammon. ◊ When you were slaves of sin, you were free in regard to righteousness. What fruit did you have then in the things of which you are now ashamed? For the end of those things is death. But now having been set free from sin, and having become slaves of God, you have your fruit to holiness, and the end, everlasting life.

Christ is the end of the law for righteousness to everyone who believes.

If anyone serves Me, let him follow Me; and where I am, there My servant will be also. If anyone serves Me, him My Father will honor. ◊ Take My yoke upon you and learn from Me, for I am gentle and lowly in heart, and you will find rest for your souls. For My yoke is easy and My burden is light.

O Lord our God, other masters besides You have had dominion over us; but by You only we make mention of Your name. ◊ I will run in the way of Your commandments, for You shall enlarge my heart.

ROM 6:18.MATT 6:24.ROM 6:20-22.ROM 10:4.JOHN 12:26.MATT 11:29-30.IS 26:13.PS 119:32

But now, thus says the Lord, who created you, O Jacob, and He who formed you, O Israel: "Fear not, for I have redeemed you; I have called you by your name; you are Mine." ◊ Can a woman forget her nursing child, and not have compassion on the son of her womb? Surely they may forget, yet I will not forget you. See, I have inscribed you on the palms of My hands; your walls are continually before Me.

The steps of a good man are ordered by the Lord, and He delights in his way. ◊ My delight was with the sons of men. ◊ The Lord takes pleasure in those who fear Him, in those who hope in His mercy. ◊ "They shall be Mine," says the Lord of hosts, "on the day that I make them My jewels. And I will spare them as a man spares his own son who serves him."

You, who once were alienated and enemies in your mind by wicked works, yet now He has reconciled in the body of His flesh through death, to present you holy, and blameless, and irreproachable in His sight.

IS 62:4.IS 43:1.IS 49:15-16.PS 37:23.PROV 8:31.PS 147:11.MAL 3:17.COL 1:21-22

The LORD delights in you.

## November 27

The glory which You gave Me I have given them.

I saw the Lord sitting on a throne, high and lifted up, and the train of His robe filled the temple. Above it stood seraphim. . . . And one cried to another and said: "Holy, holy, holy is the Lord of hosts; the whole earth is full of His glory!" ◊ These things Isaiah said when he saw His glory and spoke of Him. ◊ On the likeness of the throne was a likeness . . . of a man high above it. . . . Like the appearance of a rainbow in a cloud on a rainy day, so was the appearance of the brightness all around it. This was the appearance of the likeness of the glory of the Lord.

"Please, show me Your glory." . . . But He said, "You cannot see My face; for no man shall see Me, and live." ◊ No one has seen God at any time. The only begotten Son, who is in the bosom of the Father, He has declared Him. ◊ God who commanded light to shine out of darkness who has shone in our hearts to give the light of the knowledge of the glory of God in the face of Jesus Christ.

JOHN 17:22.IS 6:1-3.JOHN 12:41.EZEK 1:26,28.EX 33:18,20.JOHN 1:18.2 COR 4:6

Not everyone who says . . . , "Lord, Lord," shall enter the kingdom of heaven, but he who does the will of My Father in heaven. ◊ Pursue . . . holiness, without which no one will see the Lord. ◊ Add to your faith virtue, to virtue knowledge, to knowledge self-control, to self-control perseverance, to perseverance godliness, to godliness brotherly kindness, and to brotherly kindness love. For if these things are yours and abound, you will be neither barren nor unfruitful in the knowledge of our Lord Jesus Christ. For he who lacks these things is shortsighted, even to blindness, and has forgotten that he was purged from his old sins. Therefore, brethren, be even more diligent to make your calling and election sure, for if you do these things you will never stumble.

By grace you have been saved through faith, and that not of yourselves; it is the gift of God, not of works, lest anyone should boast.

JAMES 2:26.MATT 7:21.HEB 12:14.2 PET 1:5-10.EPH 2:8-9

## November 28

As the body without the spirit is dead, so faith without works is dead also.

We shall be satisfied with the goodness of Your house.

One thing I have desired of the Lord, that will I seek: that I may dwell in the house of the Lord all the days of my life, to behold the beauty of the Lord, and to inquire in His temple. . . .

Blessed are those who hunger and thirst for righteousness, for they shall be filled. ◊ He has filled the hungry with good things, and the rich He has sent away empty.

He satisfies the longing soul, and fills the hungry soul with goodness. ◊ I am the bread of life. He who comes to Me shall never hunger, and he who believes in Me shall never thirst.

How precious is Your lovingkindness, O God! Therefore the children of men put their trust under the shadow of Your wings. They are abundantly satisfied with the fullness of Your house, and You give them drink from the river of Your pleasures. For with You is the fountain of life; in Your light we see light.

PS 65:4.PS 27:4.MATT 5:6.LUKE 1:53.PS 107:9.JOHN 6:35.PS 36:7-9

Peace from Him who is and who was and who is to come. ◊ The peace of God, which surpasses all understanding, will guard your hearts and minds through Christ Jesus.

Jesus Himself stood in the midst of them, and said to them, "Peace to you." ◊ Peace I leave with you, My peace I give to you; not as the world gives do I give to you. Let not your heart be troubled, neither let it be afraid.

The Helper . . . the Spirit of truth. ◊ The fruit of the Spirit is love, joy, peace. ◊ The Spirit Himself bears witness with our spirit that we are children of God.

My Presence will go with you, and I will give you rest. . . . Then he said to Him, "If Your Presence does not go with us, do not bring us up from here. For how then will it be known that Your people and I have found grace in Your sight, except You go with us?"

2 THESS 3:16.REV 1:4.PHIL 4:7.LUKE 24:36.JOHN 14:27.JOHN 15:26.GAL 5:22.ROM 8:16.EX 33:14-16

The Lord of peace Himself give you peace always in every way. The Lord be with you all.

## December 1

*A man will be as a hiding place from the wind, and a cover from the tempest.*

Inasmuch . . . as the children have partaken of flesh and blood, He Himself likewise shared in the same. ◊ "The Man who is My Companion," says the Lord of hosts. ◊ I and My Father are one.

He who dwells in the secret place of the Most High shall abide under the shadow of the Almighty. ◊ There will be a tabernacle for shade in the daytime from the heat, for a place of refuge, and for a shelter from storm and rain. ◊ The Lord is your shade at your right hand. The sun shall not strike you by day, nor the moon by night.

When my heart is overwhelmed; lead me to the rock that is higher than I. ◊ You are my hiding place; You shall preserve me from trouble. ◊ You have been a strength to the poor, a strength to the needy in his distress, a refuge from the storm, a shade from the heat; for the blast of the terrible ones is as a storm against the wall.

IS 32:2.HEB 2:14.ZECH 13:7.JOHN 10:30.PS 91:1.IS 4:6.PS 121:5-6.PS 61:2.PS 32:7.IS 25:4

God anointed Jesus of Nazareth with the Holy Spirit and with power. ◊ It pleased the Father that in Him all the fullness should dwell. ◊ Of His fullness we have all received, and grace for grace.

You anoint my head with oil. ◊ The anointing which you have received from Him abides in you, and you do not need that anyone teach you; but as the same anointing teaches you concerning all things, and is true, and is not a lie, and just as it has taught you, you will abide in Him.

The Helper, the Holy Spirit, whom the Father will send in My name, He will teach you all things, and bring to your remembrance all things that I said to you.

The Spirit also helps in our weaknesses. For we do not know what we should pray for as we ought, but the Spirit Himself makes intercession for us with groanings which cannot be uttered.

1 JOHN 2:20.ACTS 10:38.COL 1:19.JOHN 1:16.PS 23:5.
1 JOHN 2:27.JOHN 14:26.ROM 8:26

## December 2

You have an anointing from the Holy One, and you know all things.

## December 3

I would seek God, and to God I would commit my cause.

Is anything too hard for the Lord? ◊ Commit your way to the Lord, trust also in Him, and He shall bring it to pass. ◊ Be anxious for nothing, but in everything by prayer and supplication, with thanksgiving, let your requests be made known to God. ◊ [Cast] all your care upon Him, for He cares for you.

Hezekiah received the letter from the hand of the messengers, and read it; and Hezekiah went up to the house of the Lord, and spread it before the Lord. Then Hezekiah prayed to the Lord.

It shall come to pass that before they call, I will answer; and while they are still speaking, I will hear. ◊ The effective, fervent prayer of a righteous man avails much.

I love the Lord, because He has heard My voice and my supplications. Because He has inclined His ear to me, therefore I will call upon Him as long as I live.

JOB 5:8.GEN 18:14.PS 37:5.PHIL 4:6.1 PET 5:7.IS 37:14-15.IS 65:24.JAMES 5:16.PS 116:1-2

If any of you lacks wisdom, let him ask of God, who gives to all liberally and without reproach, and it will be given to him. But let him ask in faith, with no doubting. ◊ Trust in the Lord with all your heart, and lean not on your own understanding; in all your ways acknowledge Him, and He shall direct your paths. ◊ God . . . alone is wise. ◊ Do not be wise in your own eyes.

"Ah, Lord God! Behold, I cannot speak, for I am a youth." But the Lord said to me: "Do not say, 'I am a youth,' for you shall go to all to whom I send you, and whatever I command you, you shall speak. Do not be afraid of their faces, for I am with you to deliver you," says the Lord.

Whatever you ask the Father in My name He will give you. Until now you have asked nothing in My name. Ask, and you will receive, that your joy may be full. ◊ And all things, whatever you ask in prayer, believing, you will receive.

JOB 28:12.JAMES 1:5-6.PROV 3:5-6.1 TIM 1:17.PROV 3:7.JER 1:6-8.JOHN 16:23-24.MATT 21:22

## December 5

Though He was a Son, yet He learned obedience by the things which He suffered. ◊ We suffer with Him, that we may also be glorified together. For I consider that the sufferings of this present time are not worthy to be compared with the glory which shall be revealed in us.

He knows the way that I take; when He has tested me, I shall come forth as gold. My foot has held fast to His steps; I have kept His way and not turned aside.

You shall remember that the Lord your God led you all the way these forty years in the wilderness, to humble you and test you, to know what was in your heart, whether you would keep His commandments or not. . . . So you should know in your heart that as a man chastens his son, so the Lord your God chastens you. Therefore you shall keep the commandments of the Lord your God, to walk in His ways and to fear Him.

PS 119:71.HEB 5:8.ROM 8:17-18.JOB 23:10-11.DEUT 8:2,5-6

Not that we are sufficient of ourselves to think of anything as being from ourselves, but our sufficiency is from God. ◇ A man can receive nothing unless it has been given to him from heaven. ◇ No one can come to Me unless the Father who sent Me draws him; and I will raise him up at the last day. ◇ I will give them one heart and one way, that they may fear Me forever.

Do not be deceived, my beloved brethren. Every good gift and every perfect gift is from above, and comes down from the Father of lights, with whom there is no variation or shadow of turning. Of His own will He brought us forth by the word of truth, that we might be a kind of firstfruits of His creatures.

For we are His workmanship, created in Christ Jesus for good works, which God prepared beforehand that we should walk in them.

Lord, You will establish peace for us, for You have also done all our works in us.

## December 6

**It is God who works in you.**

PHIL 2:13.2 COR 3:5.JOHN 3:27.JOHN 6:44.JER 32:39.JAMES 1:16-18.EPH 2:10.IS 26:12

## December 7

He made Him who knew no sin to be sin for us, that we might become the righteousness of God in Him.

The Lord has laid on Him the iniquity of us all. ◊ [He] Himself bore our sins in His own body on the tree, that we, having died to sins, might live for righteousness by whose stripes you were healed. ◊ As by one man's disobedience many were made sinners, so also by one Man's obedience many will be made righteous.

But when the kindness and the love of God our Savior toward man appeared, not by works of righteousness which we have done, but according to His mercy He saved us, through the washing of regeneration and renewing of the Holy Spirit, whom He poured out on us abundantly through Jesus Christ our Savior, that having been justified by His grace we should become heirs according to the hope of eternal life. ◊ There is therefore now no condemnation to those who are in Christ Jesus, who do not walk according to the flesh, but according to the Spirit.

THE LORD OUR RIGHTEOUSNESS.

2 COR 5:21.IS 53:6.1 PET 2:24.ROM 5:19.TITUS 3:4-7.ROM 8:1.JER 23:6

Brethren, if a man is overtaken in any trespass, you who are spiritual restore such a one in a spirit of gentleness, considering yourself lest you also be tempted. Bear one another's burdens, and so fulfill the law of Christ.

Brethren, if anyone among you wanders from the truth, and someone turns him back, let him know that he who turns a sinner from the error of his way will save a soul from death and cover a multitude of sins. ◊ Since you have purified your souls in obeying the truth through the Spirit in sincere love of the brethren, love one another fervently with a pure heart. ◊ Owe no one anything except to love one another, for he who loves another has fulfilled the law. ◊ Be kindly affectionate to one another with brotherly love, in honor giving preference to one another. ◊ Yes, all of you be submissive to one another, and be clothed with humility, for "God resists the proud, but gives grace to the humble."

We then who are strong ought to bear with the scruples of the weak, and not to please ourselves.

## December 8

Through love
serve one another.

GAL 5:13.GAL 6:1-2.JAMES 5:19-20.1 PET 1:22.ROM 13:8.ROM 12:10.1 PET 5:5.ROM 15:1

## December 9

To do righteousness and justice is more acceptable to the LORD than sacrifice.

He has shown you, O man, what is good; and what does the Lord require of you but to do justly, to love mercy, and to walk humbly with your God? ◊ Has the Lord as great delight in burnt offerings and sacrifices, as in obeying the voice of the Lord? Behold, to obey is better than sacrifice, and to heed than the fat of rams. ◊ To love Him with all the heart, with all the understanding, with all the soul, and with all the strength, and to love one's neighbor as oneself, is more than all the whole burnt offerings and sacrifices.

So you, by the help of your God, return; observe mercy and justice, and wait on your God continually. ◊ Mary . . . sat at Jesus' feet and heard His word. . . . One thing is needed, and Mary has chosen that good part, which will not be taken away from her.

It is God who works in you both to will and to do for His good pleasure.

PROV 21:3.MIC 6:8.1 SAM 15:22.MARK 12:33.HOS 12:6.LUKE 10:39, 42.PHIL 2:13

I know whom I have believed and am persuaded that He is able to keep what I have committed to Him until that Day. ◊ The Lord will deliver me from every evil work and preserve me for His heavenly kingdom. ◊ We are more than conquerors through Him who loved us. For I am persuaded that neither death nor life, nor angels nor principalities nor powers, nor things present nor things to come, nor height nor depth, nor any other created thing, shall be able to separate us from the love of God which is in Christ Jesus our Lord. ◊ Your life is hidden with Christ in God.

Has God not chosen the poor of this world to be rich in faith and heirs of the kingdom which He promised to those who love Him?

Our Lord Jesus Christ Himself, and our God and Father, who has loved us and given us everlasting consolation and good hope by grace, comfort your hearts and establish you in every good word and work.

JOHN 10:29.2 TIM 1:12.2 TIM 4:18.ROM 8:37-39.COL 3:3.JAMES 2:5.2 THESS 2:16-17

## December 10

No one is able to snatch them out of My Father's hand.

## December 11

**Do not let your good be spoken of as evil.**

Abstain from every form of evil. ◊ [Provide] honorable things, not only in the sight of the Lord, but also in the sight of men. ◊ For this is the will of God, that by doing good you may put to silence the ignorance of foolish men.

But let none of you suffer as a murderer, a thief, an evildoer, or as a busybody in other people's matters. Yet if anyone suffers as a Christian, let him not be ashamed, but let him glorify God in this matter.

For you, brethren, have been called to liberty; only do not use liberty as an opportunity for the flesh, but through love serve one another. ◊ Beware lest somehow this liberty of yours become a stumbling block to those who are weak. ◊ Whoever causes one of these little ones who believe in Me to sin, it would be better for him if a millstone were hung around his neck, and he were drowned in the depth of the sea. ◊ Inasmuch as you did it to one of the least of these My brethren, you did it to Me.

ROM 14:16.1 THESS 5:22.2 COR 8:21.1 PET 2:15.1 PET 4:15-16.GAL 5:13.1 COR 8:9.MATT 18:6.MATT 25:40

Fear not, for I am with you; be not dismayed, for I am your God. I will strengthen you, yes, I will help you, I will uphold you with My righteous right hand. ◊ Strengthen the weak hands, and make firm the feeble knees. Say to those who are fearful-hearted, "Be strong, do not fear! Behold, your God will come with vengeance, with the recompense of God; He will come and save you." ◊ The Lord your God in your midst, the Mighty One, will save; He will rejoice over you with gladness, He will quiet you in His love, He will rejoice over you with singing. ◊ Wait on the Lord; be of good courage, and He shall strengthen your heart.

I heard a loud voice from heaven saying, "Behold, the tabernacle of God is with men, and He will dwell with them, and they shall be His people, and God Himself will be with them and be their God." And God will wipe away every tear from their eyes; there shall be no more death, nor sorrow, nor crying; and there shall be no more pain.

ZEPH 3:15.IS 41:10.IS 35:3-4.ZEPH 3:17.PS 27:14.REV 21:3-4

## December 12

The LORD is in your midst.

## December 13

Be strong in the grace that is in Christ Jesus.

[Be] strengthened with all might, according to His glorious power. ◊ As you have therefore received Christ Jesus the Lord, so walk in Him, rooted and built up in Him and established in the faith, as you have been taught, abounding in it with thanksgiving.

They may be called trees of righteousness, the planting of the Lord, that He may be glorified. ◊ You are . . . built on the foundation of the apostles and prophets, Jesus Christ Himself being the chief cornerstone, in whom the whole building, being joined together, grows into a holy temple in the Lord, in whom you also are being built together for a habitation of God in the Spirit.

I commend you to God and to the word of His grace, which is able to build you up and give you an inheritance among all those who are sanctified. ◊ [Be] filled with the fruits of righteousness which are by Jesus Christ, to the glory and praise of God.

Fight the good fight of faith. ◊ Not in any way terrified by your adversaries.

2 TIM 2:1.COL 1:11.COL 2:6-7.IS 61:3.EPH 2:19-22.ACTS 20:32.PHIL 1:11.1 TIM 6:12.PHIL 1:28

This people I have formed for Myself; they shall declare My praise. ◊ I will cleanse them from all their iniquity by which they have sinned against Me, and I will pardon all their iniquities by which they have sinned and by which they have transgressed against Me. Then it shall be to Me a name of joy, a praise, and an honor before all nations of the earth. ◊ Therefore by Him let us continually offer the sacrifice of praise to God, that is, the fruit of our lips, giving thanks to His name.

I will praise You, O Lord my God, with all my heart, and I will glorify Your name forevermore. For great is Your mercy toward me, and You have delivered my soul from the depths of Sheol. ◊ Who is like You, O Lord, . . . glorious in holiness, fearful in praises, doing wonders? ◊ I will praise the name of God with a song, and will magnify Him with thanksgiving. ◊ They sing the song of Moses, the servant of God, and the song of the Lamb, saying: "Great and marvelous are Your works, Lord God Almighty!"

PS 66:2.IS 43:21.JER 33:8-9.HEB 13:15.PS 86:12-13.EX 15:11.PS 69:30.REV 15:3

December 14

Make His praise glorious.

**Bear one another's burdens, and so fulfill the law of Christ.**

Let each of you look out not only for his own interests, but also for the interests of others. Let this mind be in you which was also in Christ Jesus, who . . . made Himself of no reputation, taking the form of a servant. ◊ Even the Son of Man did not come to be served, but to serve, and to give His life a ransom for many. ◊ He died for all, that those who live should live no longer for themselves, but for Him who died for them and rose again.

When Jesus saw her weeping, and the Jews who came with her weeping, He groaned in the spirit and was troubled. . . . Jesus wept. ◊ Rejoice with those who rejoice, and weep with those who weep.

All of you be of one mind, having compassion for one another; love as brothers, be tenderhearted, be courteous; not returning evil for evil or reviling for reviling, but on the contrary blessing, knowing that you were called to this, that you may inherit a blessing.

GAL 6:2.PHIL 2:4-7.MARK 10:45.2 COR 5:15.JOHN 11:33,35.ROM 12:15.1 PET 3:8-9

I pray for them. I do not pray for the world but for those whom You have given Me, for they are Yours. And all Mine are Yours, and Yours are Mine, and I am glorified in them. . . . I do not pray that You should take them out of the world, but that You should keep them from the evil one. They are not of the world, just as I am not of the world.

As the Father loved Me, I also have loved you; abide in My love. ◊ Greater love has no one than this, than to lay down one's life for his friends. You are My friends if you do whatever I command you. ◊ A new commandment I give to you, that you love one another; as I have loved you, that you also love one another.

He who has begun a good work in you will complete it until the day of Jesus Christ. ◊ Christ . . . loved the church and gave Himself for it, that He might sanctify and cleanse it with the washing of water by the word.

JOHN 13:1.JOHN 17:9-10,15-16.JOHN 15:9.JOHN 15:13-14.JOHN 13:34.PHIL 1:6.EPH 5:25-26

Having loved His own who were in the world, He loved them to the end.

## December 17

Revive us, and
we will call upon
Your name.

It is the Spirit who gives life. ◊ The Spirit also helps in our weaknesses. For we do not know what we should pray for as we ought, but the Spirit Himself makes intercession for us with groanings which cannot be uttered. Now He who searches the hearts knows what the mind of the Spirit is, because He makes intercession for the saints according to the will of God. ◊ [Pray] always with all prayer and supplication in the Spirit, being watchful to this end with all perseverance.

I will never forget Your precepts, for by them You have given me life. ◊ The words that I speak to you are spirit, and they are life. ◊ The letter kills, but the Spirit gives life. ◊ If you abide in Me, and My words abide in you, you will ask what you desire, and it shall be done for you. ◊ This is the confidence that we have in Him, that if we ask anything according to His will, He hears us.

No one can say that Jesus is Lord except by the Holy Spirit.

PS 80:18.JOHN 6:63.ROM 8:26-27.EPH 6:18.PS 119:93.JOHN 6:63.2 COR 3:6.JOHN 15:7.1 JOHN 5:14.1 COR 12:3

Be anxious for nothing, but in everything by prayer and supplication, with thanksgiving, let your requests be made known to God; and the peace of God, which surpasses all understanding, will guard your hearts and minds through Christ Jesus. ◊ You did not receive the spirit of bondage again to fear, but you received the Spirit of adoption by whom we cry out, "Abba, Father."

I did not say to the seed of Jacob, "Seek Me in vain." ◊ Therefore . . . having boldness to enter the Holiest by the blood of Jesus, by a new and living way which He consecrated for us, through the veil, that is, His flesh, and having a High Priest over the house of God, let us draw near with a true heart in full assurance of faith, having our hearts sprinkled from an evil conscience and our bodies washed with pure water. ◊ We may boldly say: "The Lord is my helper; I will not fear. What can man do to me?"

HEB 4:16.PHIL 4:6-7.ROM 8:15.IS 45:19.HEB 10:19-22.HEB 13:6

Let us therefore come boldly to the throne of grace, that we may obtain mercy and find grace to help in time of need.

## December 19

Unto the upright there arises light in the darkness.

Who among you fears the Lord? Who obeys the voice of His Servant? Who walks in darkness and has no light? Let him trust in the name of the Lord and rely upon his God. ◊ Though he fall, he shall not be utterly cast down; for the Lord upholds him with His hand. ◊ The commandment is a lamp, and the law is light.

Do not rejoice over me, my enemy; when I fall, I will arise; when I sit in darkness, the Lord will be a light to me. I will bear the indignation of the Lord, because I have sinned against Him, until He pleads my case and executes justice for me; He will bring me forth to the light, and I will see His righteousness.

The lamp of the body is the eye. If therefore your eye is good, your whole body will be full of light. But if your eye is bad, your whole body will be full of darkness. If therefore the light that is in you is darkness, how great is that darkness!

PS 112:4.IS 50:10.PS 37:24.PROV 6:23.MIC 7:8-9.MATT 6:22-23

That we should be holy and without blame before Him in love.

God from the beginning chose you for salvation through sanctification by the Spirit and belief in the truth, to which He called you . . . for the obtaining of the glory of our Lord Jesus Christ. ◊ Whom He foreknew, He also predestined to be conformed to the image of His Son, that He might be the firstborn among many brethren. Moreover whom He predestined, these He also called; whom He called, these He also justified; and whom He justified, these He also glorified. ◊ Elect according to the foreknowledge of God the Father, in sanctification of the Spirit, for obedience and sprinkling of the blood of Jesus Christ.

I will give you a new heart and put a new spirit within you; I will take the heart of stone out of your flesh and give you a heart of flesh. ◊ God did not call us to uncleanness, but in holiness.

EPH 1:4.EPH 1:4.2 THESS 2:13-14.ROM 8:29-30.1 PET 1:2.EZEK 36:26.1 THESS 4:7

He chose us in Him before the foundation of the world.

## December 21

The days of your mourning shall be ended.

In the world you will have tribulation. ◊ The whole creation groans and labors with birth pangs together until now. And not only they, but we also who have the firstfruits of the Spirit, even we ourselves groan within ourselves, eagerly waiting for the adoption, the redemption of our body. ◊ We who are in this tent groan, being burdened, not because we want to be unclothed, but further clothed, that mortality may be swallowed up by life.

These are the ones who come out of the great tribulation, and washed their robes and made them white in the blood of the Lamb. Therefore they are before the throne of God, and serve Him day and night in His temple. And He who sits on the throne will dwell among them. They shall neither hunger anymore nor thirst anymore; the sun shall not strike them, nor any heat; for the Lamb who is in the midst of the throne will shepherd them and lead them to living fountains of waters. And God will wipe away every tear from their eyes.

IS 60:20.JOHN 16:33.ROM 8:22-23.2 COR 5:4.REV 7:14-17

This is the work of God, that you believe in Him whom He sent.

Faith . . . if it does not have works, is dead. ◇ Faith working through love. ◇ He who sows to his flesh will of the flesh reap corruption, but he who sows to the Spirit will of the Spirit reap everlasting life. ◇ We are His workmanship, created in Christ Jesus for good works, which God prepared beforehand that we should walk in them. ◇ [He] gave Himself for us, that He might redeem us from every lawless deed and purify for Himself His own special people, zealous for good works.

We are bound to thank God always for you, brethren, as it is fitting, because your faith grows exceedingly, and the love of every one of you all abounds toward each other. . . . Therefore we also pray always for you that our God would count you worthy of this calling, and fulfill all the good pleasure of His goodness and the work of faith with power. ◇ It is God who works in you both to will and to do for His good pleasure.

1 THESS 1:3.JOHN 6:29.JAMES 2:17.GAL 5:6.GAL
6:8.EPH 2:10.TITUS 2:14.2 THESS 1:3,11.PHIL 2:13

Your work of faith.

## December 23

Let him take hold of My strength, that he may make peace with Me; and he shall make peace with Me.

I know the thoughts that I think toward you, says the Lord, thoughts of peace and not of evil. ◊ "There is no peace," says the Lord, "for the wicked."

In Christ Jesus you who once were far off have been made near by the blood of Christ. For He Himself is our peace.

It pleased the Father that in Him all the fullness should dwell, and by Him to reconcile all things to Himself, . . . having made peace through the blood of His cross. ◊ Christ Jesus, whom God set forth to be a propitiation by His blood, through faith, to demonstrate His righteousness . . . over the sins that were previously committed, . . . that He might be just and the justifier of the one who has faith in Jesus. ◊ If we confess our sins, He is faithful and just to forgive us our sins and to cleanse us from all unrighteousness.

Trust in the Lord forever, for in YAH, the Lord, is everlasting strength.

IS 27:5.JER 29:11.IS 48:22.EPH 2:13-14.COL 1:19-20.ROM 3:24-26.1 JOHN 1:9.IS 26:4

Now the works of the flesh are evident, which are: adultery, fornication, . . . and the like; of which I tell you beforehand, just as I also told you in time past, that those who practice such things will not inherit the kingdom of God. But the fruit of the Spirit is love, joy, peace, longsuffering, kindness, goodness, faithfulness, gentleness, self-control. Against such there is no law. And those who are Christ's have crucified the flesh with its passions and desires. If we live in the Spirit, let us also walk in the Spirit.

The grace of God that brings salvation has appeared to all men, teaching us that, denying ungodliness and worldly lusts, we should live soberly, righteously, and godly in the present age, looking for the blessed hope and glorious appearing of our great God and Savior Jesus Christ, who gave Himself for us, that He might redeem us from every lawless deed.

ROM 8:13.GAL 5:19,21-25.TITUS 2:11-14

## December 24

If you live according to the flesh you will die; but if by the Spirit you put to death the deeds of the body, you will live.

## December 25

The kindness and the love of God our Savior toward man appeared.

I have loved you with an everlasting love.

In this the love of God was manifested toward us, that God has sent His only begotten Son into the world, that we might live through Him. In this is love, not that we loved God, but that He loved us and sent His Son to be the propitiation for our sins.

When the fullness of the time had come, God sent forth His Son, born of a woman, born under the law, to redeem those who were under the law, that we might receive the adoption as sons. ◊ The Word became flesh and dwelt among us, and we beheld His glory, the glory as of the only begotten of the Father, full of grace and truth. ◊ Great is the mystery of godliness: God was manifested in the flesh.

As the children have partaken of flesh and blood, He Himself likewise shared in the same, that through death He might destroy him who had the power of death, that is, the devil.

TITUS 3:4.JER 31:3.1 JOHN 4:9-10.GAL 4:4-5.JOHN 1:14.1 TIM 3:16.HEB 2:14

Your labor is not in vain in the Lord.
◊ As you have . . . received Christ Jesus the Lord, so walk in Him, rooted and built up in Him and established in the faith, as you have been taught, abounding in it with thanksgiving. ◊ He who endures to the end shall be saved. ◊ The ones that fell on the good ground are those who, having heard the word with a noble and good heart, keep it and bear fruit with patience.

By faith you stand.

I must work the works of Him who sent Me while it is day; the night is coming when no one can work.

He who sows to his flesh will of the flesh reap corruption, but he who sows to the Spirit will of the Spirit reap everlasting life. And let us not grow weary while doing good, for in due season we shall reap if we do not lose heart. Therefore, as we have opportunity, let us do good to all, especially to those who are of the household of faith.

1 COR 15:58.1 COR 15:58.COL 2:6-7.MATT 24:13.LUKE 8:15.2 COR 1:24.JOHN 9:4.GAL 6:8-10

## December 26

Be steadfast, immovable, always abounding in the work of the Lord.

## December 27

We do not look at the things which are seen, but at the things which are not seen. For the things which are seen are temporary, but the things which are not seen are eternal.

Here we have no continuing city. ◊ You have a better and an enduring possession for yourselves in heaven. ◊ Do not fear, little flock, for it is your Father's good pleasure to give you the kingdom. ◊ Now for a little while, if need be, you have been grieved by various trials. ◊ There the wicked cease from troubling, and there the weary are at rest.

We who are in this tent groan, being burdened. ◊ God will wipe away every tear from their eyes; there shall be no more death, nor sorrow, nor crying; and there shall be no more pain, for the former things have passed away.

The sufferings of this present time are not worthy to be compared with the glory which shall be revealed in us. ◊ Our light affliction, which is but for a moment, is working for us a far more exceeding and eternal weight of glory.

2 COR 4:18.HEB 13:14.HEB 10:34.LUKE 12:32.1 PET 1:6.JOB 3:17.2 COR 5:4.REV 21:4.ROM 8:18.2 COR 4:17

I will forgive their iniquity, and their sin I will remember no more. ◊ Who can forgive sins but God alone?

I, even I, am He who blots out your transgressions for My own sake; and I will not remember your sins. ◊ Blessed is he whose transgression is forgiven, whose sin is covered. Blessed is the man to whom the Lord does not impute iniquity. ◊ Who is a God like You, pardoning iniquity.

God in Christ . . . forgave you. ◊ The blood of Jesus Christ His Son cleanses us from all sin. If we say that we have no sin, we deceive ourselves, and the truth is not in us. If we confess our sins, He is faithful and just to forgive us our sins and to cleanse us from all unrighteousness.

As far as the east is from the west, so far has He removed our transgressions from us. ◊ Sin shall not have dominion over you, for you are not under law but under grace. . . . Having been set free from sin, you became slaves of righteousness.

MARK 2:5.JER 31:34.MARK 2:7.IS 43:25.PS 32:1-2.MIC 7:18.EPH 4:32.1 JOHN 1:7-9.PS 103:12.ROM 6:14,18

## December 28

**Your sins are forgiven you.**

**Understand what
the will of the
Lord is.**

This is the will of God, your
sanctification. ◊ Now acquaint yourself
with Him, and be at peace; thereby
good will come to you. ◊ This is
eternal life, that they may know You,
the only true God, and Jesus Christ
whom You have sent. ◊ We know that
the Son of God has come and has given
us an understanding, that we may know
Him who is true; and we are in Him
who is true, in His Son Jesus Christ.
This is the true God and eternal life.

We . . . do not cease to pray for you,
and to ask that you may be filled with
the knowledge of His will in all wisdom
and spiritual understanding. ◊ The God
of our Lord Jesus Christ, the Father of
glory, . . . give to you the spirit of
wisdom and revelation in the knowledge
of Him, the eyes of your understanding
being enlightened; that you may know
what is the hope of His calling, what
are the riches of the glory of His
inheritance in the saints, and what is
the exceeding greatness of His power
toward us who believe, according to the
working of His mighty power.

EPH 5:17.1 THESS 4:3.JOB 22:21.JOHN 17:3.1 JOHN
5:20.COL 1:9.EPH 1:17-19

You, who once were alienated and enemies in your mind by wicked works, yet now He has reconciled in the body of His flesh through death, to present you holy, and blameless, and irreproachable in His sight—if indeed you continue in the faith, grounded and steadfast, and are not moved away from the hope of the gospel. ◊ That you may become blameless and harmless, children of God without fault in the midst of a crooked and perverse generation, among whom you shine as lights in the world.

Therefore, beloved, looking forward to these things, be diligent to be found by Him in peace, without spot and blameless. ◊ Be sincere and without offense till the day of Christ.

Now to Him who is able to keep you from stumbling, and to present you faultless before the presence of His glory with exceeding joy, to God our Savior, who alone is wise, be glory and majesty, dominion and power, both now and forever.

1 COR 1:8.COL 1:21-23.PHIL 2:15.2 PET 3:14.PHIL 1:10.JUDE 1:24-25

# December 30

**Blameless in the day of our Lord Jesus Christ.**

## December 31

The Lord your God carried you, as a man carries his son, in all the way that you went until you came to this

I bore you on eagles' wings and brought you to Myself. ◊ In His love and in His pity He redeemed them; and He bore them and carried them all the days of old. ◊ As an eagle stirs up its nest, hovers over its young, spreading out its wings, taking them up, carrying them on its wings, so the Lord alone led him.

Even to your old age, I am He, and even to gray hairs I will carry you! I have made, and I will bear; even I will carry, and will deliver you. ◊ This is God, our God forever and ever; He will be our guide even to death.

Cast your burden on the Lord, and He shall sustain you. ◊ Do not worry about your life, what you will eat or what you will drink; nor about your body, what you will put on. . . . For your heavenly Father knows that you need all these things.

Thus far the Lord has helped us.

DEUT 1:31.EX 19:4.IS 63:9.DEUT 32:11-12.IS 46:4.PS 48:14.PS 55:22.MATT 6:25,32.1 SAM 7:12

The Lord is good to all, and His tender mercies are over all His works. ◊ He makes His sun rise on the evil and on the good, and sends rain on the just and on the unjust.

Oh, how great is Your goodness, which You have laid up for those who fear You, which You have prepared for those who trust in You in the presence of the sons of men! ◊ My people shall be satisfied with my goodness.

The Lord, the Lord God, merciful and gracious, long-suffering and abounding in goodness and truth. ◊ The goodness of God endures continually. ◊ Oh, give thanks to the Lord . . . Oh, give thanks to the God of gods . . . Oh, give thanks to the Lord of lords!

In everything give thanks; for this is the will of God in Christ Jesus for you. . . . He who calls you is faithful.

PS 65:11.PS 86:5.PS 145:9.MATT 5:45.PS 31:19.JER 31:14.EX 34:6.PS 52:1.PS 136:1-3.1 THESS 5:18,24

## Thanks-giving

You crown the year with Your goodness, and Your paths drip with abundance.

## Thanksgiving

Then they cried out to the Lord in their trouble, and He saved them out of their distresses.

Oh, that men would give thanks to the Lord for His goodness, and for His wonderful works to the children of men! ◊ Were there not ten cleansed? But where are the nine? ◊ Forget not all His benefits. ◊ God, who answered me in the day of my distress.

I sought the Lord, and He heard me, and delivered me from all my fears. ◊ I love the Lord, because He has heard my voice and my supplications. Because he has inclined His ear to me, therefore I will call upon Him as long as I live. ◊ My heart trusted in Him, and I am helped; therefore my heart greatly rejoices, and with my song I will praise Him.

Call upon Me in the day of trouble; I will deliver you. ◊ Whoever offers praise glorifies Me.

Giving thanks always for all things to God the Father in the name of our Lord Jesus Christ.

PS 107:19.PS 107:21.LUKE 17:17.PS 103:2.GEN 35:3.PS 34:4.PS 116:1-2.PS 28:7.PS 50:15,23.EPH 5:20

I looked for . . . comforters, but I found none. ◇ His brethren came to comfort him. ◇ My soul refused to be comforted.

I will come. ◇ I will turn their mourning to joy, will comfort them. ◇ I, even I, am He who comforts you. ◇ Your comforts delight my soul.

You shall . . . comfort me on every side. ◇ Your rod and Your staff, they comfort me. ◇ You, Lord, have helped me and comforted me.

Blessed be the God and Father of our Lord Jesus Christ, the Father of mercies and God of all comfort, who comforts us in all our tribulation, that we may be able to comfort those who are in any trouble, with the comfort with which we ourselves are comforted by God.

IS 66:13.PS 69:20.1 CHR 7:22.PS 77:2.JOHN 14:18.JER 31:13.IS 51:12.PS 94:19.PS 71:21.PS 23:4.PS 86:17.2 COR 1:3-4

## Bereave-ment

**As one whom his mother comforts, so I will comfort you.**

## Bereavement

Father, I desire that they also whom You gave Me may be with Me where I am.

While we are at home in the body we are absent from the Lord. . . . We are confident, yes, well pleased rather to be absent from the body and to be present with the Lord. ◊ I am hard pressed between the two, having a desire to depart and be with Christ, which is far better. ◊ Whether we live or die, we are the Lord's.

You have a better and an enduring possession for yourselves in heaven. ◊ It has not yet been revealed what we shall be, but we know that when He is revealed, we shall be like Him, for we shall see Him as He is. ◊ Now we see in a mirror, dimly, but then face to face. ◊ I will see your face in righteousness; I shall be satisfied when I awake in Your likeness.

We shall always be with the Lord. Therefore comfort one another with these words.

JOHN 17:24.2 COR 5:6,8 PHIL 1:23.ROM 14:8.HEB 10:34.1 JOHN 3:2. 1 COR 13:12.PS 17:15.1 THESS 4:17-18

Surely He has borne our griefs and carried our sorrows. ◊ He Himself took our infirmities and bore our sickness. ◊ He, being full of compassion. ◊ As a father pities his children, so the Lord pities those who fear him. For He knows our frame.

Who shall separate us from the love of Christ? Shall tribulation, or distress? ◊ Whom the Lord loves He chastens. ◊ Now no chastening seems to be joyful for the present, but grievous; nevertheless, afterward it yields the peaceable fruit of righteousness to those who have been trained by it. ◊ We know that all things work together for good to those who love God.

And He said to me, "My grace is sufficient for you, for My strength is made perfect in weakness." Therefore most gladly I will boast in my infirmities, that the power of Christ may rest upon me.

JOHN 11:3.IS 53:4.MATT 8:17.PS 78:38.PS 103:13,14.ROM 8:35.HEB 12:6.HEB 12:11.ROM 8:28. 2 COR 12:9

## Sickness

**Lord, behold, he whom You love is sick.**

## Sickness

Shall we indeed accept good from God, and shall we not accept adversity?

The sufferings of this present time are not to be compared with the glory which shall be revealed in us. ◇ Have mercy on me, O Lord, for I am weak; O Lord, heal me. ◇ The prayer of faith will heal the sick.

When my heart is overwhelmed; lead me to the rock that is higher than I. ◇ The Lord is the strength of my life. ◇ The eternal God is your refuge.

You are near, O Lord. ◇ You have heard my voice . . . You drew near on the day I called You, and said, "Do not fear!" A very present help in trouble.

Bless the Lord . . . who forgives all your iniquities, who heals all your diseases, who redeems your life from destruction.

Be anxious for nothing, but in everything by prayer and supplication, with thanksgiving, let your requests be made known to God; and the peace of God, which surpasses all understanding, will guard your hearts and minds through Christ Jesus.

JOB 2:10.ROM 8:18.PS 6:2.JAMES 5:15.PS 61:2.PS 27:1.DEUT 33:27.PS 119:151.LAM 3:56-57.PS 46:1.PS 103:2-4.PHIL 4:6-7

The Lord who made heaven and earth bless you. ◇ Our God and Father. ◇ The living God, who gives us richly all things to enjoy.

For your heavenly Father knows that you need all these things. ◇ For the Father Himself loves you.

No good thing will He withhold from those who walk uprightly. ◇ He stores up sound wisdom for the upright; He is a shield to those who walk uprightly. ◇ Blessed are those who keep His testimonies, who seek Him with the whole heart!

He who keeps you will not slumber. Behold, He who keeps Israel shall neither slumber nor sleep. ◇ For the Lord will be your confidence, and will keep your foot from being caught. ◇ You will keep him in perfect peace, whose mind is stayed on you, because he trusts in you.

The Lord of peace Himself give you peace always in every way.

NUM 6:24.PS 134:3.2 THESS 2:16.1 TIM. 6:17.MATT 6:32.JOHN 16:27.PS 84:11.PROV 2:7.PS 119:2.PS 121:3-4. PROV. 3:26.IS 26:3. THESS 3:16

## For a Birthday

The Lord bless you and keep you.

## For a Birthday

So teach us to number our days, that we may gain a heart of wisdom.

Are not my days few? ◊ Man who is born of woman is of few days. ◊ As for man, his days are like grass . . . but the mercy of the Lord is from everlasting to everlasting. ◊ Oh, satisfy us early with Your mercy, that we may rejoice and be glad all our days!

Behold, the fear of the Lord, that is wisdom. ◊ The wisdom that is from above is first pure, then peaceable, gentle, willing to yield, full of mercy and good fruits.

A wise man will hear. ◊ Whoever hears these sayings of Mine, and does them, I will liken him to a wise man who built his house on the rock. ◊ That Rock was Christ.

PS 90:12.JOB 10:20.JOB 14:1.PS 103:15,17.PS 90:14.JOB 28:28.JAMES 3:17.PROV 1:5.MATT 7:24.1 COR 10:4

Be tenderhearted, be courteous; not returning evil for evil or reviling for reviling, but on the contrary blessing, knowing that you were called to this. ◊ Be kindly affectionate . . . , in honor giving preference to one another.

Love one another as I have loved you. ◊ Love suffers long and is kind; love does not envy; love does not parade itself, is not puffed up; does not behave rudely, does not seek its own, is not provoked, thinks no evil; does not rejoice in iniquity, but rejoices in the truth; bears all things, believes all things, hopes all things, endures all things.

If we love one another, God abides in us, and His love has been perfected in us. . . . And we have known and believed the love that God has for us. God is love, and he who abides in love abides in God, and God in him.

1 PET 3:8.1 PET 3:8.ROM 12:9.JOHN 15:2.1 COR 13:4-7.1 JOHN 4:12,16

## Marriage

Be of one mind, having compassion for one another.

## Marriage

Unless the Lord builds the house, they labor in vain who build it.

Beware, lest you forget the Lord. . . . You shall fear the Lord your God and serve Him. . . . You shall do what is right and good in the sight of the Lord, that it may be well with you. ◊ You shall have no other gods before me.

But seek first the kingdom of God and His righteousness. ◊ As for me and my house, we will serve the Lord. ◊ And as the bridegroom rejoices over the bride, so shall your God rejoice over you.

Marriage is honorable among all. ◊ The Lord God said, "It is not good that man should be alone; I will make him a helper comparable to him."

I will walk within my house with a perfect heart. ◊ But there shall by no means enter it anything that defiles or causes an abomination.

The Lord our God we will serve, and His voice we will obey.

PS 127:1.DEUT 6:12,13,18.EX 20:3.MATT 6:33.JOSH 24:15.IS 62:5.HEB 13:4.GEN 2:18.PS 101:2.REV 21:27.JOSH 24:24